D1609511

NEW HANOVER COUNTY
PUBLIC LIBRARY

In honor of

David M. Paynter

Library Director
1982 - 2008

GREAT MONUMENTS
OF
INDIA

NEW HANOVER COUNTY
PUBLIC LIBRARY
201 CHESTNUT STREET
WILMINGTON, NC 28401

DORLING KINDERSLEY
London, New York, Melbourne,
Munich, and Delhi

DK INDIA
Editorial Team	Suchismita Banerjee, Glenda Fernandes, Kingshuk Ghoshal, Alka Ranjan, Ankush Saikia, Rohan Sinha, Dipali Singh, Saloni Talwar, Rima Zaheer
Design Team	Neha Ahuja, Aparajita Barai, Romi Chakraborty, Tannishtha Chakraborty, Mahua Mandal, Neerja Rawat, Ivy Roy, Malavika Talukder
DTP Designers	Harish Aggarwal, Dheeraj Arora, Jagtar Singh, Preetam Singh
DTP Co-ordinators	Sunil Sharma, Balwant Singh
Production Manager	Pankaj Sharma
Design Manager	Arunesh Talapatra
Art Director	Shefali Upadhyay
Head of Publishing Operations	Aparna Sharma

DK LONDON
Project Art Editor	Anna Hall
Managing Art Editor	Karen Self
Managing Editor	Camilla Hallinan
Art Director	Bryn Walls
Associate Publisher	Liz Wheeler
Publisher	Jonathan Metcalf
Production Editor	Luca Frassinetti
Production Controller	Inderjit Bhullar

First American Edition, 2009

Published in the United States by
DK Publishing
375 Hudson Street
New York, New York 10014

09 10 11 12 13 10 9 8 7 6 5 4 3 2 1
GD136—November 2009

Copyright © 2009 Dorling Kindersley Limited
All rights reserved

Contains content from the Eyewitness Travel
monuments series: Amber Fort (2008), Fatehpur Sikri
(2008), Humayun's Tomb (2008), Qutb Minar (2008),
Red Fort (2008), and Taj Mahal (2008).

Without limiting the rights under copyright reserved
above, no part of this publication may be reproduced,
stored in or introduced into a retrieval system, or
transmitted, in any form, or by any means (electronic,
mechanical, photocopying, recording, or otherwise),
without the prior written permission of both the
copyright owner and the above publisher of this book.

Published in Great Britain by Dorling Kindersley Limited.

A catalog record for this book
is available from the Library of Congress.

ISBN 978-0-75665-907-3

Printed and bound by Hung Hing, Hong Kong

**Discover more at
www.dk.com**

Content

SUHAG MANDIR, AMBER FORT
*The topmost storey of the Ganesh Pol (gateway),
the Suhag Mandir, is a small pavilion with
delicately carved marble screens and windows.*

Imprints of Time

India is a young country with an ancient history, where the ancient and the modern exist side by side. Successive waves of invasions and migrations over time have created a society characterized by kaleidoscopic variety. The seventh largest country in the world, with a population second only to China, India stretches from the Himalayas in the north to a tropical peninsula in the south, containing within it a dazzling mosaic of languages, dialects, religions, castes, and customs. It is only natural that India's great monuments paint a similarly diverse and vibrant picture. *Great Monuments of India* is a selection of 11 sites that best capture – in sandstone and granite and marble – the story of India's past and its people. This book is not meant to be a comprehensive survey of every significant historical structure found in India; even so, its selected monuments encompass the period from the 3rd century BCE to the middle of the 17th century, presenting an architectural history of India that also explains key religious and political developments. The monuments have a wide geographical spread too, from Buddhist funerary mounds in central India to temples in a south Indian port city and a hilltop citadel in western India. All are masterpieces, encapsulating India's rich legacy to our shared global heritage.

Red Fort
DELHI — Humayun's Tomb
JAIPUR — Qutb Minar
Amber Fort — AGRA
Taj Mahal
Fatehpur Sikri
BHOPAL
Khajuraho
Sanchi
BHUBANESHWAR
Konark
BENGALURU
Hampi
CHENNAI
Mamallapuram

◊ ANCIENT MOSQUE
At the Qutb complex in Delhi, the pillared cloisters of the late 12th century Quwwat-ul-Islam mosque are richly decorated with Hindu motifs such as tasselled ropes and bells.

MAP KEY
● NEAREST CITY

Milestones

Ancient India

The history of Indian architecture begins with the earliest known civilization of the Indus Valley. Although archaeology records the existence of Neolithic communities, nomadic hunters, and farmers in northern India from around 7,000 BCE, planned settlements and cities only become evident in the cities of Harappa and Mohenjodaro around 2500 BCE. This great civilization ended when a nomadic warlike tribe, the Aryans, migrated from Central Asia to northern India and settled down in the fertile plains of the river Ganges.

First settlements

The first dwellings, developed as natural shelters for hunters and food gatherers, were made of mud, wattle and daub, and stone. Pit dwellings were dug and covered with thatch, and timber huts gradually emerged, along with clusters of circular houses, surrounded by mud fortifications. Evidence of these are seen in parts of central and western India. Settlements in south India, in the present states of Karnataka and Tamil Nadu, developed later, around 3000 BCE. In the Indus Valley, advances in farming methods, crafts, and tool technology heralded the emergence of the first cities in India and the beginning of urban life.

REGAL BEARDED PRIEST
This Indus Valley stone statuette is believed to depict a priest-king; his trefoil-patterned robe indicates that he may have been a ruler.

Indus Valley civilization

The "twin capitals" of the Indus Valley civilization covered nearly a square mile each. Immense in size for their time, each city housed a population of over 30,000. Both were built on a grid-iron pattern of streets running north-south and east-west, which divided each city into a higher central citadel and lower residential blocks. Another hallmark of their town planning was an elaborate and efficient sanitation system: a common well shared by a group of houses, with individual bathing areas connected to drains that ran under the streets and into large sewers and brick pits.

In the citadel of Mohenjodaro was the Great Bath, a ceremonial tank most probably used for ritual ablutions. There was also a massive granary, and a vast hall, conjectured to be either a palace or place of worship. Terraced platforms contained cells for the priests, platforms for flour-making, and rooms for workers. In the residential section, a house was the basic unit, varying in size and storeys. Timber rafters were used for the roofs, and bricks were the natural material for walls, using the rich soil provided by the river Indus. Each house had a central courtyard open to sky, a feature that is still common today.

Archaeological evidence suggests that the Indus Valley people were a prosperous society. Their government may have been a form of theocracy, consisting of a small priestly class headed by a priest-king or a council of high priests. The cities had extensive trade contacts with the Middle East, as evidenced by Indus Valley seals found in Sumeria (present-day Iraq). More than 3,000 Indus Valley inscriptions have been discovered, pointing to a highly evolved script, which has yet to be deciphered. This peaceful and advanced society was, however, vulnerable to the recurring floods of the Indus and ill-protected from invasions. By 1500 BCE, its cities had been sapped of their vigour, making way for the Aryan invasion.

The Vedic Age

By the middle of the 1st millennium BCE, the Aryans had migrated further eastwards and settled in the fertile Ganges plains. As they transformed into an agrarian society, they began to adopt new customs, beliefs, and gods. Society was now divided into four classes, headed by Brahmins (priests), followed by Kshatriyas (warriors), Vaishyas (traders), and Sudras (labourers). The Vedic religion enshrined a pantheon of gods and its philosophy is contained in the four Vedas, which later became the foundation of Hinduism. They are also the main sources of information about the Aryans. Two great epics, *Mahabharata* and *Ramayana*, were composed in this period, and richly illustrate the religious and secular life of the time.

As rulers began policies of expansion, territorial states and hereditary kingships replaced tribal chieftains. This led to the emergence of several large kingdoms such as Magadha, Kashi, and Koshala. Towns such as Ayodhya, Rajgriha, Kaushambi, and Kashi became centres of trade and urban life. Building activity largely followed the Indus Valley pattern, though frequent rebuilding over older sites has destroyed many ancient settlements. Common features included baked bricks, open courtyards, a sewage system, and planning on a grid-iron pattern – all documented in the later *Arthashastra*, a political treatise of the 2nd century BCE.

  🏛 **WELL-PLANNED CITY**
Like Mohenjodaro, the streets of Harappa were neatly laid out in an orderly, grid-like pattern.

  🏹 **THE RAMAYANA**
This scene shows Hanuman, the monkey god, bowing before Lord Rama.

Buddhist and Jain Architecture

In the 6th century BCE, as class stratification intensified, resistance to the hegemony of the Brahmins led to the emergence of two great religious leaders. Siddhartha Gautama (c.550–468 BCE) renounced a princely life to seek alternative answers to the suffering of humankind, and founded Buddhism. Similarly, Vardhamana Mahavira (c.540–476 BCE) founded Jainism. The principles of equality and *ahimsa* (non-violence) formed the bedrock of both religions.

Buddhist and Jain buildings

The main features of Buddhist architecture derive from the practice of renunciation, *dharma* (propagation of the faith), and reverence for the Buddha. The *chaitya* (sanctuary or place of worship) was a natural development of the rock-cut cave which provided shelter to itinerant monks; the *viharas* (cells) or monasteries were more permanent structures where monks lived and studied (as seen at Nalanda and Sanchi); stone pillars were inscribed with edicts; and the semi-circular brick mound, or stupa, enshrined the Buddha's relics. The grandest of these is the Great Stupa at Sanchi (see pp.22–43), constructed during the reign of King Ashoka (268–231 BCE). This was later enlarged and an elaborate stone *vedika*, or railing, replaced the original timber fence surrounding it. Its crowning glory was the four stone *toranas*, or gateways. Remains of buildings have also been excavated at Vidisha, where wood and brick shrines, with timber domes and vaults, once existed. The 2nd century BCE temples at Ajanta and Ellora in Maharashtra are stunning examples of how rock-cut caves continued to develop and became increasingly sophisticated in style.

The Jains were mainly bankers and traders, and their temples (also evolved from rock-cut caves) were richly endowed. Brick was rarely used, but marble was popular,

YAKSHI
This Didarganj Yakshi (a symbol of fertility) statue is at the Patna Museum.

MAHABODHI TEMPLE
Constructed by Emperor Ashoka in Gaya, the temple is 55m (180.5ft) high.

ASHOKA'S EDICTS
This is a copy of a stone edict of King Ashoka. These edicts, carved on stone pillars, reflected Ashoka's thoughts on morality, war, kingship, and religion.

often transported from long distances. Temple clusters, such as those at Palitana in Gujarat, and Ranakpur and Dilwara in Rajasthan, combined Hindu iconography and aspects of the life and teachings of Mahavira Jain.

Mauryas

Little is known about Indian architecture in the period between the Indus Valley civilization and the rise of the Mauryan empire, since most building materials used were perishable wood or brick. But excavations at Rajgir and Kaushambi, in modern Bihar and Uttar Pradesh, testify to the existence of fortified cities, with stupas, monasteries, and temples of the type found at the later Mauryan sites of Nagari and Vidisha in Madhya Pradesh. There is evidence of the use of dressed stone in a palace excavated at Kaushambi. By the end of the 3rd century BCE, Ashoka embarked on an ambitious policy of expansion, which culminated in the annexation of Kalinga (modern Orissa). Appalled by the carnage of war, he adopted Buddhism and thereafter spread its teachings through religious inscriptions and edicts, which were carved on *stambhas* (pillars) erected all over his empire. The Mauryan economy was driven by agriculture. Trade and crafts also flourished.

After the Mauryas

Following Ashoka's death, the Mauryan empire disintegrated and several smaller kingdoms arose, such as those of the Sungas and Kushanas in the north and the Satavahanas in the west and south. There is evidence of prayer halls and small monasteries for monks – a gigantic hall with a magnificent façade was carved at Karle in the Western Ghats. Greek invasions also influenced the architecture of the time, especially rock-cut art. Two types developed: the Mathura school of art, which was strictly Indian in spirit and did not borrow from Greek styles; and the Gandhara school, which incorporated Greek elements.

The Sungas reconstructed the railings around the Bharhut Stupa, in the state of Madhya Pradesh, and built *toranas* to other stupas. The Satavahanas constructed a large number of stupas, of which the Great Stupa at Amaravati in the 2nd century BCE is the most famous example.

During the Kushana period in the 2nd century CE, the Buddha began to be represented in human form instead of through symbols such as the lotus and footprint, as was the practice earlier. Another feature of this age was that the emperor himself was represented as divine.

Jain ascetics preferred to live in forests, caves, and rock-shelters away from cities. Man-made caves date from the 2nd century BCE to the 7th century CE. The earliest of these are near Rajgir in Bihar, and at Karle, a magnificent example from the c.1st century BCE with horseshoe windows, great pillars, and finely carved reliefs. Jain scriptures refer to temples which perhaps existed before the 6th century BCE in Mathura, Kampila, and other places – but they no longer survive.

⚜ **GANDHARA BUDDHA**
Gandharan art, dated between 1st and 5th centuries CE, was the first school of sculpture to show the Buddha in human form, as may be seen in this carving of Buddha.

⚜ **A BUDDHIST STUPA RELIEF**
This is a depiction of the dream of Maya, from a Buddhist stupa from Bharhut (modern Madhya Pradesh), dating back to the late Mauryan period .

The Golden Age

A new dynasty, the Guptas, emerged in the 4th century CE. Historians have described the Gupta period as a golden age when every aspect of life reached a peak of excellence. Meanwhile, in the Deccan and southern India, several small but powerful kingdoms also established themselves. In the Deccan, the Vakatakas, Chalukyas, and Rashtrakutas created striking works of art and sculpture, while in the south, the Cholas, Pallavas, and Pandyas flourished.

The Guptas

The Gupta rulers were great administrators, who, like the Mauryas, consolidated an empire by conquering and uniting warring kingdoms and establishing political and economic stability. The Gupta kingdom expanded into a vast empire in the north under Samudra Gupta (c.335–380), who then swept into the southern peninsula as far as Kanchipuram. This period witnessed a resurgence of Hinduism after its decline during Mauryan rule, when Buddhism had assumed greater importance. The reign of Chandra Gupta II (c.375–415) marks a high point of Indian culture. Sanskrit language and literature were at their peak. Poets such as Kalidasa, Shudraka, and Bhasa wrote what are now considered Indian classics. Vatsyayana composed the famous *Kamasutra*. Many *puranas*

and *shastras* (ancient Hindu texts) were also written down along with commentaries on sacred works. The famous mathematician Aryabhatta and the astronomer Varahamihira belong to this age.

The preeminence of Hinduism in the Gupta empire is reflected in the architecture of innumerable temples built to honour Hindu gods such as Shiva, Vishnu, and Krishna, and goddesses such as Durga and Lakshmi. Earlier temples of the period had a flat slab-roof, often monolithic, but the gradual development of a superstructure over the *garbha-griha* (cell sanctuary), in brick or stone, gave rise to the *shikhara*. This curvilinear tapering tower (inspired by its bamboo prototype) probably

☙ **CELESTIAL DANCER**
The Vishnu temple at Deogarh is adorned with sumptuous carvings.

☙ **VISHNU TEMPLE**
This lively relief comes from the temple of Vishnu at Deogarh, in Uttar Pradesh.

☙ **ELLORA CAVE NO. 2**
Ellora caves 1-12 are essentially Buddhist caves carved out to form viharas *or monasteries.*

originated with the Vishnu temple at Tigawa (Madhya Pradesh), and the temples of Bhitargaon and the Dasavatara at Deogarh (Uttar Pradesh).

Rock-cut cave temples

Buddhism and Jainism continued to receive royal patronage and had a major influence on the architecture of the early Gupta period and for a while thereafter. A fine example of the merging of architecture with iconography is the Udaigiri caves (Madhya Pradesh), which house a colossal image of the god Vishnu. Another example is the cave temple at Elephanta near Mumbai, which contains a massive statue of the three-headed Shiva. Artistically and sculpturally, the most stunning achievements are the caves at Ajanta and Ellora, carved into the hills of the Western Ghats. Primarily classified as Buddhist, the Ajanta caves of the 1st to 7th century are decorated with exquisite murals and sculptures depicting the life of Buddha. Ellora, too, is famous for its sculptures. Its 8th-century Kailashnath temple is a masterpiece of the Rashtrakuta dynasty.

The Pallavas

The Pallavas came to power in the 6th century and ruled over northern Tamil Nadu and Andhra Pradesh with their capital at Kanchipuram. They encouraged music, painting, literature, and architecture. They were also great maritime traders travelling as far as Java, Malaysia, and China. Early in the 7th century, the Pallava ruler Mahendravarman II converted to Hinduism from Jainism and was a keen poet and dramatist. Under his patronage, some of the most unusual rock-cut temples were built. The port city of Mamallapuram (see pp.44–65), built by Narasimhavarman I in the 7th century on the eastern coast, was a centre of building activity. Its boulder-strewn landscape provided a dramatic setting for a cluster of Pallava architectural masterpieces: the free-standing Shore Temple and the five monolithic rock-cut shrines called *rathas* ("chariots"). The Shore Temple, perched on a promontory by the sea, is one of the gems of southern temple architecture. The Pancha Pandava Rathas, named after the five Pandava brothers in the epic *Mahabharata*, are ingenious interpretations of the rural portable wooden shrine. A spectacular display of bas-reliefs carved on giant-sized rocks also illustrates the perfection achieved by Pallava stone masons.

The Kailasanatha Temple in Kanchipuram was built by Rajasimha, the last great Pallava king, and is a fine example of an early structural temple, reflecting the rapidly emerging south Indian style: *gopurams* (gateways), pilastered walls, a pyramidal *shikhara*, and a wall enclosing the complex. Other Pallava masterpieces in Kanchipuram include the Kamakshi Temple, with four colourful *gopurams*, and the Vaikuntha Perumal Temple, which is unique for its three sanctums, built on top of one another and dedicated to Lord Vishnu.

⚜ FRESCO FROM KAILASANATHA TEMPLE
A detailed fresco painting of the Hindu deity Shiva adorns the inner walls of the 8th-century Kailasanatha Temple in Kanchipuram.

⚜ KAILASANATHA TEMPLE
Built almost entirely in sandstone, the Kailasanatha Temple in Kanchipuram is dedicated to Lord Shiva. Statues of Nandi the bull, Shiva's mount, stand guard at the entrance.

The Chalukyas

As kings and priests jointly ruled the lives of ordinary people, temples were given prominence and permanence by being built in stone. Secular architecture was given secondary status and made of durable materials. Crafts guilds developed with a hereditary system of authority, in which the master craftsman dictated the rules of building.

The Chalukyas, originally local chieftains, formed a separate kingdom in the Deccan under Pulakesin I in 543 CE. Under Pulakesin II they became a dominant power in peninsular India and even sent an ambassador to the court of Persia (modern-day Iran). During their rule spanning five centuries, they built a large number of spectacular temples in their capitals at Badami and Pattadakal, and at Aihole in the state of Karnataka. Chalukya temples evolved from Gupta shrines, but in their mature period they showed links with both the northern (Nagara) and southern (Dravida) styles of architecture.

Prominent in the early phase are the temples at Aihole and Badami. Early craftsmen, not quite versed with the visual form of Hindu temples, could only emulate the rural model of a village council built on a platform at Aihole. The Lad Khan

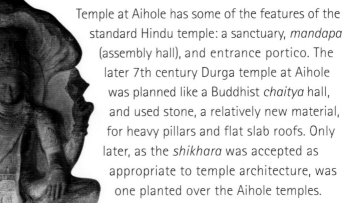

SEATED VISHNU
Relief from Badami cave temple built during the 6th century.

Temple at Aihole has some of the features of the standard Hindu temple: a sanctuary, *mandapa* (assembly hall), and entrance portico. The later 7th century Durga temple at Aihole was planned like a Buddhist *chaitya* hall, and used stone, a relatively new material, for heavy pillars and flat slab roofs. Only later, as the *shikhara* was accepted as appropriate to temple architecture, was one planted over the Aihole temples.

Most spectacular among the Badami group are the temples carved into red sandstone cliffs overlooking a lake. A steep flight of steps leads to magnificently carved caves. The entrance to each temple is through a pillared verandah, into a columned hall and then a small inner sanctum containing an idol of the deity to which the temple was dedicated. There are both Hindu and Jain temples here, the former with impressive images of Vishnu and Shiva carved into the rock face. The Bhutanatha group of temples, built in successive phases on the same lake features the typical pyramidal, tiered towers common to the Chalukya style.

The 8th-century free-standing temples at Pattadakal mark the mature phase of Chalukyan architecture. The sacred complex of 10 temples was mainly used for royal

BHUTANATHA TEMPLE
This temple has a superstructure that resembles the early south Indian style with its open mandapa.

functions. They include influences of both the southern Dravida style and the northern Nagara style. Well known among the former are the Virupaksha and Mallikarjuna temples. Virupaksha closely resembles the Kailasanatha Temple at Kanchipuram and represents a fully developed stage of Dravidian architecture. The Nagara-style temples at the entrance to the complex are more modest.

West India, Deccan, and Bengal

Western India saw the rise of the Pratiharas, a Rajput clan, in the 8th century. At its peak, the dynasty ruled over the states of Gujarat, Rajasthan, and Madhya Pradesh. At the same time, the Rashtrakutas were predominant in the northern Deccan, primarily in the Western Ghats (the Kailashnath Temple at Ellora being a high point of their artistic achievements), while the Palas, a Buddhist dynasty, dominated the east. All three kingdoms regularly fought one another for control over Kannauj, a strategically placed city in the plains of the river Ganges. The city of Kannauj controlled practically the whole of northern India. None were completely successful and Kannauj eventually fell to the Turks in the 10th century.

The Cholas

The Cholas emerged in south India in the late 10th century and became a prominent military, economic, and cultural power not only in the peninsula but across Asia. Rajaraja Chola (r.985–1014) annexed parts of Sri Lanka and Maldives. Rajendra Chola I (r.1014–1044) sent an expedition to north India and defeated the Pala ruler of Pataliputra (now called Patna). The reign of the later Cholas was marked by prosperity and high culture. The Brihadishvara Temple of Thanjavur, completed around 1009, typifies the grandeur of the Chola tradition. Dedicated to Shiva, it was constructed in granite, and its main structure topped by a lofty *shikhara* of 13 storeys rising to a height of nearly 70m (230ft). Covered with sculptures and mouldings, the beautifully balanced proportions of the different components enhanced the structure's aesthetic quality. The second of the great imperial temples of the dynasty is at Gangaikondacholapuram, which Rajendra Chola I made his capital. Chola temples evolved as complex institutions, assuming political, fiscal, and cultural roles, and were the hub of authority and power. Exquisite bronze sculptures – mainly images of deities – were kept in the inner shrine of these temples.

Between the 8th and 11th centuries, India's golden age saw several other developments in temple architecture. In Kashmir in the north, the Temple of the Sun was built at Martand with Hellenic style columns, pyramidal roofs, and arches. In the east, at Bhubaneshwar in Orissa, the *shikhara* developed the so-called "shoulder spire", converging near the apex in the circular *kalasha* or crowning stone as seen at Parasurameshvar, Mukteshvara, and Lingaraja temples.

⚜ **STONE LINTEL OF SHIVA AND SAPTAMATRIKAS**
A 10th-century Pratihara stone relief from Allahabad, Uttar Pradesh, features Lord Shiva and the Saptamatrikas or seven mother goddess representing seven basic sounds.

⚜ **ENTRANCE TO BRIHADISHVARA TEMPLE**
The picture shows the elaborate gateway, or gopuram, leading to the royal temple complex. The temple is dedicated to Lord Shiva.

A Period of Change

Between the 10th and 11th centuries constant internal warfare between kingdoms in both north and south weakened resistance to outside forces. Turkic invaders from Central Asia paved the way for Islamic rule in north India. They brought their own culture but were also influenced by indigenous traditions, especially in art and architecture. As successive Muslim dynasties were founded in the north, a powerful Hindu empire emerged at Vijayanagara in the south.

The Rajputs

Rulers of feudal kingdoms in north and central India, the Rajputs ("sons of kings") were Hindu Kshatriya clans, one of the most powerful among them being the Chauhans. The Rajputs built impressive forts perched on rocky outcrops – the ramparts of Amber Fort (see pp.194–211) follow the contours of the hill on which it stands. The forts were symbols of royalty, with luxurious palaces, halls, and temples within. Inter-feudal rivalry weakened the Rajputs, making them vulnerable to repeated attacks, first by Mahmud of Ghazni, a Turkish chieftain, and Muhammad of Ghur, an Afghan warlord.

Sultans of Delhi

Before returning to Afghanistan, Muhammad of Ghur left his slave general, Qutbuddin Aibak, in charge of his conquered territories, founding the Mamluk (Slave) dynasty. The Mamluk, the Khilji, Tughlaq, Sayyid, and Lodi sultans ruled successively for over three and a half centuries. The new rulers were Muslim and paved the way for the Great Mughals. Aibak converted the Rajput stronghold of Qila Rai Pithora into his capital at Delhi. He built the magnificent Quwwat-ul-Islam Masjid on the ruins of 27 temples, using elements dismantled from them. He also began building the five-storey Qutb Minar (see pp.92–109), which was completed by his successor Iltutmish, whose tomb was the first to be covered with a dome in India. Red sandstone and marble became the favourite materials in architecture; stylized and geometric patterns were added

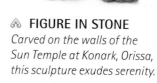

⚜ FIGURE IN STONE
Carved on the walls of the Sun Temple at Konark, Orissa, this sculpture exudes serenity.

⚜ JAISALMER FORT
Built in the 12th century by Maharawal Jaisal, a Rajput warrior of the Bhatti clan, the magnificent Jaisalmer Fort rises from a hill in the Thar Desert; it encloses palaces and temples.

⚜ STATELY TOMB
A fine example of the funerary architecture of the Delhi Sultanate is the octagonal tomb of Sikander Lodi, with its tall arches. Built in 1517, its lofty silhouette was achieved by a double dome.

to the ornate floral designs of Hindu masons; and mosque building began with *minars* (towers) and open courtyards lined by colonnades. The old structural forms and techniques of Hindu builders were transformed into a new vision by Muslim architects and overseers. The Hindu form of construction with straight horizontal beams or lintels now became primarily arched; the first true arch (see p.96) was built in the tomb of the 13th-century sultan, Ghiyasuddin Balban, in Delhi.

During Khilji rule, the vocabulary of architecture was further enhanced by the increasing use of arches, *jaalis* (filigreed screens in stone), and the construction of splendid domes. In the Tughlaq period that followed, there was vigorous experimentation in construction techniques, as displayed in the Tughlaqabad Fort and the tomb of Ghiyasuddin Tughlaq, both in Delhi. Sloping walls and a strongly militant appearance typified Tughlaq palaces, tombs, and forts. The power of the sultanate spread under Muhammad-bin-Tughlaq (c.1325). The Sayyids came next, followed by the Lodis (1451-1526). After the death of the second Lodi sultan, Sikander Lodi, who also founded the city of Agra, the Delhi Sultanate declined and finally gave way to Mughal power. Meanwhile several independent Muslim states had been set up in the Deccan, including ones at Bijapur, Golconda, and Bidar, where individual, often florid, regional styles added to the overall Islamic vocabulary of architecture.

Empire of the south

During the rule of the Delhi sultans in the north, the dominant power in south India was the Vijayanagara empire (c.1336–1565). Vast and prosperous, it lasted for more than two centuries. At the zenith of its power, it was ruled by Krishnadeva Raya and Achyutaraya. A sacred and royal centre spread over the boulder-strewn site of Hampi (see pp.130–51). Though largely in ruins now, the elaborate *mandapas* (columned halls) and *vimanas* (towers) are still impressive. The Vitthala Temple is a high point of Hampi's architecture.

Other kingdoms

Throughout this period of change, temple architecture continued to thrive in east and central India, where independent kingdoms held sway. The Hindu Chandella kings of central India built the Khajuraho temples (see pp.66–91), remarkable for their sculptural virtuosity. The Eastern Ganga dynasty ruled Kalinga (present-day Orissa) from the 11th to the 15th centuries and left a lasting architectural legacy of spectacular temples such as the Sun Temple in Konark (see pp.110–29) and the Jagannath Temple in Puri.

ORNATE TEMPLE
A series of stepped spires rise over the porches and halls of the Vishvanath Temple at Khajuraho.

HAUZ KHAS
This madrasa, a centre of Islamic learning in Hauz Khas, Delhi, was built in 1352 by Firoz Shah Tughlaq; he built 30 madrasas in all.

The Mughal Era

Babur's victory over the Delhi Sultanate in 1526 laid the foundations for the vast and glorious empire of the Mughals, bringing with him a passion for the arts. A unique Indo-Islamic style was created and found prolific expression in architecture, painting, and crafts. By the 18th century, the great empire had weakened. The Marathas in the west, Sikhs in the north, and ambitious European powers brought Muslim rule to an end.

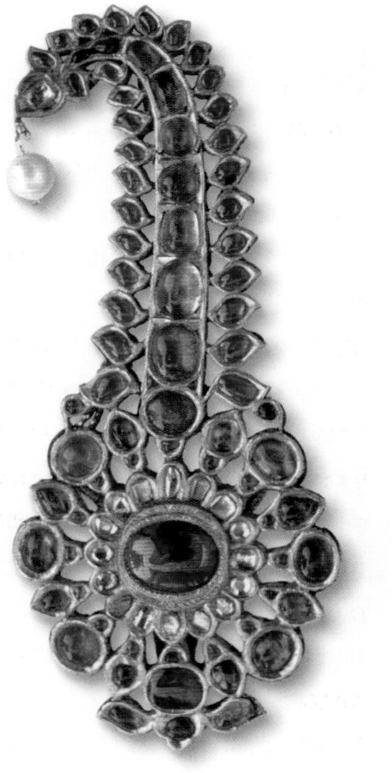

MUGHAL JEWELLERY
The Mughals introduced exquisite jewellery, such as this turban ornament, to display their gems.

Founding an empire

Zahiruddin Muhammad Babur lived an extraordinary life. A descendant of the Mongols Genghis Khan and Tamerlaine, he was born in Fergana, Central Asia, in 1483 was and proclaimed king at the age of twelve. He conquered Kabul and marched into India, challenging and defeating the Delhi Sultan, Ibrahim Lodi, whose army was much larger than his. Babur was not only tactically superior and battle-hardened, but also enjoyed the advantage of superior weaponry. He brought with him a sophisticated and cultured tradition, with a preference for the arts. Tragically, he did not live long enough to enjoy the fruits of his success and died in 1530. Legend has it he pledged his own life in order to save that of his sick son, Humayun. Miraculously, Humayun recovered but Babur contracted a mysterious fever which claimed his life.

A brilliant and charismatic ruler, Babur took considerable interest in architecture. Inspired by the lush scenery of his beautiful homeland, he commissioned three gardens at Agra, his capital. Laid out along geometric lines, these were the precursors of the famous *charbagh* (Persian paradise garden), which epitomized Mughal landscape design. Babur summoned craftsmen all the way from Persia and Samarkand to work on his projects. Although few buildings survive from his reign, the remains of a mosque he built in Panipat to celebrate his victory can still be seen today. His own tomb is in Kabul.

BABUR'S TOMB, KABUL
It is said that Babur was happiest in a tent pitched in a garden. After his death, his remains were laid to rest in a simple grave in his favourite garden at Kabul.

AKBAR'S TOMB, SIKANDRA
Although Akbar started the construction of his own tomb, it was completed by Jahangir. Its imposing gateway has a colossal arch made of red sandstone inlaid with marble and black slate.

Reinforcing a culture

Humayun, Babur's successor, lost his throne in 1540 to Sher Shah Suri, an Afghan vassal of the Mughals. Homeless and stateless, he sought refuge at the court of Shah Tahmasp, the ruler of Persia. With the help of his host, Humayun eventually put together an army, and regained his empire in 1555. However, six months later, he tripped on the stairs of his library in Purana Qila, the fort that enclosed his citadel, Dinpanah, and died. He was succeeded by his eldest son, Jalaluddin, who, at thirteen, was not old enough to rule. Jalaluddin assumed the title of Akbar ("Great"), and ruled for some time under the guardianship of a regent.

Humayun's brief reign marked a turning point in India's history. It not only re-established the supremacy of the Mughals, but also led to important innovations in the field of art and culture. The emperor was a keen enthusiast of painting, music, poetry, and architecture, and was deeply inspired by the prevailing culture of the Persian court during his exile there. On his return, he invited several Persian artists – painters, calligraphers, and architects – who contributed their skills to create a glorious mix of Persian and indigenous architectural traditions. Among the first Mughal monuments to display this synthesis was the spectacular Humayun's Tomb (see pp.152–169), commissioned after the emperor's death by his senior wife Haji Begum.

Consolidating the empire

Akbar assumed full power at the age of 20, and began to consolidate and expand the kingdom bequeathed to him. Although he was illiterate, he had a sharp intellect and a prodigious memory. An astute administrator and military strategist, he created an efficient government and promoted a secular phililosopy of life, the Din-i-Ilahi, which honoured people of all faiths. Akbar's administration was based on a remarkable system of revenue collection, called the *mansabdari* system, which gave the ruler a sound financial base to fund the expansion of his empire, and also enabled him to continue the building traditions of his forefathers.

Eclectic builder

The genius of Akbar as a builder, both of empire and great architecture, flowered in the city of Agra, his capital. His numerous war campaigns had taken him all over India, exposing him to differences in architectural style and form, and being a man of liberal outlook he gave free reign to his builders to express their creativity under his guiding hand. Red sandstone was favoured, as seen in his fortress-palace known as the Lal Qila (Red Fort, see pp.212–235), which is said to have been influenced by the Gwalior Fort, and at his most ambitious project, Fatehpur Sikri (see pp.170–193). A unique example of urban planning, the city of Fatehpur Sikri was entered through

❦ MUGHAL HAREM
The harem (women's quarters), accessible only to the emperor, was a self-contained world where Mughal women lived in pomp and splendour.

a monumental gateway and was built on a system of multiple axes, culminating in the grand mosque at one end. Akbar had to ultimately abandon the city, possibly due to a shortage of water, and he moved to Lahore. The rest of his life was spent in consolidating his empire, effectively bringing the whole of India, except the far south, under his control. Akbar's architecture was elegant and eclectic. Domes and arches, key features of Persian architecture, were used alongside *chajjas* (overhanging canopies) and chhatris (umbrella-like roof pavilions), common features of Rajput Hindu architecture. In terms of decoration, marble inlay was common, and complemented by brightly coloured designs on walls and ceilings.

Fine arts and gardens

After Akbar's death in 1605, his son Salim ascended the imperial throne, taking the title Jahangir ("Conqueror of the World"). Highly literate and with wide-ranging cultural interests, he became emperor when Mughal military and economic might was at its peak. The resulting peace and stability allowed Jahangir to distance himself from the task of governance and concentrate on painting and poetry. He later became addicted to alcohol and opium, and more or less handed over power to his Persian-born wife, Nur Jahan, who is credited as the main inspiration behind the design of this era's buildings. Despite Jahangir's single-minded devotion to the fine arts, some important monuments were completed during his reign – Akbar's mausoleum at Sikandra, and the highly decorative tomb of Itmad-ud-Daulah, Nur Jahan's father, at Agra. Mughal gardens flourished, and one of the loveliest of these – the Shalimar Garden – was laid out against the stunning landscape of Kashmir. This was where Jahangir held court in summer.

EMPEROR JAHANGIR
Jahangir's portraits depicted his affection for his pets – including his prized falcon.

JAMA MASJID, DELHI
Built by Shah Jahan in 1656, the construction of this imposing mosque, the largest in India, took six years and 5,000 workers to complete.

SHALIMAR GARDEN, LAHORE
Shah Jahan commissioned the Shalimar Garden in 1637 as a series of descending rectangular terraces and cascades on a rigid symmetrical plan.

Reign of marble

Jahangir died in 1627, and Khurram, his favourite son, succeeded him with the title of Shah Jahan ("Ruler of the Universe"). Shah Jahan ruled with a stern hand for three decades, aided by an efficient military-administrative machinery. Towards the end of his rule there were signs of the decline of the empire. But the flowering of Indian architecture reached its zenith under his patronage.

Shah Jahan was a consummate builder. It was during his reign that the form of Mughal buildings achieved excellence in standards of workmanship and detail. Marble was now used extensively. His first major project was Shahjahanabad, a new capital city in Delhi. At its heart lay the Red Fort (see pp.212–235), a formidable palace-fortress, which remained the Mughal seat of power until the end of the dynasty. The Diwan-i-Khas and the later Moti Mahal inside were built completely in marble. The Jama Masjid was another of his achievements, but none could surpass the scale and beauty of the Taj Mahal (see pp.236–255), built in memory of Shah Jahan's beloved wife, Mumtaz Mahal. The magic of its architecture derives from its perfect proportions, exquisite craftsmanship, and the inherent lustre of its white marble.

The end of Shah Jahan's reign was marked by dynastic strife. His son Aurangzeb wrested the throne from Dara Shikoh, Shah Jahan's favourite son and heir apparent.

Decline of the empire

Aurangzeb, who ruled India for nearly 50 years, was the last of the great Mughals. Rigid and often ruthless, he waged constant wars in the Deccan and Afghanistan to extend his territory, besides quelling rebellions that surfaced in different parts of his empire. These campaigns, however, took a severe toll on his exchequer, already bankrupted by Shah Jahan's building projects. In the end Aurangzeb had little time and money to continue the grand building traditions of his predecessors. Inspired by the Taj Mahal, his son Azam Shah built the Bibi-ka-Maqbara, the tomb of his mother, at Aurangabad in Maharashtra, but it was a poor replica of the original. Mughal architecture was now diluted by a shift from powerful form to overly elaborate decorative details.

In 1615, Sir Thomas Roe became the first official British envoy to Jahangir's court. The East India Company which began trading in 1600 slowly enlarged its commercial and military interests. Though the First Anglo-Indian War ended in a decisive victory for the Mughals in 1689, Aurangzeb's death in 1707 marked the beginning of the decline of the Mughal empire. His successors were weak, with little inclination to pursue the interests of their predecessors. The empire began to fracture as local warlords broke free from Mughal control. Gradually, all the skilled architects, builders, and stonemasons dispersed to the courts of these provincial rulers, bringing to an end a glorious chapter in the history of Indian architecture.

⚜ IMITATING THE TAJ
Bibi-ka-Maqbara, known as the poor man's Taj Mahal, is an imitation of its famous predecessor. It was built in Aurangabad by Aurangzeb's son Azam Shah for his mother.

⚜ FRENCH EAST INDIA COMPANY WAREHOUSE
Vying with the English and the Dutch for a share in the lucrative Indian trade, the French set up a base in Pondicherry, in modern-day Tamil Nadu, during Aurangzeb's reign.

Colonial Era

In the 16th century, the arrival of Europeans, notably the English East India Company, changed the course of India's history. A major revolt in 1857-58 was crushed as the governance of India was taken over by the British Crown. Increasing opposition to colonial rule led to a unique non-violent form of resistance spearheaded by Mahatma Gandhi; British rule finally ended in 1947 and the independent nations of India and Pakistan were born.

⚜ **SIR DAVID BAIRD**
An engraving of a British officer in India belonging to the late 18th century.

Anglo-Indian confluence

With colonization began a new chapter in Indian architecture. Early French and Portuguese colonizers had settled in various parts of India and styled buildings on classical European models. Fort St George in Chennai is an example of early colonial forts. The new architecture included both public and private buildings, the former laying emphasis on large dimensions, and conveying the idea of authority. Gothic and Italianate styles became popular, especially in churches. Colonial architecture evolved into what is called the Indo-Saracenic style, or a combination of the Hindu, Islamic, and western elements, and was used for institutional and civic buildings – government offices, railway stations, universities, and museums. Several noted British architects assimilated and adopted native Indian styles. A significant example is the Maharaja's Palace at Mysore. Colonial bungalows became a genre by themselves and commemorative architecture was epitomized by the Victoria Memorial in Calcutta (now Kolkata), the Gateway of India in Mumbai, and the War Memorial Arch in New Delhi. The new capital of India after Calcutta, New Delhi represents the zenith of British Raj architecture. Sir Edward Lutyens planned the city with the Viceroy's Residence at its centre– now called Rashtrapati Bhawan – official home to the President of India. Herbert Baker added the two Secretariat blocks and other buildings. The commercial centre of New Delhi, Connaught Place, was designed by Robert Tor Russel.

⚜ **VICTORIA MEMORIAL**
Designed by Sir William Emerson, the Victoria Memorial in Calcutta is among the most imposing of all British structures in India.

⚜ **RASHTRAPATI BHAWAN**
Formerly the Viceroy's Residence, this majestic building was designed by Sir Edward Lutyens who harmonized Indian stylistic devices with Western architecture.

Post-independence

Independent India saw a complete break with tradition. The Modernist movement that was sweeping through Europe inspired the first generation of Indian architects to, in Nehru's words, design "unfettered by the traditions of the past". Modern Indian architecture has since been shaped by a debate between those who favour the universal language of modernity, and those who believe in adapting the modern to indigenous, regional styles and materials.

Breaking free

When Indian professionals took over the running of the Public Works Departments (PWDs), this resulted in little architectural change because most had been trained under the British. Ganesh Deolalikar, the first Indian to head the Central Public Works Departments (CPWD) in New Delhi, designed the Supreme Court in Lutyens' style. However, many others went abroad to learn from masters such as Le Corbusier and Walter Gropius. This led to new directions in architecture through the works of A.P. Kanvinde, Habib Rahman, Balkrishna Doshi, and Charles Correa. A completely new aesthetic emerged with the arrival of Le Corbusier, who in the 1950s was invited by Jawaharlal Nehru, the first prime minister of independent India, to design a new city in Punjab, which had lost Lahore to Pakistan. Chandigarh was the first modern city of post-independence India. Strong and bold new forms in concrete now endorsed the modernist theme of form following function. Other foreign architects who settled in India and made their mark were Louis Kahn in Ahmedabad, Joseph Allen Stein in Delhi, and Laurie Baker in Kerala. Iranian architect, Fariburz Sahba, designed the iconic Baha'i Temple in Delhi. However, as urban Indian architecture rapidly moves to a global vision with the emergence of glitzy new city malls and high-rise hotels, Indian architects such as Correa and Raj Rewal are also leaving their imprint through mature and elegant works abroad.

🪨 **GUARDIAN**
This sculpture is outside the Reserve Bank of India, Delhi.

🦢 **BAHA'I TEMPLE**
This lotus-shaped temple in Delhi, designed by Fariburz Sabha, was completed in 1986.

Sanchi

Radiantly glowing in the sunlight, the gentle contours of the stupas at Sanchi exude an almost unearthly tranquillity. Here, on a hill-top, the stupas (hemispherical funerary mounds in which the relics of the Buddha or his disciples were interred) have stood as beacons of Buddhism since the 3rd century BCE. In the 6th century BCE, Siddhartha Gautama, later called the Buddha (the Enlightened One), preached the principle of the Middle Path. The great Mauryan emperor Ashoka converted to Buddhism after repenting the carnage of battles fought to extend his empire. His zeal for Buddhism inspired him to enshrine the relics of the Buddha at Sanchi, near the ancient city of Vidisha. The site was strategically located along a trade route linking his capital, Pataliputra (modern Patna) with the western ports. This made it viable for Buddhist monks to live here, as they depended on the generosity of rich merchants who lived nearby. Ashoka initially commissioned a monolithic pillar and a small stupa made of brick, which forms the core of the Great Stupa, the main monument in the Sanchi site. Temples, gateways, and monasteries continued to be built here until the 7th century CE. Although the Buddha had never been to Sanchi, the monuments here constitute one of the most revered Buddhist pilgrimage sites. With the decline of Buddhism in India, the site gradually lost its importance. It was re-discovered, in 1818, by General Taylor of the Bengal Cavalry. Between 1912 and 1919, the stupas were extensively restored by the Archaeological Survey of India (ASI) under Sir John Marshall, who numbered all the structures. The site was declared a World Heritage Site by UNESCO in 1989.

⚶ **SACRED HILL**
Sanchi, a small town, lies in Vidisha, a district in the state of Madhya Pradesh.

The Middle Path

A prince of the Sakya clan, Siddhartha Gautama was born between 550 and 468 BCE. Saddened by the suffering around him, he renounced his princely legacy and embarked on a spiritual quest, practising penances and deep meditation. After he attained *nirvana* (enlightenment), he travelled to preach the tenets of Buddhism, a religion of compassion and practical wisdom. Righteousness and prudence, he said, were the means to avoid misery. He outlined the Four Great Truths: suffering exists; it is caused by desire; removal of desire brings release from misery; this is possible by following the Middle or Eightfold Path, the "middle way" of right conduct between asceticism and pleasure, aimed at *moksha* (release from suffering). The Sanchi stupas were built in homage to the Buddha from the 3rd century BCE to the 7th century CE. Below are the dates of some rulers associated with the site.

- c.320–298 BCE **Chandragupta Maurya** establishes the first empire in India, with its capital at Pataliputra.

- c.268–231 BCE **Ashoka**, Chandragupta Maurya's son, rules; Buddhism becomes the official religion.

- c.185–73 BCE **Sunga dynasty** holds sway over the Ganga plain in the north.

- c.50 BCE–250 CE **Satavahana dynasty** reigns over an independent kingdom in northern India.

- c.320–550 CE **Gupta emperors** dominate northern India; a great cultural flowering takes place.

- c.606–647 CE **Harshavardhana** achieves political unity in northern India.

Royal Patrons of Buddhism

Ruthless and strong-willed at first, Ashoka wrested the Mauryan throne from his brothers after fierce strife. The conquest of Kalinga, a neighbouring kingdom (modern Orissa), was a turning point in Ashoka's life. Deeply affected by this battle, which claimed more than 100,000 lives, Ashoka renounced war and sought solace in Buddhism. After this radical change, he began to set out his ethical code on rocks and tall, free-standing pillars all over his vast empire. These inscriptions ordered his subjects to respect all religions, to be honest, to practise charity, and to avoid killing animals. Ashoka also built many stupas enshrining Buddhist relics, including a small brick mound, which was later encased in stone to be transformed into the Great Stupa. It is said that he chose the site not only for its strategic position but because the nearby city of Vidisha was the parental home of Devi, his favourite queen.

ROYAL PROCESSION ⊱
This bas-relief on a gateway at Sanchi shows a royal personage, identified by experts as Emperor Ashoka, on a horse, and accompanied by his queens.

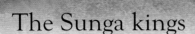

The Sunga kings

The Mauryan empire continued for some decades after Ashoka's death until, in a dramatic move, Pushyamitra Sunga, a general in the Mauryan army, assassinated Emperor Brihadratha and usurped the throne. This signalled the end of the Mauryan empire and the beginning of the Sunga dynasty, which ruled over the Ganga plains until the 1st century BCE. Buddhism continued to flourish and Ashoka's brick stupa was reconstructed, with additions of a circumambulatory path, a terrace, a flight of stairs to the terrace, and balustrades.

BALUSTRADE OF GREAT STUPA'S STAIRCASE

The Satavahanas

Numerous dynasties arose after the decline of the Mauryas, one of the most powerful being the Satavahanas. They reigned over northern-central India, with their kingdom extending to the river Krishna in the south. Splendid *toranas* (ceremonial gateways) were added to the Great Stupa during this period, as stated in an inscription on the South Torana, recording the offerings of Ananda, chief artisan in the court of Gautamiputra Satakarni (c.106–130 CE), the greatest Satavahana ruler.

The Gupta emperors

Named after Chandra Gupta I, who was crowned emperor in the old Mauryan capital of Pataliputra, the Gupta dynasty ruled for over two centuries. This period was marked by fine sculpture, vibrant Sanskrit poetry and drama, and revolutionary advances in mathematics and astronomy. The empire covered most of the Ganga plain and central India under Samudra Gupta and Chandra Gupta II. Royal patronage of Buddhism continued and statues of the Buddha were installed in Sanchi. The Guptas declined after 450 CE.

BUDDHIST SYMBOLS

Before the Gupta age, the Buddha was represented only by symbols – the lotus symbolizing his divine birth, the Bodhi tree, his enlightenment, and the *dharmachakra* (Wheel of Law), his First Sermon. An important Buddhist symbol is the footprint, which signifies his eternal presence. It also represents the first step that he took after enlightenment.

FOOTPRINTS IN STONE

Sacred Symmetry

The stupa represents the teachings and practices of Buddhism. Intended as a replica of the universe, it is imbued with cosmic significance. The *anda* (hemispherical mound), which rises from a low, cylindrical base, represents the dome of heaven. On its summit is the *yasti* (finial), which represents the ascending heavens. Reaching skywards, it is often in the form of one or more *chhatras* (umbrella-like tiers) and fenced in by a square *harmika* (railing). The cosmic symbolism is reinforced by four free-standing *toranas* (gateways), which mark the axial points on the path around the structure, indicating the rotational movement of celestial bodies. Built initially of bricks and packed earth, and encircled by balustrades, the stupa was eventually clad in finely finished stone. The structure is perfect in its symmetry, signifying balance, constancy, unity, and strength.

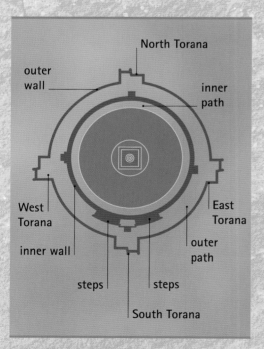

⚜ STUPA STRUCTURE
This aerial view shows the essential features of the Great Stupa; the relic chamber in the heart of the stupa was filled in by archaeologists in 1881.

The Great Stupa

Majestic and serene, the Great Stupa (numbered Stupa 1 by John Marshall) has witnessed the passage of centuries. It stands on a flat-topped hill within a monastic complex, which includes several other stupas and monasteries. The Great Stupa is 40m (131ft) in diameter and 16.5m (55ft) high, its plain façade contrasting with the exuberantly carved posts and railings of its balustrades. It can be approached through four grand *toranas*, also richly embellished with emblems and narrative scenes.

North entrance

A pathway from the main gate to the stupa runs past a peepul tree (*Ficus religiosa*) – it is said to have grown from a sapling taken from the original Bodhi ("Wisdom") tree under which the Buddha sat when he attained enlightenment. The pathway leads to the North Torana from where the Great Stupa can be entered. From here, the processional path winds around the stupa. Steps from the South Torana lead up to a second, inner path on the terrace.

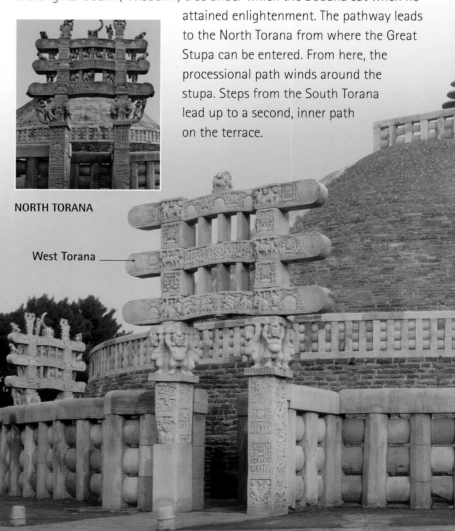

NORTH TORANA

West Torana

PINNACLE OF PIETY
The finial, a three-tiered stone parasol, symbolizing the layers of heaven, rises above the harmika (square railing).

Walking around the stupa

Meant for *pradakshina* (ritual circumambulation), two circular paths, the outer one at ground level and the inner one on the terrace, were built around the stupa during the Sunga period. This ritual holds a special significance for pilgrims, who focus on the heart of the stupa, where the relics of the Buddha once lay. They walk in a clockwise direction, with the right shoulder towards the stupa. Images of the Buddha, each facing one of the gateways, stand on the stone-paved path at ground level. A flight of steps leads up to the second path on the circular terrace. The paths and the staircase are encircled by balustrades, which are richly carved with flower, bird, and animal motifs within medallions and with inscriptions recording donations of individual balustrade panels by rich merchants.

square railing

circular terrace

ground–level balustrade

PATH ON TERRACE
This processional path on the terrace encircles the stupa, between the wall of the mound and the vedika *(balustrade). Visible from here is the North Torana.*

MEDITATING BUDDHA
This statue is one of the four life-sized sandstone images of the Buddha on the ground-level path. They were added in the 5th century BCE, in the Gupta age.

SYMBOLIC SHAPE
The oval shape of the Great Stupa rises above the balustrades and toranas; its form also represents the final deliverance of the Buddha from earthly misery.

Layout of the Sanchi complex

The Archaeological Museum stands at the bottom of the hill on which the Sanchi complex lies. A path leads up from here to an enclosure ringed by a stone wall (10th or 11th century), which contains most of the buildings of Sanchi. The complex is divided up into the Main Terrace, the Eastern Area, the Southern Area, and the Western Slope. On the Main Terrace are the Great Stupa, Stupas 3 to 16, Pillars 10 and 35, and Temples 17, 18, and 31. In the Eastern Area lie Temple and Monastery 45 with other monasteries and Buildings 32, 43, 49, and 50 (not shown in the diagram below). The Southern Area includes only remains of structures, such as Temple 40. Another path from the West Torana of the Great Stupa leads to the Western Slope, where Monastery 51 and Stupa 2 stand. Below this is an ancient track paved with stone slabs, which begins from Stupa 7, passes by Stupa 2, and descends to the plains.

♥ **BUILT ON A PLATFORM**
Constructed on the base of an earlier brick structure, the Great Stupa stands on a platform that is 40m (131ft) in diameter.

West Torana

South Torana

COMPLEX PLAN

N

→ Path
☐ Area illustrated to the right

Western Slope

Main Terrace

Eastern Area

Southern Area

1. Entrance
2. Great Stupa
3. North Torana
4. East Torana
5. South Torana
6. West Torana
7. Stupa 3
8. Stupa 4
9. Stupa 5
10. Temple 31
11. Stupas 26, 27
12. Temple and Monastary 45
13. Stupas 12, 13, 14, 16
14. Temple 17
15. Temple 18
16. Pillar 10
17. Stupa 7
18. Pillar 35
19. Monastary 51
20. The Great Bowl
21. Stupa 2

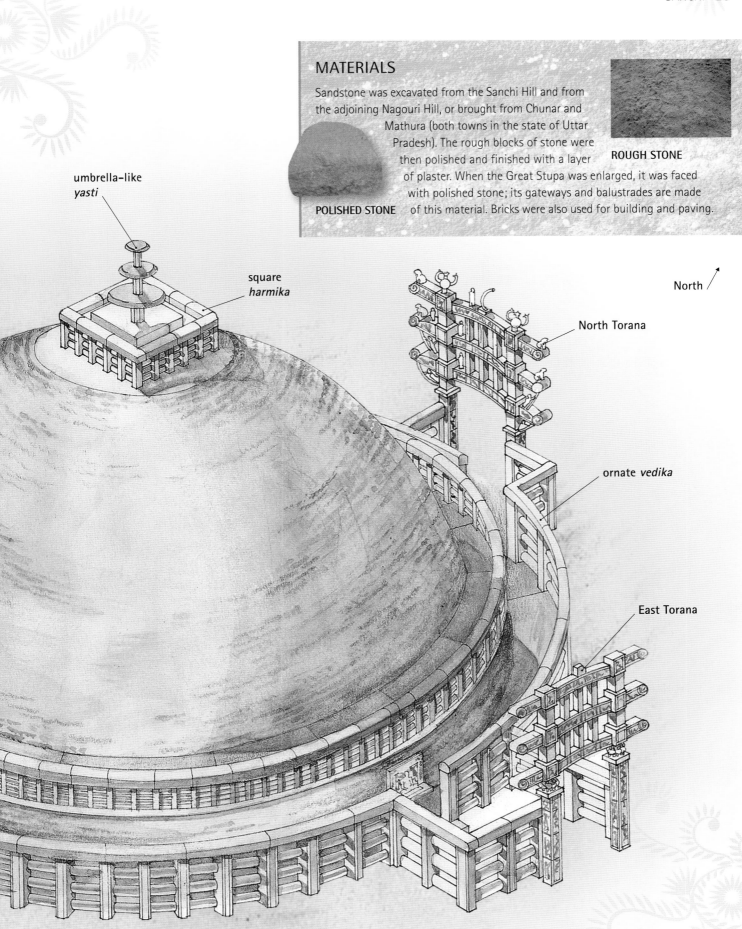

umbrella–like
yasti

square
harmika

North

North Torana

ornate *vedika*

East Torana

MATERIALS

Sandstone was excavated from the Sanchi Hill and from the adjoining Nagouri Hill, or brought from Chunar and Mathura (both towns in the state of Uttar Pradesh). The rough blocks of stone were then polished and finished with a layer of plaster. When the Great Stupa was enlarged, it was faced with polished stone; its gateways and balustrades are made of this material. Bricks were also used for building and paving.

ROUGH STONE

POLISHED STONE

North Torana

The Great Stupa's main charm lies in its four stone *toranas*, each bearing lively sculptures. Like the other three, the North Torana is 9m (30ft) in height, and consists of two square pillars and three architraves with scrolled ends. The carvings on this *torana* show the Buddha leaving his palace, preaching in a grove, and performing miracles. They also include grand royal processions and life-like animal figures, such as horses, lions, elephants, and a monkey offering the Buddha honey.

— ornate bracelets

⟨ GATE GUARDIAN
This turbanned, bejewelled dwarapala (doorkeeper) poses gracefully on the North Torana.

ETERNAL SYMBOLS ⟩
Crowning the North Torana are triratnas, tridents symbolizing the Buddha and his teachings.

South Torana

Although the South Torana is the most damaged of the gates, many exquisite carvings remain intact. Among these, on the west pillar, are reliefs portraying devotees paying homage to the Wheel of Law and worshipping the Buddha's turban. Stupas and trees, representing the Manushi Buddhas, predecessors of the Buddha, cover the upper architrave, while a raging battle over the Buddha's relics can be seen on the lowest one.

MAURYAN CAPITAL ⟩
Majestic lions stand as emblems of royal authority on a South Torana pillar.

CELESTIAL NYMPH ❧
Supporting the lowest architrave of the East Torana is this yakshi, a symbol of fertility, posing under a mango tree.

East Torana

The carvings on this gateway include scenes portraying worship of the stupa, and events in the Buddha's life, such as a royal retinue at the palace of Kapilavastu, his home before he renounced his princely life. Across the middle architrave is a depiction of the "Great Departure" when the Buddha, shown as a riderless horse, leaves his home. In a continuous narrative, the carvings from right to left show the ride away from the palace using three successive horse images. The episode ends when the Buddha, now a parasol above footprints, dismounts from his horse. Also depicted is Maya, the Buddha's mother, and her dream of a white elephant, signifying the imminent birth of her son.

West Torana

This gateway had collapsed by the mid-19th century, but was then restored by British archaeologists. Like the other gateways, its architraves portray the Buddha in various scenes. The topmost one shows him in seven different incarnations, while the lowest one shows panic-stricken demons fleeing in disarray, their expressions of fear vividly recreated. They are confronted by a parasol, a symbol of the Buddha's enlightenment, which seems to terrify them.

expressive faces

POT-BELLIED DWARFS ❧
The capitals are supported by quartets of dwarfs with grimacing faces and grotesquely fat stomachs.

Stories in stone

The *Jataka* stories are vibrant morality tales revolving around the 550 incarnations of the Buddha before he attained enlightenment. They offer practical wisdom linked to the Buddha's Four Noble Truths and the Middle Path of right understanding, thought, speech, action, effort, livelihood, mindfulness, and concentration. In his previous incarnations as a Bodhisattva (enlightened being), the Buddha is believed to have been born as a human or an animal, such as a deer or an elephant. Each architrave of the Great Stupa's four *toranas* bears sculptures narrating these stories, which are related to Bodhisattvas, such as Chhaddanta, an elephant who helped a hunter to saw off his own tusks, which the queen of Varanasi (Chhaddanta's jealous wife from a previous birth) ordered. The queen then died of remorse. The other stories include those of Sama (who represents filial love), Mahakapi, Vessantra, and Alambasa (a hermit). It is believed that the Buddha accumulated virtue by good deeds in his earlier lives, which helped him to achieve *nirvana* (enlightenment) in his final life.

⚜ CHHADDANTA JATAKA
This frieze on the South Torana's middle architrave shows Chhaddanta , a Bodhisattva born as the six-tusked king of elephants, with his herd in a forest.

⚜ MAHAKAPI JATAKA
Narrated on the top architrave of the West Torana is the story of Mahakapi, the chief of 80,000 monkeys, who selflessly gave up his life for his subjects.

Vessantara Jataka

Featured on the lowest architrave of the North Torana is the tale of Vessantara, a prince renowned for his charity. He was banished from his palace when he gave away his father's auspicious royal elephant, who was believed to bring rain. Vessantara left the palace in a chariot with his family and lived as a hermit in a forest. On the right of the architrave is the scene of Vessantara sitting with his wife, Maddi, in the hermitage. He gave his wife and children away as well, but the story ended happily, for the gods had wanted only to test the prince's generosity.

Animated scenes

Carved on the pillars of each *torana* are bas-reliefs depicting the great events in the Buddha's life – his birth, enlightenment, the First Sermon, and his *parinirvana* (demise). The Sanchi sculptors recreated a pulsating world of human beings – dancing, singing, forming processions, and carrying out household tasks, such as pounding rice and fetching water from a river

⚘ MIRACLE OF WOOD AND FIRE

The ascetics of Uruvela could not cut wood or light a fire because the Buddha had quenched the flames. This scene is portrayed on the south pillar of the East Torana.

– each scene vibrantly portraying everyday life in the 1st century BCE. Many scenes show the miracles the Buddha performed to win over the Kashyapa brothers, ascetics who lived in the jungle of Uruvela and refused to follow his teachings. These miracles include the Buddha walking on air and across a flooded river.

⚘ MIRACLE OF THE SERPENT

This scene on the south pillar of the East Torana shows a fire temple inhabited by a poisonous snake. When the Buddha went inside, the snake meekly crawled into his begging bowl.

THE FIRST SERMON

One of the most significant events in the Buddha's life was his First Sermon at Sarnath, in eastern India, in which he outlined the Four Noble Truths. The First Sermon is represented by the Wheel of Law, set in motion when the newly enlightened Buddha pronounced his first doctrine. The wheel, a recurring motif on the *toranas*, also symbolizes the sun of knowledge, which relieves spiritual darkness. The relief (below) from a pillar on the South Torana, shows disciples and deer paying homage to it.

symbolic parasol

THE WHEEL OF LAW

STUPA IN HOMAGE TO THE BUDDHA'S DISCIPLES

Stupa 3

In the main area, to the northeast of the Great Stupa, is Stupa 3 of the Sunga era (c.185–73 BCE). Reached through a single *torana* and capped by a stone umbrella, it once enshrined the relics of Sariputra and Moudgalyayana, the Buddha's earliest disciples. This stupa is modelled on the Great Stupa, but its dome is more hemispherical. Carvings on the upper architraves of the gateway depict stories about the Bodhisattvas. On the lowest architrave are scenes in paradise, with images such as tortoises and *makara*s (mythical beasts).

☙ GOD OF THUNDER AND RAIN
Portrayed in stone on the lowest architrave of the gateway is Indra, god of thunder and rain, sitting in paradise (Nandavan) with his wife Sachi, while minstrels stand in attendance.

Stupa 4

Behind Stupa 3, amid the ruins of several masonry stupas from the 2nd century BCE to the 7th century CE, is Stupa 4, probably built in the 2nd century BCE. Near it is a stone panel that may have been part of the stupa's balustrade. It bears carvings of lotus buds and flowers, leaves, and birds.

☙ ANCIENT MOUND
Looking unfinished, Stupa 4 stands forlornly, a plain, circular mound of masonry, without gateways or any embellishment.

Stupa 5

A number of stupas, temples, and monasteries were added to the Sanchi complex during the reign of Emperor Harshavardhana, a Buddhist, who ruled northern India from Kanauj during the 7th century CE. Among them is Stupa 5, a flattened structure built on a circular plinth, which is located to the south of Stupa 3.

◈ LONE PEDESTAL
On the southern side of Stupa 5 is a stone pedestal on which an image of the Buddha (now in the Sanchi ASI Museum) once stood.

Temple 31

Built first in the 6th or 7th century and reconstructed in the 10th or 11th century, Temple 31 belongs to the Satavahana period. To the left of the steps leading to its platform is a magnificent 4th-century statue of a *nagini* (snake deity) in human form with snake coils as a backdrop. The inner sanctum is now closed to protect a statue of the Buddha belonging to the Gupta period, which has a richly carved halo and is seated on a double-petalled lotus.

cobra hood

♥ TEMPLE RUINS
Rectangular in shape and flat-roofed, Temple 31 now has a bare appearance.

SNAKE DEITY

Temple and Monastery 45

Opposite the East Torana of the Great Stupa is a flight of steps that leads to the terrace of the Eastern Area. Here are several structures and ruins of the medieval period (7th to 11th centuries), numbered 43 to 50 by Sir John Marshall, and an array of detached carvings, small votive stupas, and statues. Monastery 45, once a monastic complex, lies here and within its square courtyard is Temple 45 (only the ruins of Monastery 45 are now visible to the east of Temple 45). Although Temple 45 still stands proudly, only vestiges of its original splendour and exuberance of decoration can be seen. It was rebuilt in the 9th or 10th century, on the remains of an earlier temple that was destroyed in a fire. Planned as a courtyard, its square *garbha-griha* (sanctum), crowned by the ruins of a hollow *shikhara* (spire in the northern Indian style), is surrounded by a passageway on three sides. To the west are traces of a columned hall.

DOORWAY PILLARS ✣
The pillars flanking the doorway to the sanctum are decorated with human figures, statues of lions, and lotus motifs.

✿ **THE BUDDHA OF WISDOM**
Sitting on a lotus in a niche on the southern outer wall of Temple 45 is this 10th-century statue of Manjusri, the Wisdom Buddha.

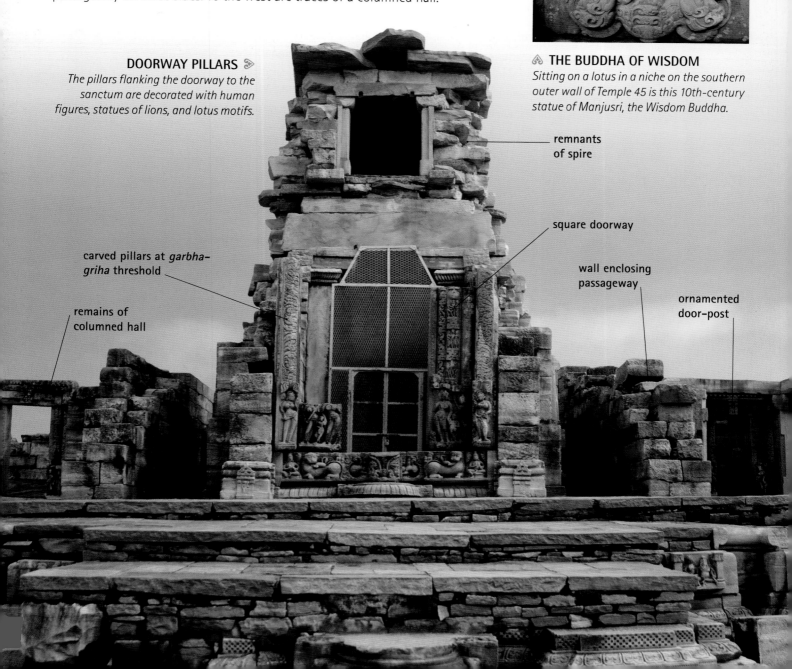

remnants of spire

square doorway

wall enclosing passageway

ornamented door-post

carved pillars at *garbha-griha* threshold

remains of columned hall

Verandah and chambers of Temple 45

To the right of the main structure of Temple 45 are the remains of a
wall enclosing a passageway, next to which are three chambers and
a verandah. In the verandah is a statue of the Buddha, dated to
around the 10th century. It is seated on a double-petalled lotus
and is crowned by a halo. The chambers are entered through richly
carved door-posts.

✸ BUDDHA WITH A HALO
*This statue of the Buddha in the verandah
of Temple 45 sits in a meditative pose; the
oval halo, lavishly carved with floral motifs,
enhances its quiet serenity.*

✸ DOOR-POST
*This ornamental entrance
to a chamber of Temple 45
is decorated with exquisite,
detailed sculptures.*

floral motifs

finely sculpted
human figures

goddess holding
a mace

diaphanous
attire

TIMELESS FIGURES ✸
*Still posing on the door-post
are the river goddesses,
Ganga and Yamuna*

Temple 17

A significant architectural structure of the Gupta period (5th century CE) is the flat-roofed Temple 17, which stands on a moulded basement to the south of the Great Stupa. It is one of the earliest well-preserved stone temples in India, but its sanctum is empty today. Captain F. C. Maisey, a British army officer who excavated the site in 1851, described a Buddhist image that existed there, but it had disappeared by the time John Marshall arrived at the site in 1912. The temple has a flat roof, a four-columned porch, and a square sanctuary. The doorway bears vertical bands with leaf and rosette patterns carved on them. Temple 17 is remarkable for its symmetrical proportions and stark grandeur.

SQUARE CAPITALS
Surmounting each column of Temple 17 is a square stone capital composed of four double-bodied lions seated at the corners.

FREE-STANDING COLUMNS
Four grand columns support the porch of Temple 17, each crowned by inverted lotuses, which, in turn, are capped by a capital with sculpted lions.

Other stupas

Several remains of other stupas, dating from the 2nd century BCE to the 7th century CE, dot the Main Terrace. Among them are Stupas 12, 13, 14, and 16. A fragment of an inscribed image of Maitreya (the "future Buddha") was excavated near Stupa 12, while a Buddha statue was found on a wall of Stupa 14. A short distance away (near Stupa 5), Stupas 28 and 29 have interesting square bases, with mouldings characteristic of the early Gupta age. A highly polished fragment of a vase – probably of the Mauryan or Sunga era – was found near Stupa 29.

SMALLER MOUNDS
Composed of masonry, these stupas convey an idea of what the original Great Stupa must have looked like when its core was constructed by Ashoka.

♥ SANDSTONE PILLARS
The tall pillars of Temple 18 are topped by octagonal capitals, each framed by medallions and carved petals.

SYMBOL OF PERFECTION

The neck of each column in the porch of Temple 17 is in the shape of an inverted lotus, with deeply etched stylized petals. An emblem of perfection and of Buddha's teaching, the flower is a recurring motif in Buddhist art and architecture. This exquisite symmetrically shaped flower, which rises from mud, signifies the purity of the soul transformed by enlightenment.

INVERTED LOTUS

Temple 18

Facing the South Torana of the Great Stupa are the imposing sandstone pillars of Temple 18 (only nine out of the original 12 survive), each 5.18m (17ft) high and decorated with medallions framing the capitals. The structure was built in the 7th century CE, on the foundations of an earlier *chaitya-griha* (prayer hall), and consists of an apse, a central nave, and aisles. The floor level was raised in the 10th–11th century CE and door-jambs were added, decorated with an image of Ganga, the river goddess, and her attendants as well as bands of floral motifs. These are now in the Archaeological Museum at the site.

Pillar 10

To the right of the South Torana of the Great Stupa is Pillar 10, or rather, only its rounded lower portion, with a glistening surface of polished sandstone. Erected by Emperor Ashoka in the 3rd century BCE, it is the oldest free-standing pillar in Sanchi, and was once crowned by a fine capital (right), now in the ASI Museum on the Sanchi site. Remarkable for its aesthetic proportion and structural balance, the capital is composed of four sculpted lions seated back-to-back, similar to the more famous capital of the Sarnath "Pillar of Law" (the emblem of the Republic of India). Unlike the Sarnath Pillar, the pillar at Sanchi does not support a Wheel of Law; instead, flower motifs can be seen above the lions.

carvings of geese and flowers _____

inverted lotus _____

REGAL LIONS ✎
Exuding a timeless vigour, these lions sit on a pedestal composed of a bell-shaped lotus and a circular stone slab adorned with fine carving.

✎ BROKEN SHAFT
Cut from Chunar sandstone, this highly polished monolithic pillar, now broken, exemplifies the skill and artistry of Mauryan sculpture. The pillar was used as a sugarcane press by a local landlord in the 19th century CE.

✎ ASHOKA'S EDICT
This inscription on the pillar records a warning to Buddhist monks of punishment if they caused a schism in the sangha (brotherhood of monks).

Pillar 35

A short walk from the South towards the North Torana of the Great Stupa leads to the pedestal of Pillar 35 (the Vajrapani Pillar), which was once surmounted by an exquisite figure of the Bodhisattva Vajrapani, who represents the energy of the enlightened mind. Now exhibited in the Archaeological Museum at Sanchi, the figure is identifiable by the fragmented *vajra* (thunderbolt) on the right hip. It is dressed in a *dhoti* (loin cloth) and heavy jewellery – earrings, necklace, and bracelets. A halo rising above the richly ornamented *kirtimukha* (head-dress) has 24 small holes around it.

MASSIVE PEDESTAL
The lower portion of the pillar, with its lotus-shaped base, still stands solidly on a square stone pedestal, with a balustrade carved in relief.

Stupa 7

From the West Torana of the Great Stupa, a path stretching about 30m (90ft) towards the southwest leads to another small stupa. This is Stupa 7, similar in structure to Stupas 12, 13, 14, and 15, in its square plinth and mound-like appearance. However, it stands apart from these stupas due to the presence of a finial, a feature missing in the other small structures. Also built of masonry, the stupa, probably built later than the 7th century, is surrounded by the ruins of a terrace, and rises to a height of about 2.15m (8ft). An ancient path, which is flanked by ruins, begins near Stupa 7 and leads to Stupa 2.

VOTIVE STUPAS

A cluster of 24 votive stupas (replicas of actual stupas, left as offerings by pilgrims), was excavated in 1993–94, when excavators of the Archaeological Survey of India worked on restoring the site. Miniature in size – only 1m (3ft) high – they stand on the Sanchi Hill, within an enclosure, and date back to the 3rd century BCE.

image of the Buddha
bell-shaped form
STUPA REPLICA

STONE PARASOL
Standing tall on the flat roof of Stupa 7 is this finial; its umbrella shape symbolizes the Buddha's protection of his devotees.

Monastery 51

Leading down to the third group of monuments, which lie on the Western Slope, is a flight of steps just opposite the West Torana of the Great Stupa. Here, on a rocky ledge on the lowest slope, is the most interesting monastic building in the Sanchi complex – the 7th-century Monastery 51. Fairly well preserved, it is enclosed by stone walls faced with flat bricks. The monastery is entered through two massive buttresses, from which the central courtyard opens out. The courtyard itself is paved with bricks. In the centre of the west side is a large chamber, which may have been used as a chapel, but seems more like a passageway now. Excavations around this chamber revealed that a Buddha statue may have been enshrined here.

⚜ MONASTERY 51
The plan of Monastery 51 is a central courtyard enclosed by a colonnaded verandah; behind the verandah is a line of 22 monks' cells.

❦ WINGED BEAST
Carved on the balustrade of Stupa 2 is a plethora of fanciful creatures, such as this mythical hybrid animal.

THE GREAT BOWL

Just a short walk from the west gateway of Stupa 2 (and southeast from Monastery 51) is a gigantic begging bowl carved out of a single block of rock, perhaps from a boulder. Excavations of the area around it in 1996 revealed that it was deeply embedded in soil, which was surrounded by boulders to hold the loose earth. The monks of Sanchi used it as a container to deposit foodgrains given to them as alms. At one time, there must have been

hundreds of monks living in Sanchi, which explains the size of the bowl, and may have also been a point of convergence for all the pilgrims who visited the Sanchi complex over the centuries.

ALMS CONTAINER

Stupa 2

Below the Great Stupa, on the Western Slope, is Stupa 2, which was built in the 2nd century BCE. Although it has a plain appearance, its balustrade, with four L-shaped passages leading to the circumambulatory path, is lavishly decorated. Among the motifs on the balustrade are scenes with animal figures, such as a deer and elephant being attacked by lions, and hybrid creatures, such as a horse-headed female. Other images of note are those of Goddess Lakshmi, a crocodile eating a fish, and *yakshas*. The reliefs of Stupa 2 are in the style of the moulded terracotta plaques typical of the Sunga period.

✦ HOODED SNAKE
The sinuous curves of this stone serpent coil within a medallion on the balustrade that encircles Stupa 2.

✦ MOTIFS AND INSCRIPTIONS
The balustrade of Stupa 2 bears a rich variety of floral and figural motifs and inscriptions recording donations.

flat-topped structure

stone balustrade

Mamallapuram

Mamallapuram, named after Mamalla, as the Pallava king Narasimhavarman I (630-668 CE) was also known, was used as a harbour by the Pallavas, south India's first imperial power. Today, it is a quiet fishing town, also known as Mahabalipuram, 60km (37 miles) from the city of Chennai (earlier known as Madras). Its architecture has earned it the status of a UNESCO World Heritage Site. Mamallapuram is also a popular tourist spot offering a combination of sun, surf, and ruins. Scattered among the rocky hillocks are the dramatic Shore Temple, magnificent rock-cut temples, and detailed tableaux that recreate familiar Hindu legends. Hindu mythology comes alive with dramatic depictions of popular stories – the descent of the river Ganges, the struggle for power between goddess Durga and a demon, and the miracle of Lord Krishna lifting a mountain with one finger. Built largely during the reigns of Narasimhavarman and his successor Rajasimhavarman, these temples show the evolution from rock-cut architecture to structured building. They represent some of the finest examples of early temple art in India. It has been suggested that some of these temples were not built for worship but this site served as a school for young sculptors and a platform to showcase the talents of local artists. Today, 14 centuries after the rocks of Mamallapuram were transformed into beautiful masterpieces, the legacy continues on every street corner where artists and sculptors may be found chipping away at lumps of stone to produce remarkable likenesses to the Hindu gods and godesses.

ROCKY LEGACIES
The Mamallapuram monuments lie along the coast of Tamil Nadu.

Chennai

The Pallavas

The Pallava kings ruled over the Deccan region of south India for about 600 years, from the 4th to the 9th centuries CE, rising to prominence under Simhavarma. While one school of thought states they were rivals of the Satavahanas who ruled in what became the modern state of Andhra Pradesh, another theory traces their origins to the Pahlavas from Persia. Pallava culture reached a high point under King Mahendravarman I, who was a painter, musician-composer, and architect. Later, King Narasimhavarman II constructed the Shore Temple at Mamallapuram. The Pallavas fought many wars with other rulers of the Deccan such as the Chalukyas and the Pandyas. The Pallavas flourished till the 8th century, after which they began to decline due to the combined onslaught of the Pandyas and the Cholas.

- c.535–580 **Simhavarma II**

- c.580 **Simhavishnuvarman**

- c.580–630 **Mahendravarman I**

- c.630–668 **Narasimhavarman I (Mamalla)**

- 668–672 **Mahendravarman II**

- 672–700 **Parmesvaravarman I**

- 700–728 **Narasimhavarman II (Rajasimha)**

- **Mahendravarman III** (co-ruler)

- 728–731 **Parmesvaravarman II**

- 731–796 **Nandivarman II Pallavamalla**

- 894 Pallava rule comes to an end.

A Magnificent Heritage

It was the Pallavas who put Mamallapuram on the map of India's great architectural heritage. Although their capital was at Kanchipuram — about 70km (44 miles) west of Chennai — it was at Mamallapuram that they created their most exquisite works of art. The earliest patrons of Tamil art, they helped establish a distinct Tamil identity through the development of music, dance, poetry, and sculpture. The greatest achievement of these pioneering rulers of south India was in architecture – they created a style so fresh and daring that it influenced Tamil temple-building for centuries to come.

KING MAMALLA
King Narasimhavarman I is portrayed in one of the panels of the Dharmaraja Ratha (see p.53).

Kings and queens

There are two royal sculptures in the Adi Varaha rock-cut *mandapa* (pillared hall) in Mamallapuram. One of these (left), shows a king with his two queens next to him. An inscription in the Pallava Grantha script declares that this is "The illustrious Mahendra-Pallava, Supreme King". The other sculpture (below) is of a seated king flanked by his queens, with an inscription that identifies the king as "The illustrious Simhavishnu-Pallava, Supreme King". After much debate, it is now accepted that these represent Mahendravarman and Narasimhavarman I (Mamalla) respectively.

⚜ REGAL PORTRAIT
King Mahendravarman is gesturing and appears to be leading his queens somewhere. Note the lively postures in contrast to the formality of the group in the picture to the right.

KING NARASIMHAVARMAN I SEATED

Maritime trade

Mamallapuram was a prominent sea port from the beginning of the 1st century CE. The discovery of 4th century Roman coins indicates that Mamallapuram had trade contacts with the Roman world. The Pallavas were great seafarers and had overseas contacts with Ceylon (now Sri Lanka), China, and some Southeast Asian countries. King Narasimhavarman had the foresight to build a naval base here.

⚓ SEA PORT
Using their extensive trading network, the Pallavas also transported culture and Hinduism across the seas.

Rocky Splendour

The finest examples of temple architecture in south India belong to the Pallava period. The temple architecture of the Pallavas is divided into two groups: rock-cut (610–690) and structural (690–900). The greatest accomplishments of Pallava architecture are the rock-cut temples at Mamallapuram. These temples are further divided into *mandapas* (pillared halls) and *rathas* (chariots). Some common stylistic features of Pallava architecture include the following:

- **Dwarapalas**: armed doorkeepers on either side of the sanctum.
- **Pillars**: ornamented, both massive and slender.
- **Lions**: squatting or rearing, serving to support the pillars.
- **Somaskanda**: a family panel consisting of god Shiva with goddess Uma (Parvati) and their baby Skanda (Kartikeya).

Draupadi Ratha
Arjuna Ratha

THE LION PILLAR
Heraldic lions supporting pillars became a signature motif of southern architecture from Pallava times.

Kingdom by the Sea

The monuments at Mamallapuram may be categorized as *rathas* or chariot-shaped monolith temples; *mandapas* or pillared halls covered with bas-reliefs; open-air rock reliefs; and structural temples, constructed with slabs of stone. The Pancha Pandava Rathas (above) are named after the five Pandava brothers, heroes of the epic *Mahabharata*, and their wife Draupadi. Although *ratha* means "chariot", these *rathas* have been constructed without wheels.

Draupadi Ratha

Named after Draupadi, this is the smallest and simplest of all the *rathas*. In Hindu mythology, Draupadi was the shared wife of the Pandavas. The square temple has a simple roof, similar to a thatched hut, with decorated corners. This *ratha* is a shrine to goddess Durga. In front of the *ratha* is Durga's lion, which is the *vahana* (vehicle) of the goddess.

DURGA
Durga is surrounded by attendants in this ratha. *On the left, a devotee is kneeling before her, preparing to cut off his own head as a sacrifice.*

Bhima Ratha

Nakula–Sahadeva Ratha

Durga's lion

⚜ THE PANCHA PANDAVA RATHAS
Despite their names, these rathas *have no connection with the storyline of the epic* Mahabharata *or its heroes, and their naming was simply a local tradition.*

Arjuna Ratha

The Arjuna and the Draupadi Rathas share a platform, held up on the backs of elephants and lions. The Arjuna Ratha is dedicated to Shiva and almost replicates the Dharmaraja Ratha. The two-storeyed Arjuna Ratha resembles a small palace or pavilion, with sculpted pilasters, miniature roof shrines, and an octagonal dome, all characteristic features of later south Indian temples. The sanctum (innermost shrine) is empty except for a pedestal carved on the back wall. There is a veritable gallery of sculptures adorning the other three walls. These include both divine and human figures. A deity riding an elephant adorns one of the central niches and may be indentified as Subramanya, a son of Shiva. A life-size monolithic sculpture of Shiva's mount Nandi kneels behind the Arjuna Ratha, on the shrine's eastern side.

⚜ SHIVA LEANING ON NANDI
A sculpture of a four-armed Shiva leaning on Nandi, his bull, can be seen on one of the outer walls.

Layout of the Mamallapuram site

A visitor to Mamallapuram has a choice of starting the tour with any one of the three independent sites: the Shore Temple on the beach, the Pancha Pandava Rathas in a sandy compound, or the other temples that are grouped together on a rocky hillock. There are nine *rathas* in total in Mamallapuram. The illustration on the right shows the five Pancha Pandava Rathas – Draupadi Ratha, Arjuna Ratha, Bhima Ratha, Dharmaraja Ratha, and the Nakula-Sahadeva Ratha. These five *rathas* were built by Narasimhavarman I and are considered architectural wonders even today, though sea-erosion has taken its toll on the structures. It is conjectured that the *rathas* were never used for worship. The Ganesha Ratha is found with the *mandapas* on the hillock. The other three *rathas* are located outside the complex, on the outskirts of the town – they are the Valayankuttai Ratha and the two Pidari Rathas.

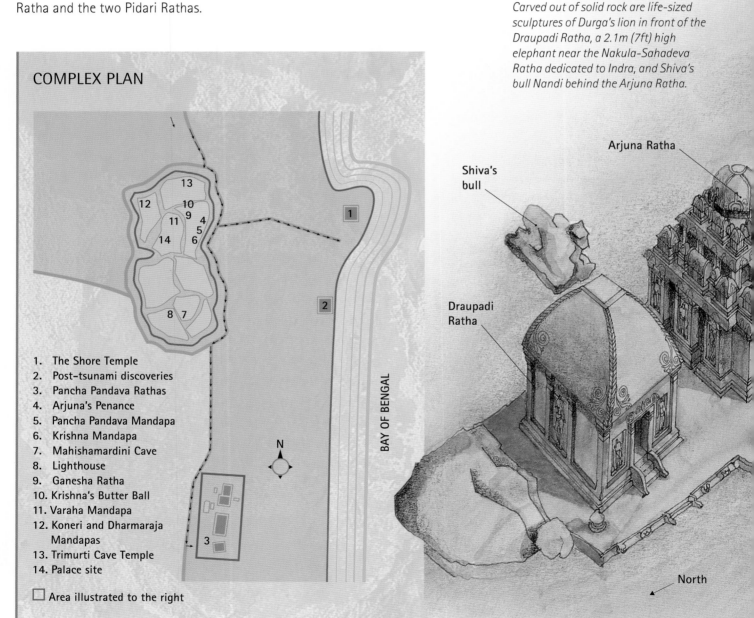

◈ VEHICLES FOR THE GODS
Carved out of solid rock are life-sized sculptures of Durga's lion in front of the Draupadi Ratha, a 2.1m (7ft) high elephant near the Nakula-Sahadeva Ratha dedicated to Indra, and Shiva's bull Nandi behind the Arjuna Ratha.

COMPLEX PLAN

1. The Shore Temple
2. Post-tsunami discoveries
3. Pancha Pandava Rathas
4. Arjuna's Penance
5. Pancha Pandava Mandapa
6. Krishna Mandapa
7. Mahishamardini Cave
8. Lighthouse
9. Ganesha Ratha
10. Krishna's Butter Ball
11. Varaha Mandapa
12. Koneri and Dharmaraja Mandapas
13. Trimurti Cave Temple
14. Palace site

☐ Area illustrated to the right

BAY OF BENGAL

N

Shiva's bull

Arjuna Ratha

Draupadi Ratha

North

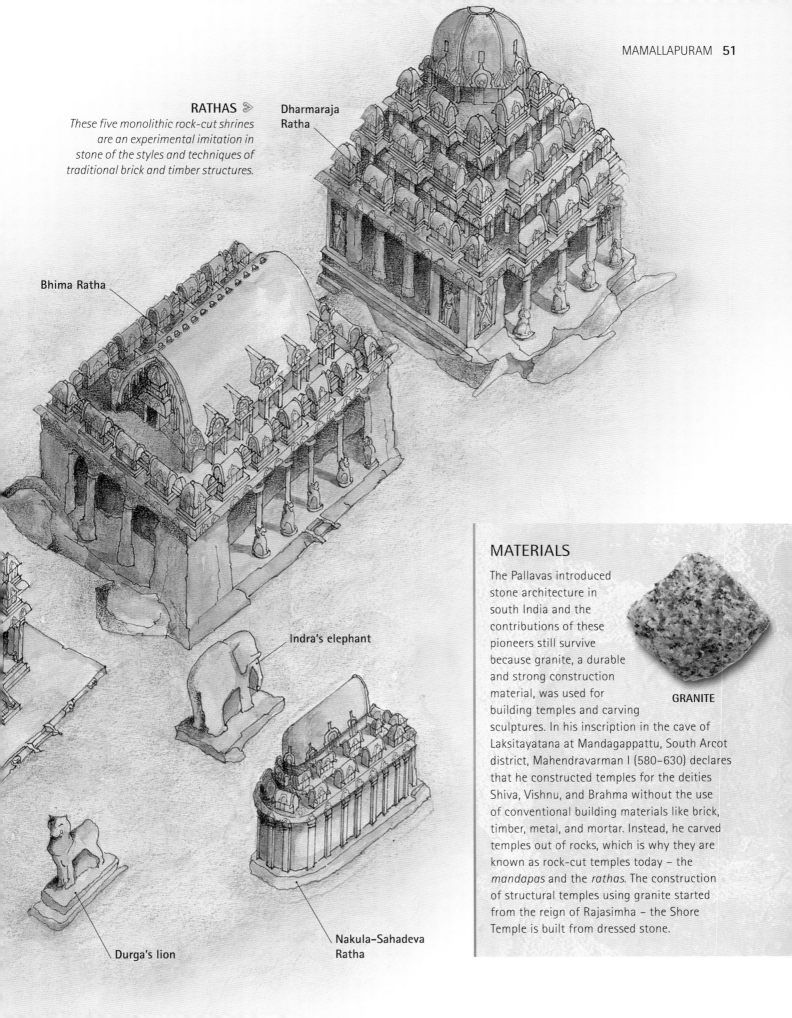

RATHAS 🔊
These five monolithic rock-cut shrines are an experimental imitation in stone of the styles and techniques of traditional brick and timber structures.

Dharmaraja Ratha

Bhima Ratha

Indra's elephant

Durga's lion

Nakula–Sahadeva Ratha

MATERIALS

The Pallavas introduced stone architecture in south India and the contributions of these pioneers still survive because granite, a durable and strong construction material, was used for building temples and carving

GRANITE

sculptures. In his inscription in the cave of Laksitayatana at Mandagappattu, South Arcot district, Mahendravarman I (580–630) declares that he constructed temples for the deities Shiva, Vishnu, and Brahma without the use of conventional building materials like brick, timber, metal, and mortar. Instead, he carved temples out of rocks, which is why they are known as rock-cut temples today – the *mandapas* and the *rathas*. The construction of structural temples using granite started from the reign of Rajasimha – the Shore Temple is built from dressed stone.

barrel-vaulted roof

elaborately-carved porch

Nakula–Sahadeva Ratha

This temple faces south and is named after the twins, Nakula and Sahadeva, the youngest Pandava brothers of the *Mahabharata*. There are no figure carvings on this temple, but the presence of the elephant confirms that the temple was consecrated to Indra whose mount was an elephant called Airavata. The temple is built in the *Gajaprishthakara* shape, resembling the rear end of an elephant.

elephant sculpture

☙ INDRA'S ABODE
This south-facing shrine has a curved rear similar to that of the 2.1m (7ft) elephant adjacent to it.

☙ APSIDAL SHAPE
The visual pun on the elephant's shape is best seen from the rear.

Bhima Ratha

Next to the Arjuna Ratha is the large Bhima Ratha, named after the strongest of the Pandava brothers. Reminiscent of palace architecture, the lower part of the shrine rests on an oblong base and is unfinished. The long, columned porch has a seated lion at the base of each pillar. The temple has a roof shaped like a wagon-top, and its single upper storey features false windows. What is noticeable in this shrine is the absence of carved figures on its walls. Though the sanctum is devoid of an idol, it was probably meant for the reclining form of Vishnu.

LARGEST RATHA

Dharmaraja Ratha

This unfinished *ratha* is named after Yudhishthira, the eldest of the Pandava brothers, who was also known as Dharmaraja. It is the southernmost temple in the group, and also the tallest. The upper part consists of three diminishing storeys. Topped by an octagonal-shaped dome, this *ratha* is about 13m (43ft) high and its square base is supported by figures of squatting lions. Its outer walls display an entire catalogue of Shiva iconography, including Shiva as Ardhanarisvara (half man, half woman). One of the figures depicted is the Pallava King Narasimhavarman I (see p.46).

ARDHANARISVARA
This four-armed half-man, half-woman figure balances the masculine strength of Shiva and the feminine grace of his consort Parvati.

octagonal-shaped dome

horseshoe-shaped arches

⚘ PALLAVA SCRIPT
Of the 18 Pallava Grantha inscriptions found in this ratha, 16 are single-word titles given mostly to Narasimhavarman I.

TALLEST RATHA

The temple on the shore

The Shore Temple complex was constructed in the 7th century during the reign of Narsimhavarman II (c.700-728). It consists of two shrines – one facing east and the other facing west – both of which are dedicated to Shiva. In between these two is an oblong, flat-roofed shrine housing Vishnu, who is represented as reclining on his serpent. The temple's *vimana* (towered roof of a sanctum) is four-tiered with an octagonal *shikhara* (spire above the sanctuary). Visitors are allowed access only to the external structures of the complex as the three inner shrines are cut off from public access by locked grill doors, permitting views of the interiors only through the grill. There is a large open court at the western end of the complex.

SOMASKANDA
The family panel consisting of Shiva and Parvati with their baby Skanda is on the inner rear wall of the temple facing east.

shikhara

IMPOSING SPIRE
This five-storeyed monument is a pyramidal structure 18m (60ft) high, and 15m (50 ft) square at the base.

vimana

temple facing east

temple facing west

MAJESTIC LION
A miniature Mahishamardini showing Durga as the demon slayer is carved on this lion sculpture in the courtyard of the temple.

Around the temple

The wall enclosing the temple has a series of Nandi bulls carved on it. The large open court at the western end has a *bali-pittha* (sacrificial altar), a large sculpture of Durga's lion, and a carved deer with a mutilated head. There is a damaged inscription consisting of six verses on the *bali-pittha*. The verses sing the praises of Rajasimha (Narasimhavarman II), extolling his qualities such as beauty, valour, and piety. One of these verses is identical to the last verse of the inscription found in the Kailasanatha Temple at Kanchipuram. According to popular belief, there were seven pagodas or temples along the shore but all barring one have been submerged; recent underwater archaeological explorations in the area have revealed many other structural remains.

THE BALI-PITTHA

RECENT EXCAVATIONS

Several buried structures around the Shore Temple were uncovered in the 1990s. One of the discoveries is a unique stepped structure, running north to south parallel to the Bay of Bengal, though its purpose is unknown. The steps consist of granite slabs with a core of laterite rock. The interlocking method used here prevented the slabs from collapsing. Other finds include a miniature shrine dedicated to Shiva and a sculpture of Varaha (the boar, which is one of the incarnations of Vishnu).

STEPPED STRUCTURE

boar form of Vishnu

VARAHA ⬙
The remains of a Varaha and a miniature shrine are enclosed in a small well on the north side of the temple.

Arjuna's Penance

A tour of the cave temples begins with this stunning open-air bas-relief (right) carved out of a monolith. A lively cast of characters from the celestial, temporal, and animal worlds has been depicted with masterly skill. A figure in yogic posture is believed by some to be Arjuna, the third of the Pandava brothers. Arjuna's Penance is a story from the *Mahabharata* that how Arjuna undertook rigorous penance in order to obtain Shiva's most powerful weapon. Most of the figures of animals and celestial beings are carved either facing or approaching the rock's central cleft.

THE PENANCE PANEL

⚜ THE PENANCE
The sage standing on one leg is said to be either Arjuna or King Bhagiratha doing penance to please Shiva.

UNFOLDING OF A LEGEND ⚜
Commissioned by Narasimhavarman I, this beautifully preserved open-air tableau is 29m (96ft) long and 13m (43ft) high in total.

Descent of the Ganges

Central to the theme of this panel (below) is the legend of the sacred river Ganges coming to earth, depicted by a natural cleft or fissure in the rock face. The yogic figure on one leg to the left of the river is believed by some scholars to be King Bhagiratha, who wanted to bring the river Ganges to earth to purify the souls of his ancestors. The legend relates that Shiva agreed to allow the sacred river to flow through his hair to break the force of its fall. In Pallava times, water may have flowed down the fissure from what was once a collecting pool above. To the right of the cleft, life-sized elephants protect their young.

female *naga*

CLEFT IN THE ROCK
The descent of the celestial river is represented by a natural cleft, which is filled with reverential nagas (snakes).

THE MONKEY GROUP
This realistic composition can be seen to the right of the tableau.

MAHISHAMARDINI PANEL
This panel in the Mahishamardini cave depicts the mythological story of Goddess Durga, the mother of the universe, vanquishing the demon Mahisha. The goddess has eight arms and is riding her ferocious lion while battling the buffalo-headed demon who is seen retreating with his army.

seated lion pillar

Cave temples

Sixteen man-made caves in different stages of completion are found scattered through the hilly area behind Arjuna's Penance. These cave sanctuaries were hewn out of the granite rock face. Most of the cave temples have an inner and outer *mandapa* (pillared hall). The outer *mandapa* has pillars, usually adorned with lions, and graceful columns. The inner *mandapa* contains one or more cells, usually decorated with exquisite sculptures of gods, goddesses, and mythological figures.

☙ PANCHA PANDAVA MANDAPA

Left of Arjuna's Penance is this cave temple of which only six lion pillars and pilasters (shallow rectangular columns) are finished. Lions and griffins with human riders decorate the brackets in the pillars.

Krishna Mandapa

The huge bas-relief in this cave, adjacent to the Pancha Pandava *mandapa*, depicts the story of Krishna lifting the Govardhana Hill to protect its cowherds and their cattle from a wrathful Indra. The figure of Krishna is surrounded by scenes of village life: a cowherd is milking a cow which is fondly licking its calf; another cowherd is playing a flute while the *gopis* (milkmaids) carry a pile of pots; a woodcutter is strolling with an axe; a child is taking a ride on the shoulder of an old man.

RAISING THE HILL ☙
Krishna is believed to have lifted the hill with his little finger, demonstrating his divine power and supremacy over Indra.

☙ PASTORAL SCENE
The elaborate bas-relief in the Krishna Mandapa was carved in the mid-7th century, probably predating the Arjuna's Penance panel.

Mahishamardini cave and the lighthouse

This triple-celled cave sanctuary has a central cell which has a carved Somaskanda panel. This is flanked by the Durga panel (see pp.58–59) and the Seshayi Vishnu panel. The Durga panel depicts the goddess defeating the Mahisha, the buffalo demon, which is why she is known as Mahishamardini (the destroyer of Mahisha). On the opposite side is a carving of Vishnu reclining on the great serpent Adisesha. The Olakaneswara (the flame-eyed Shiva) Temple, next to the New Lighthouse and just above the Mahishamardini cave, affords a splendid 360-degree view of the sea. A primitive lighthouse was set up on the roof of this temple during colonial times.

OLAKANESWARA TEMPLE

⚜ SESHASAYI VISHNU PANEL
A recumbent Vishnu resting under the protective hood of the five-headed serpent in this panel of enduring beauty is a Pallava masterpiece.

⚜ SOMASKANDA
The Somaskanda sculpture radiates peace, power, and wisdom. The idea behind the Somaskanda family panel is to depict the union of male and female energies.

Ganesha Ratha

Originally dedicated to Shiva, this two-storeyed rectangular shrine (right) is now dedicated to Ganesha. Said to have been built by Paramesvaravarman I (672-700), the temple features beautifully carved inscriptions listing his royal titles. The columned verandah has a *dwarapala* (doorkeeper) on either side. Between the *dwarapalas* are two lion pillars and two pilasters. It is the only shrine in Mahabalipuram where devotees actually offer prayers. Its sanctum originally had a *lingam* (the phallic symbol of Shiva), which is said to have been removed by the British in the late 18th century. The local people then probably put an image of Ganesha in the shrine.

dwarapala

WAGON ROOF ▷
The large barrel-vaulted and elaborately decorated roof with arched ends resembles the Bhima Ratha.

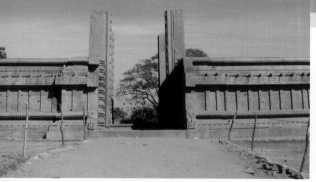

INCOMPLETE ORNATE GATEWAY

Raya Gopuram

Beyond the Varaha Mandapa (see p.63) is an unfinished *gopuram* (entrance tower). This incomplete yet impressive gateway is embellished with the ornate style of carvings typical of the Raya kings of the Vijayanagara empire in the 14th century. The Raya Gopuram is the second unfinished Vijayanagara *gopuram* that can be seen in Mamallapuram, the first being in the Sthala-Sayana temple, opposite Arjuna's Penance.

KRISHNA'S BUTTERBALL

Named after the mischievous god Krishna's fondness for butter, this gigantic monolith rests precariously on a narrow rock base to the right of the Ganesha Ratha and seems to defy the rules of gravity. Could it be one of Krishna's pranks? Legend has it that several Pallava kings attempted to move the stone, but neither the kings nor their elephants could shift the boulder by even an inch. Recent attempts to do so have failed as well.

natural granite rock

SIDE PROFILE ▷
Despite its massive size, this boulder lies perfectly balanced on a slender rock base.

Varaha Mandapa

This rock-cut hall built during the time of Narasimhavarman I has four impressive carvings of Vishnu, Trivikrama, Durga, and Gajalakshmi. Vishnu is shown in the Varaha *avatara* (form) saving the earth goddess, Bhumi Devi, from the clutches of a demon and being submerged in the ocean. The myth of Bhumi Devi also signifies the saving of mankind from the ocean of ignorance. Vishnu is also presented in the form of Trivikrama, the conqueror of the three worlds. The rear wall of the cave has a carving of Gajalakshmi (a form of Lakshmi) who is Vishnu's consort. In another panel, Durga riding her lion is engaged in a fierce battle with the buffalo-headed demon, Mahisha.

TRIVIKRAMA PANEL
In his Vamana form as a Brahmin dwarf, Vishnu subdues the demon Mahabali.

VARAHA CAVE ENTRANCE
Heraldic lions support the ornamental pillars, and the four panels of the famous Pallava doorkeepers are particularly noteworthy here.

GAJALAKSHMI PANEL
The goddess Lakshmi sits erect on a lotus while an elephant squirts holy water on her.

VARAHA PANEL
The gigantic figure of Varaha is holding aloft the tiny Bhumi Devi (earth goddess) to save her from drowning.

Koneri and Dharmaraja Mandapas

These two *mandapas* face west and share a wall. The Koneri Mandapa is an unfinished five-celled rock-cut temple with a central cell. It has four pillars supported by crouching lions and is flanked by pilasters. The Dharmaraja Mandapa contains an inscription in Pallava Grantha which gives the name of the temple as Atyantakama Pallavesvara–griham. This cave has three cells and massive pillars adorn its exterior.

⚜ SCHOOL FOR SCULPTORS?
The fact that most of these mandapas are unfinished gives credence to the theory that this site was perhaps a school for budding artisans.

Trimurti Cave Temple

Located towards the north of the Ganesha Ratha, this triple-celled *mandapa* is dedicated to the three prime gods of the Hindu pantheon – Lord Brahma (the Creator), Lord Vishnu (the Protector), and Lord Shiva (the Destroyer). It does not have a front portico or hall. There is a separate section in the temple for each of the gods, the entrances of

which are guarded by the typical Pallava doorkeepers or *dvarapalas*. Nearby is a small, incomplete rock-cut collection of various animals.

⚜ ELEPHANT GROUP
This is a unfinished carving of a group of elephants (the parent and its two offspring), a peacock, and a monkey.

Other mandapas

The Kotikal Mandapa is a primitive-looking shrine consisting of a hall that is 6.75m (22ft) long and 2.5m (8ft) wide. This shrine is devoted to Durga and has two massive pillars and pilasters on either side of the façade. The cell in the centre of the rear wall is guarded by female doorkeepers on either side. There is also an inscription in the Pallava Grantha script. The incomplete Ramanuja Mandapa is a triple-celled cave devoted to Shiva. Further down to the south lies an unfinished attempt at depicting Arjuna's Penance on another smaller boulder, known as the Smaller Penance.

BATHING POOL

PALACE SITE AND THRONE

The Lion Throne on top of a hill further west is a large rectangular seat with a beautifully carved seated lion, and was discovered near piles of brick rubble thought to be the remains of the palace of the Pallava kings. The lion resembles Durga's lion in the Mahishamardini Cave. There is also a rock-cut bath (above) nearby.

reclining lion

ROYAL SEAT

Reclaimed from the sea

The fate of an ancient temple on the beach near the Tiger's Cave, which is 5km (3 miles) from Mamallapuram, has been decided by three tsunamis over a period of possibly 2,000 years. The temple dedicated to Muruga (Tamil deity, also known as Subramanya) was discovered after the December 2004 tsunami which hit the coast of Mamallapuram. According to the Archaeological Survey of India (ASI), the temple may date back to between the 1st century BCE and 2nd century CE. The original brick temple was damaged by what may have been a tsunami or a massive tidal wave. Subsequently, the Pallava kings converted it into a granite temple in the 8th and 9th centuries, which also fell to tidal waves or a tsunami. The ASI team has found coins, stucco figurines, terracotta lamps, beads, and roofing tiles at the site. Excavatory work is still in progress but these discoveries have revived interest in the theory that the area was originally home to seven pagodas, six of which were submerged by the sea. As the waves receded in 2004, three rocky structures with elaborate carvings of animals (right) emerged near the Shore Temple: an elaborately carved head of an elephant, a horse in flight, and a granite lion. Above the elephant's head is a small square niche with a carved statue of a deity.

⚜ ROCKY DISCOVERIES
According to archaeologists, the lion and elephant motifs were commonly used to decorate walls and temples during the Pallava period in the 7th and 8th centuries.

SUBRAMANYA TEMPLE

Khajuraho

The temples of Khajuraho, in the state of Madhya Pradesh, are amongst the most beautiful works of art and architecture of medieval India. Built between the 10th and 12th centuries CE, these exquisite temples are renowned for their erotic sculptures that have captured the imagination of millions across the world, evoking wonder, speculation, and sometimes criticism in equal measure. According to local tradition there were once over 85 temples in the city, but only about 20 or so remain, in varying degrees of preservation. Most are dedicated to Hindu deities, while a few belong to the Jain faith, one of the oldest religions of India. How these temples came about remains shrouded in obscurity, as not much is known about the Chandellas – the builders of these spectacular

AXIAL SETTING
Khajuraho lies in the central state of Madhya Pradesh, in the Chattarpur district.

monuments. Local legends say that the unwed mother of the first Chandella king gave birth to the child after having an affair with the moon god. After growing up, the king commissioned the temples to appease the gods and absolve his unwed mother of her social stigma. The Chandellas ruled over Khajuraho, then known as Jejakabhukti, from the 10th century and made the city a hub of cultural and architectural activities. This continued for nearly 300 years, but by the end of the 13th century, the Chandellas mysteriously abandoned Khajuraho.

The temples miraculously escaped destruction during the Muslim invasions of the 13th and 14th centuries, and survive today as the best-preserved examples of Hindu architecture and art in central India.

The Chandella dynasty

The Chandellas ruled over central India between the 10th and 13th centuries CE. Starting off as vassals of the Pratiharas, they became independent after their overlords lost power. Gradually, they consolidated their kingdom into one of the most stable in the region. This stability allowed the Chandellas to focus on art and architecture, which thrived under royal patronage. Khajuraho and its surrounding areas witnessed a remarkable flowering of architecture as successive rulers commissioned forts, palaces, water tanks, and temples throughout their lands.

❧ c.917 **Harsha**, the first notable Chandella leader to be mentioned in inscriptions, helps the Pratiharas regain control of central India. Harsha rules for nearly 25 years and extends his territory.

❧ c.940 Harsha's son, **Yasovarman**, defeats the Rashtrakutas of the Deccan and the Palas of eastern India, and soon proclaims his independence.

❧ c.950 Yasovarman is succeeded by his son **Dhanga**, who consolidates the kingdom and makes it the strongest in central India.

❧ c.1002 Dhanga's son **Ganda** takes over from his father. He enjoys a short and peaceful reign spanning 15 years.

❧ c.1017 Ganda's son, **Vidyadhara**, emerges at the helm. Chandella power reaches its zenith during his rule.

❧ c.1029 After Vidyadhara's death Chandella supremacy gradually declines. They remain confined to a few areas until the 12th century.

FRIEZE ON LAKSHMANA TEMPLE DEPICTING CHANDELLA HIGH LIFE

Mythical origins

The Chandellas, a Rajput tribe, traced their lineage from the moon. According to a popular myth, their forefather was the child of the moon god and a Brahmin girl, called Hemavati. One day, struck by her dazzling beauty, the god seduced the girl and, when she became pregnant, advised her to go to Khajuraho to deliver the baby. Hemavati did as she was told and gave birth to an exceptionally beautiful child, named Chandravarman. Due to his divine parentage, he grew up to be extremely strong and fearless, and after many military conquests went on to establish the Chandella kingdom.

RELIGIOUS SYMBOLISM

The temples of Khajuraho have been the subject of intense debate ever since their "discovery" in modern times by T. S. Burt. The debate is about the symbolism of its sculptures. Many have suggested that the erotic carvings on the temple walls highlight the decadent lifestyle of the Chandellas and their subjects. Others disagree, pointing to the large number of Hindu gods and goddesses that adorn the exterior and interior walls, and to the fact that most temples were dedicated to the powerful Hindu trinity of Brahma, Vishnu, and Shiva. Still others believe that the

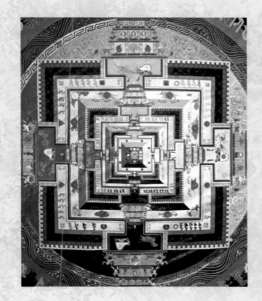

Chandellas were followers of Tantrism, ancient occult beliefs and practices that figured in the existing religions of the time – Hinduism, Buddhism, and even the puritanical Jainism. Tantrics believed in discarding conventional restraints and inhibitions, and held that any human activity, even those involving sex, could be transformed into a spiritual act. This belief found its way on to the walls of these temples.

TANTRIC YANTRA
A yantra, composed of patterns made of concentric figures, is a tantric tool of ritual and meditation.

CHANDELLA INSCRIPTION
Inscriptions etched on plaques inside some of the temples, such as this one from the Vishvanath Temple, are important records of Chandella history.

Re-discovering the past

Between the 12th and 13th century, the Chandella kingdom began to decline due to incursions made by the armies of rulers in Delhi. Unable to resist the onslaught, the Chandellas withdrew to a few fortified centres. Gradually, Khajuraho disappeared from public consciousness and remained so for over 600 years. It was re-discovered in 1838 by Captain T. S. Burt of the East India Company army, who heard about the place from his palanquin bearers. Burt's discovery attracted a large number of scholars. In 1904, the site was acquired by the Archaeological Survey of India (ASI).

HUNTING PARTY
Some of the temples have richly carved panels depicting Chandella lifestyle, such as this hunting party on a frieze.

RECENT EXCAVATIONS
Ongoing excavations by the ASI have uncovered a large number of buried structures in Khajuraho.

Nagara Style

The temples of Khajuraho represent the climax of the Nagara, or northern Indian architectural style, which was popular in central India as well. Its chief components are an *ardha-mandapa* (porch), *mandapa* (columned hall), *antarala* (vestibule), and a square *garbha-griha* (sanctum), all laid out on an east–west axis. In a few temples, especially the larger ones, the *mandapa* is expanded sideways using balconied projections, converting it into a *maha-mandapa* (large assembly hall). These temples also have an inner path enclosing the sanctum which permits devotees to walk around the chamber. The balconies attached to the *mandapa* and the inner path allow light and ventilation inside the temple. The roof rises in graded peaks over the central area, mirroring the effect of a mountain range, while a curved *shikhara* (spire) soars above the sanctum. In larger temples, smaller spires surround the *shikhara*, spreading its weight on the sanctum and providing stability to the structure.

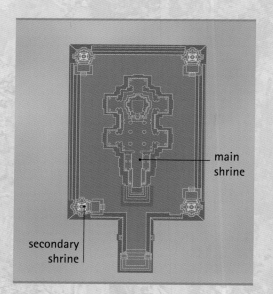

main shrine

secondary shrine

⚜ PANCHAYATANA PLAN
A few temples, notably the Lakshmana, follow a panchayatana (five-shrined) plan, with a central temple and secondary shrines at the four corners.

Entering Khajuraho

Khajuraho today is little more than a village but its ruins, spread over 21 sq km (8 sq miles), attest to the fact that it was an important centre of power under the Chandellas. Its various temples are clustered in three groups – the Western, Eastern, and Southern – of which the Western group has been declared a UNESCO World Heritage Site. The Western Group is situated on the main road, in a fenced enclosure. It contains the largest and finest of all the Khajuraho temples.

⚜ RAMPANT LION
The lion, a royal emblem of the Chandella dynasty, is a recurring theme in almost all Khajuraho temples.

kalasha (pot finial)

shikhara (spire)

entrance porch

TEMPLE GROUPS

Situated near the Shivsagar Tank, the Hindu temples of the Western Group include the Lakshmana, Varaha, Kandariya Mahadev, Jagadambi, Chitragupta, and Vishvanath temples, as well as the minor Parvati and Nandi shrines. The Eastern Group, located close to the village, have three Hindu temples – Brahma, Vamana, and Javari – and three Jain temples – Ghantai, Parsvanath, and Adinath. The Southern Group consists of the Duladeo and the Chaturbhuj, which are both Hindu temples.

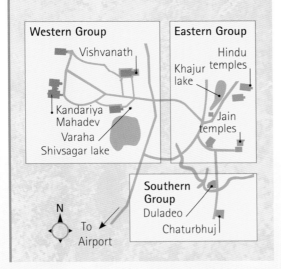

Western Group
- Vishvanath
- Kandariya Mahadev
- Varaha
- Shivsagar lake

Eastern Group
- Khajur lake
- Hindu temples
- Jain temples

Southern Group
- Duladeo
- Chaturbhuj

N
To Airport

VARAHA MANDAPA
The elevated pavilion containing the statue is built on 14 short pillars that support a pyramidal roof.

VARAHA STATUE
Carved in naturalistic detail, the boar's face has nine figures that symbolize the nine planets saved by Vishnu.

Varaha Shrine

The first structure in the Western group is a pavilion housing a huge statue of Varaha (the boar), an incarnation of the Hindu god Vishnu. According to Indian mythology, Vishnu took the form of a boar to rescue the earth goddess, Bhumi, and the nine planets from the clutches of a demon called Hiranyaksha. Made out of a single block of sandstone, the idol measures 2.6m (8.5ft) by 1.7m (5.6ft). On its massive body are carved 674 miniature figures of Hindu deities, while a pair of feminine feet in front of its legs represents Bhumi.

KANDARIYA MAHADEV TEMPLE
Undoubtedly the grandest monument in Khajuraho, the Kandariya Mahadev Temple showcases Chandella architecture at its finest.

Shiva shrine

Jagadambi Temple

Lakshmana Temple

Built around 954, the Lakshmana Temple is the earliest, and one of the best-preserved temples in Khajuraho. Dedicated to Vishnu, whose consort is Lakshmi – the Hindu goddess of wealth – the temple has a *panchayatna* plan, with the main shrine at the centre and four subsidiary shrines at the corners. It stands on a platform that can be accessed by a flight of steps. The platform itself is decorated with friezes depicting events from everyday life, hunting and battle stories, erotic motifs, as well as scenes of bestiality. The main shrine, measuring 29.8m (97.8ft) by 13.7m (45ft), has a single entrance porch, which is framed by an ornate lintel resting on the heads of two aquatic monsters called *makaras*. Along the porch wall is a Chandella stone inscription, dating to 954, which records that Yasovarman, the seventh Chandella king, constructed the temple in honour of Vishnu.

TOWER SUMMIT
The shikhara is topped with two disc-like, fluted stone structures called amalakhas. Together these imitate the shape of an earthen pot.

DANCING GANESHA

MAIN TEMPLE
The temple is approached from the east via a porch. The smaller towered shrines mark the platform's four corners.

shikhara (spire)

secondary shrine

side balcony

MATANGESHWAR TEMPLE

The Matangeshwar Temple, adjoining the Lakshmana Temple, is the only one where there is still active worship. Considered the holiest of all Khajuraho temples, it enshrines a huge *lingam*, the phallic symbol of the Hindu god Shiva.

A LIVING TEMPLE

⚜ ORNATE FAÇADE
Deeply sculpted panels enrich the Lakshmana Temple's exterior. An image of Surya, the sun god, is set in a niche above the porch entrance.

⚜ SOUTHERN BALCONY
Four high balconies, two on each side, not only illuminate the hall and the inner passageway, but also give the Lakshmana Temple its complex shape.

Exterior frieze panels

The outer walls of the Lakshmana Temple are covered with sculptural masterpieces – tiers of deeply sculpted panels displaying Hindu gods and goddesses, primarily Vishnu, but also other deities such as Shiva, accompanied by their attendants and consorts. Some of the male and female figures are coupled in sexual union, a motif that is charged with a magical significance. The base of the temple has flower and leaf motifs, a narrow panel depicting court life and erotic scenes, and ornamental niches containing images of principal Hindu deities. Above the base are two bands of sculptures that wind in and around the projections and corners of the temple, with over 230 carved figures in each band.

BEARDED GOD
The top panel on the south depicts a bearded Agni, the god of fire.

ELEPHANT TORSOS
Among the courtly themes reserved for the temple base are these majestic royal elephants with their attendants.

GARGOYLE DETAIL ON THE BASE

PORCH INTERIOR
High columns flank the passageway inside the entrance porch. An inscribed slab on the right of the doorway states the temple's history.

RELIGIOUS DISCOURSE
This frieze on the temple base shows a preacher instructing a band of seated disciples, while being attended upon by devadasis, or court dancers.

COLUMN DECORATION
The sanctum's columns depict corpulent figures, with legs kicked back as if flying.

SCULPTED BRACKETS
The elegantly carved female bracket-figures are considered masterpieces of medieval art.

Inner Sanctum

The temple's interior is cool and dark, with sunlight casting alluring shadows over the sculptured walls. The sanctum stands behind an ornamental doorway with carved panels of auspicious motifs. Within stands a four-armed and three-headed Vishnu. The central head is of a human, while the heads on either side are that of a boar and a lion, both representing incarnations of Vishnu. Around the sanctum is a narrow path. The exterior wall of the sanctum has a number of tiered sculpted panels; the topmost ones depict the life of Krishna, another incarnation of Vishnu.

Kandariya Mahadev Temple

The Kandariya Mahadev Temple is the largest and architecturally the most impressive temple in Khajuraho. Its name refers to Shiva, the powerful Hindu god, in whose honour the temple was constructed. Believed to have been built during King Ganda's reign (1017–29), the temple's design, symmetrical proportions, and sculptural detailing make it the most refined example of central Indian art. This grand monument measures about 30m (98.4ft) in length and 20m (65.6ft) in width, while its soaring *shikhara* rises 35.3m (116ft) above the ground. The temple shares its platform with a small shrine, also dedicated to Shiva, and the Jagadambi Temple.

SOUTHERN FAÇADE

rear balcony

CENTRAL TOWER
The main shikhara *looms over 84 smaller replicas that appear to be clambering up to the central tower.*

shikhara (spire)

maha-mandapa (large assembly hall)

⚶ TEMPLE ENTRANCE
The entrance is towards the east, and can be accessed by a steep flight of stairs. The doorway is intricately patterned with arabesque motifs.

MAKARA TORANA LINTEL DETAIL

Makara torana

One of the most distinctive features of the Kandariya Mahadev Temple is the *makara torana*, a ceremonial arch that adorns the temple's porch entrance. Carved out of a single stone, this exquisitely sculpted lintel is designed like a garland of flowers and is draped with loops from one side of the doorway to the other. It stems from the heads of two carved *makaras*, or mythical aquatic monsters, and within the folds of the garland are tiny celestial nymphs who seem to be carrying it across the heavens.

mandapa (columned hall)

ardha–mandapa (porch)

niched deities

SAPTAMATRIKAS

Among the nine niches in the base of the Kandariya Mahadev Temple are the *Saptamatrikas*, or seven mother goddesses, who play a protective role in Hinduism and Tantrism. Usually portrayed in a group, they include Brahmani, Vaishnavi, Maheshwari, Kaumari, Varahi, Indrani, and Chamunda.

NICHE IN SOUTHERN WALL

lion emblem

Layout of the Kandariya Mahadev Temple

The Kandariya Mahadev Temple's design consists of the same components that are present in the other large temples of Khajuraho. It has a porch, columned hall, large assembly hall, vestibule, and a sanctum with balconies on the sides and rear. All of these are aligned on an east-west axis, a hallmark of Khajuraho temples. The temple's façade has a large number of recesses that run from the bottom to the top of the walls. Although no secondary shrines now remain, the temple has a *panchayatna* plan, and would probably have had shrines in its four corners.

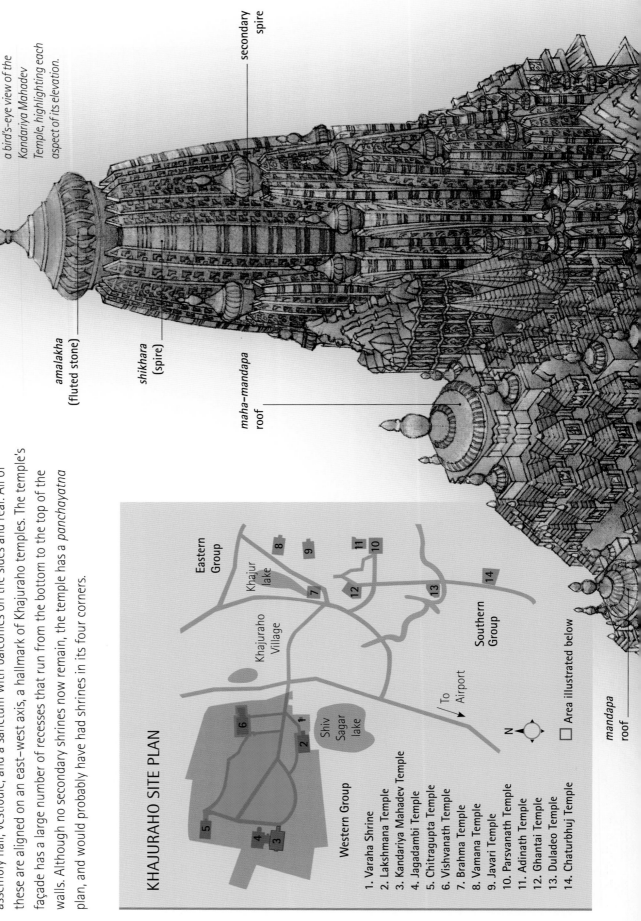

GRAND DIMENSIONS
This illustration presents a bird's-eye view of the Kandariya Mahadev Temple, highlighting each aspect of its elevation.

secondary spire

kalasha (pot finial)

amalakha (fluted stone)

shikhara (spire)

maha-mandapa roof

mandapa roof

KHAJURAHO SITE PLAN

Eastern Group

Khajur lake

Khajuraho Village

Shiv Sagar lake

To Airport

Southern Group

N

☐ Area illustrated below

Western Group

1. Varaha Shrine
2. Lakshmana Temple
3. Kandariya Mahadev Temple
4. Jagadambi Temple
5. Chitragupta Temple
6. Vishvanath Temple
7. Brahma Temple
8. Vamana Temple
9. Javari Temple
10. Parsvanath Temple
11. Adinath Temple
12. Ghantai Temple
13. Duladeo Temple
14. Chaturbhuj Temple

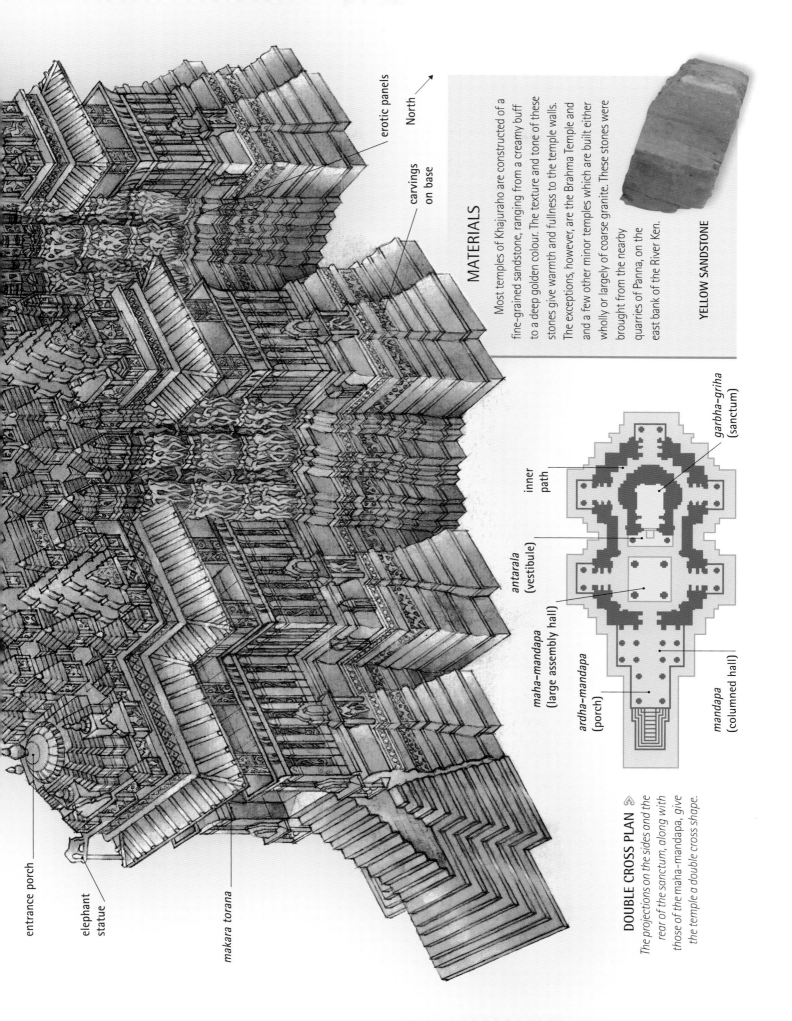

entrance porch

elephant statue

makara torana

erotic panels

North

carvings on base

MATERIALS

Most temples of Khajuraho are constructed of a fine-grained sandstone, ranging from a creamy buff to a deep golden colour. The texture and tone of these stones give warmth and fullness to the temple walls. The exceptions, however, are the Brahma Temple and and a few other minor temples which are built either wholly or largely of coarse granite. These stones were brought from the nearby quarries of Panna, on the east bank of the River Ken.

YELLOW SANDSTONE

inner path

garbha-griha (sanctum)

antarala (vestibule)

maha-mandapa (large assembly hall)

ardha-mandapa (porch)

mandapa (columned hall)

DOUBLE CROSS PLAN

The projections on the sides and the rear of the sanctum, along with those of the maha-mandapa, give the temple a double cross shape.

Temple exterior

Kandariya Mahadev's architectural design is richly complemented by its sculpture. Over 900 images of various sizes grace the temple's walls. Its lofty base, which is 3m (9.8ft) high, includes two rows of processional friezes teeming with elephants and horses, warriors, hunters, acrobats, musicians, dancers, and miscellaneous scenes of erotic couples. Above the base, the central wall space is designed with three bands of sculpture, each a metre high. These contain the largest number of sculptures – an array of gods and goddesses, *mithuna* (lovers), women engaged in everyday activities, as well as mythical animals.

MYTHICAL BEINGS ≫
The recesses in the walls house mythical creatures that give protection from evil.

 **FLORAL MOTIFS**
Intricate flower and leaf motifs have been used to embellish the temple walls.

Temple interior

Being the largest of all Khajuraho temples, the interior of the Kandariya Mahadev Temple is extremely spacious, with a wealth of carvings and sculptures unmatched in any other temple. The ceilings of the porch and the *mandapa* resemble inverted pools with floral motifs, and are supported by brackets depicting a variety of celestial nymphs in lively postures. The doorway of the sanctum is richly adorned with narrow panels of images. The central lintel carries a seated figure of Shiva holding a trident and a snake, with Vishnu on his left and Brahma on his right.

 INNER PATH
The walls of the inner path around the sanctum are lavishly adorned with sculptures.

SACRED SYMBOL ≫
The plain sanctum with a marble lingam (phallic symbol of Shiva) contrasts with the elaborately-carved doorway.

Jagadambi Temple

Dedicated to Parvati, the consort of Shiva, the Jagadambi Temple stands on the same platform as the Kandariya Mahadev. It is however much smaller, with only one set of balconies, one *mandapa*, and no inner path around the sanctum. Its sculptural embellishments are extremely refined, and most of them are easily visible because of the temple's low height. Some of the finest carvings are those of celestial nymphs, whose faces display expressions of utter bliss.

🖉 DELICATE PROPORTIONS
The refined design of the Jagadambi Temple inspired the construction of Chitragupta Temple.

🖉 SHIVA WITH CONSORT
A niche on the south side has an image of Shiva embracing his consort Parvati, also known as Uma.

AMOROUS COUPLES

The Jagadambi Temple contains some of the finest depictions of couples in amorous poses, tucked away in the temple's recesses. These lovers, known as the *mithuna*, are sensuously carved, and are distinguished by a rare sensitivity and expression of intense rapture. A celebrated example on the south side depicts a woman who climbs over her lover "as a creeper climbs a tree".

ROMANCING THE STONE

EXOTIC PANELS
These figures from the Lakshmana Temple are of Vishnu (top band) and Shiva with their consorts, flanked by attendants engaged in daily activities.

Chitragupta Temple

The Chitragupta Temple is the only one in Khajuraho dedicated to Surya, the sun god. Situated a few metres away from the Jagadambi Temple, it closely resembles the latter in its plan and decorative scheme. The temple measures 22m (72ft) in length and 13m (42.5ft) in width, and consists of a porch, columned hall, large assembly hall with balconies, vestibule, and a sanctum without an inner path. Its exterior displays fine sculptures, especially at the base, which also contains a processional frieze featuring a group of stone carvers, a hunting scene, and elephant fights. Among other noteworthy sculptures are the scene of Shiva's marriage carved in a recess on the north wall, and sensuous couples on the west and south walls.

kalasha
(pot finial)

amalakha
(fluted stone)

lion emblem

GRACEFUL CURVES

⬥ **SACRED DEITIES**
Carvings of deities appear in niches on the outside walls; in some they are shown with consorts, such as Shiva with Parvati (top).

THE SUN GOD

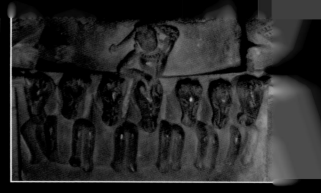

⚜ **SEVEN-HORSE CHARIOT**
The pedestal of the main idol depicts the horse drawn chariot in which the sun god is believed to travel non stop across the sky.

⚜ **GOD OF LIGHT**
This is one of the three figures of the sun god carved on the sanctum doorway

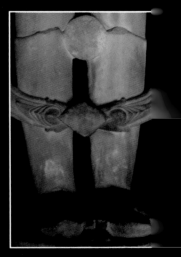

⚜ **BOOTED DEITY**
Surya is the only god in Hindu iconography to ...

Inner chambers

The inner rooms of the Chitragupta Temple are remarkable both for the innovations in design and for their sculptural detail. The octagonal ceiling of the *maha-mandapa*, for example, evolved from the square ones of the other temples, and makes this temple look more ornate. Additionally, the interior walls are carved with some of the finest figures of nymphs, erotic couples, and gods, including an eleven-headed Vishnu on the southern wall. Among other notable sculptures are royal processions and scenes of Chandella court life. The centrepiece of the temple, however, remains the sanctum's presiding deity – the majestic sun god looming

Vishvanath Temple

Constructed by King Dhanga in 1002, the Vishvanath Temple is one of the finest monuments in Khajuraho. Considered the most important Shiva temple after the Kandariya Mahadev, it closely resembles the latter in style and composition. It measures 27.5m (90ft) by 13.7m (45ft), and contains all the elements of the Nagara style, namely the porch, hall, large assembly hall, the vestibule, and sanctum. All its rooms are designed with faceted pillars and elaborately-carved brackets that support ornate roofs. The sanctum is enclosed by an inner path, with balconies on the sides and rear that allow light and ventilation. The temple originally had a *panchayatna* plan, but only two of its secondary shrines have survived – one each in the northeast and southwest corners.

lion emblem

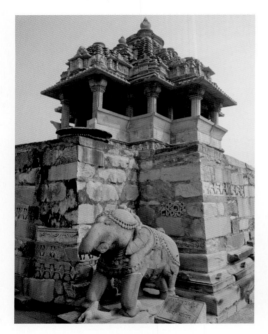

AN ELEPHANT FLANKING THE NANDI SHRINE

NANDI AND PARVATI SHRINES

Two shrines located in the vicinity of the Vishvanath Temple are closely associated with Shiva's life. Directly opposite the temple's entrance is the shrine of the Nandi bull, the deity's mount. A square pavilion, it is flanked by a pair of elephants and contains a massive statue of the bull, seated on a pedestal and gazing demurely at her master. Towards the southwest of the Vishvanath Temple lies a small shrine dedicated to Shiva's consort, Parvati. Only its sanctum and *shikhara* survive; the former holds an image of Parvati standing on an iguana, her mount.

SEATED BULL
The sandstone idol of Nandi faces its master in the Vishvanath Temple.

PARVATI SHRINE

Sculptural embellishment

The high base of the Vishvanath Temple has sculptures and narrative panels interspersed with niches. Most of the niches feature the *Saptamatrikas*, except for the first one on the south wall, which houses a lovely dancing Ganesha, the elephant-headed god. Above the base, three bands of equal size depict nymphs performing daily activities, mythical creatures, as well as gods and goddesses of the Hindu pantheon. On the north and south sides, between the balconies, are erotic scenes of amorous couples making love in a variety of positions. The temple interiors are equally stunning, with faceted pillars and elaborately carved sculpted brackets below an ornate ceiling.

⚜ SIMPLE SPIRE
The shikhara *is surrounded by minor spires, which are fewer in number than those found in the larger temples.*

⚜ WORSHIPPING WATER
Water plays a significant role in Hinduism, for purification as well as fertility. Shiva is shown here (in the centre) carrying an urn of water.

⚜ STONE LINGAM
The sanctum originally enshrined two lingams, one made of emerald and the other of stone.

⚜ LANGUID GRACE
This sculpture of a nymph on the outer south façade shows her plucking a thorn from her foot.

⚜ CELESTIAL DANCER
A nymph sculpted in a classic dance posture adorns the panel on one of the temple's walls.

⚜ FINE DETAILING
This nymph admiring herself in a mirror shows the artist's deft touch in depicting even simple activities.

Brahma Temple

Situated on the south end of the Khajur lake, the Brahma Temple, built in c.900 CE, is the first of the three Hindu temples in the Eastern Group. Its tiered roof is made of sandstone while the body is of granite. Its name is a misnomer as the lintel of the sanctum doorway features an image of Vishnu, while the sanctum itself contains a four-faced lingam representing Shiva. The walls of the temple are plain, without any figurative work.

amalakha (fluted stone)

⚜ SQUARE PLAN
The Brahma temple follows a simple square plan that consists of only a sanctum, without any mandapa.

⚜ GANGA AND YAMUNA
The deities of Ganga (the Ganges) and Yamuna – two of India's rivers – are carved on either side of the entrance.

ELEGANT SHIKHARA ⚜
The slender and soaring outline of the Javari Temple's shikhara adds to the charm of its structure.

secondary spire

Javari Temple

Dedicated to Vishnu, the Javari Temple lies to the east of the Brahma Temple. Its exterior walls are lined with miniature sculptures, which are easy to see due to the temple's relatively small size. The long entrance porch has an exquisitely-carved *makara torana*, while a projecting cornice separates the *shikhara* from the main body of the temple. The sanctum is quite small and does not have any ambulatory around it.

DETAIL OF LINTEL ABOVE THE JAVARI TEMPLE'S SANCTUM

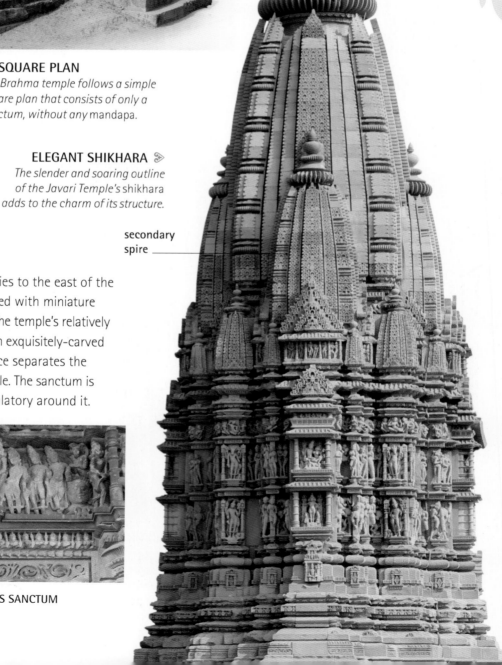

Vamana Temple

The Vamana (dwarf) Temple is said to have been built between 1050 and 1075. Its exterior walls have the typical two bands of fine sculptures, as well as erotic scenes that can be seen on the roof pediments. Although a Vishnu temple, it also has carvings of Brahma and Shiva and their consorts in the upper niches of the sanctum. A figure of the Buddha on one of the walls reflects the religious tolerance of the Chandellas.

SINGLE TOWER
The spire over the sanctum does not feature any subsidiary shikharas around it.

DWARF INCARNATION
Hindu myths say Vishnu took the form of a dwarf to teach a lesson to a haughty king.

Ghantai Temple

The Ghantai Temple, south of Khajuraho village, is poorly preserved, with only the pillars and ornate ceiling of the porch and hall intact. An elaborate doorway inside has an eight-armed goddess riding on an eagle and 16 auspicious Jain symbols. A part of the ceiling has dancers and musicians in oblong panels along the borders.

BELLED PILLARS
The temple is named after the chain-and-bell (ghanta in Hindi) carvings on its elegant pillars.

PILLAR BRACKETS
Sculpted nymphs appear on the brackets of the Ghantai Temple, but these are not very refined.

Parsvanath Temple

Built during King Dhanga's reign (950–1002), the Parsvanath Temple is the largest of all the Jain temples. Despite its Jain affiliation its design is strikingly similar to Hindu temples. It is set on an east–west axis with two projections at the front and back. The former is the vestibule, while the latter is a secondary shrine that was apparently added later. The main exterior wall of the temple is divided into two broad sculpted bands depicting Hindu gods and their consorts. These are accompanied by female figures performing routine activities. A narrow panel just above the two bands depicts musicians and flying nymphs showering flowers on the deities assembled below. A noteworthy feature is the temple's porch, which is decorated with an ornate ceiling, with a pair of flying figures hanging from it.

⚜ **PARSVANATH IDOL**
The highly-polished statue of the Jain spiritual leader Parsvanath in the main shrine is flanked by a male nude figure on the left and a female on the right.

⚜ **ORNAMENTAL TOWER**
The shikhara of the Parsvanath Temple is covered by smaller secondary towers, a feature shared by the Western temples.

CELESTIAL NYMPH

Adinath Temple

Located north of the Parsvanath Temple is the Adinath Temple, dedicated to the first Jain spiritual leader. Although only the vestibule and sanctum survive, the temple's plan indicates a close resemblance to the Hindu Vamana Temple. The Adinath Temple's exterior walls have the characteristic three rows of carvings that are considered some of the best in all of Khajuraho. Among the most outstanding are the lithe female forms, dressed in intricately-woven costumes and performing a variety of tasks.

⚜ **SOARING TOWER**
An impressive feature of the Adinath Temple is its shikhara which curves smoothly inward only at the top.

Chaturbhuj Temple

Situated approximately 3km (2 miles) south of the Western Group, the Chaturbhuj ("four-armed") Temple is the only important temple in Khajuraho that faces west. It is also the only one which does not have any erotic sculptures. The temple has three principal components – a *mandapa*, vestibule, and sanctum. An ornamental doorway leads to the sanctum, which contains a remarkable idol of a 2.7m (9ft) tall Vishnu, carved out of a single stone.

❦ FOUR-ARMED VISHNU
The richly-adorned figure stands in a relaxed pose with one leg bent behind and resting on the toes.

SHALLOW PORCH ❧
From left to right, this view shows the tiny porch, the hall, and the tall, slim shikhara above the sanctum.

Duladeo Temple

One of the last temples to be built in Khajuraho, the Duladeo Temple is associated with Shiva's marriage to Parvati (*Dula* signifying bridegroom), which is represented on the exterior walls. The well-preserved western side carries repeated images of the divine couple in three sculpted bands, along with other deities, mythical creatures, and amorous couples. A unique feature of the temple is the large, open, and octagonal *mandapa*. Its circular inner ceiling is supported by brackets with celestial nymphs. These are adorned with headdresses and ornaments that differ from those in the other temples.

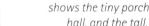

❦ CRUMBLING FAÇADE
The porch, mandapa, *and* shikhara *of the Duladeo Temple show signs of severe damage.*

❧ CELESTIAL MUSICIANS
The topmost band of the western wall is decorated with celestial musicians and garland bearers taking part in Shiva's wedding procession.

Qutb Minar

Most human beings dream of being immortal, and this is particularly true of kings, whose desire to live on is reflected in the monuments they build. The Qutb Minar, a five-storeyed structure of sandstone and marble, reaches for the sky in just such an expression of imperial might. It is believed to have been built as a symbol of victory and to celebrate the establishment of the Delhi Sultanate in the newly conquered territory in India. Towering over the city of Delhi, it is the principal monument of the Qutb complex, which has been declared a UNESCO World Heritage Site. The monuments comprising this complex (the earliest examples of the Indo-Islamic architectural style) were built from the late 12th century onwards by the rulers of the Delhi Sultanate. They were built over Qila Rai Pithora, a city founded by the Chauhan Rajput clan and the first of the fabled seven cities that made up Delhi (the others being Mehrauli, Siri, Tughlaqabad, Firozabad, Jahanpanah, and Shahjahanabad). The Chauhans were forced to cede it to Muhammad of Ghur in 1193. Qutbuddin Aibak, Muhammad's general, became the first sultan of Delhi and commenced the construction of the Qutb Minar (the word *qutb* means "axis", while *minar* means "tower"). The building of the tower cannot be attributed to a single ruler – Aibak died after completing just one storey, while the rest were added by subsequent kings. Surrounding the Minar is the Mehrauli area, which is steeped in history, with numerous monuments dotting the landscape.

⚜ SYMBOL OF TRIUMPH
The Qutb complex lies in the south of Delhi, the capital city of India.

Rulers of Delhi

Marking a new era in Indian history, the Delhi Sultanate was established in 1206 by Qutbuddin Aibak, who founded the first of many Muslim dynasties, collectively known as the Delhi Sultanate. The Mamluk (formerly known as the Slave kings), the Khilji, Tughlaq, Sayyid, and Lodi sultans ruled successively for more than three centuries, changing the political and cultural milieu of the Indian subcontinent. The foundations of the great Mughal empire were laid by Babur who overthrew the Lodis at the historic battle of Panipat. Its might declined rapidly in the early eighteenth century, making way for the European powers. The British then gained control and rose as a political force; their forces dethroned the last Mughal emperor in 1857. Below are some important dates relating to the different dynasties that ruled over Delhi.

- **1206–1290 Mamluk sultans**
  1206–1210 Qutbuddin Aibak
  1211–1236 Shamsuddin Iltutmish
  1266–1286 Ghiyasuddin Balban

- **1290–1321 Khilji sultans**
  1296–1316 Alauddin Khilji

- **1321–1414 Tughlaq sultans**
  1351–1388 Firoz Shah Tughlaq

- **1414–1451 Sayyid sultans**

- **1451–1526 Lodi sultans**
  1488–1517 Sikander Lodi

- **1526–1857 The Mughal emperors**
  1526–1530 Zahiruddin Babur
  1530–1556 Nasiruddin Humayun
  1556–1605 Jalaluddin Akbar
  1605–1717 The other Great Mughals
  1836–1857 Bahadur Shah Zafar

Looking Back in Time

The strategic location of Delhi made it an attractive prospect for invaders from Central Asia. In 1193, Muhammad of Ghur (in what is now central Afghanistan) swept into north India and sacked Delhi, setting the stage for his general, Qutbuddin Aibak, to establish his rule in the city. The Delhi Sultanate expanded, surviving into the early 16th century. In 1526, another invader from Central Asia – Zahiruddin Babur – took over Delhi and laid the foundation of the Mughal empire that was to dominate the subcontinent for over 200 years.

MINARET OF JAM
The Qutb Minar was inspired by a minaret – 65m (214ft) high – in the remote valley of Jam in western Afghanistan. This minaret was built between 1193 and 1194 by Ghiyasuddin, the sultan of Ghur (brother of Muhammad of Ghur).

The Mamluk sultans

The first Muslim rulers of India, the Mamluk sultans, reigned for 84 years. When Muhammad of Ghur died in 1206, Qutbuddin Aibak, a former slave, stayed on in Delhi and was crowned as the sultan. Shamsuddin Iltutmish, Aibak's son-in-law, and Ghiyasuddin Balban, both Il-bari Turks – were also slaves before they ascended the throne (their tombs lie in the Qutb complex). Iltutmish expanded the Delhi Sultanate till Sind in the west and Bengal in the east. Balban, the eighth sultan, ruled with an iron hand, quelling rebellions to bring peace to his kingdom. As the empire expanded, the sultans sought to demonstrate their power by building grand monuments around the Qutb Minar.

QUTB MINAR

ALAI DARWAZA

The Khilji rulers

Jalaluddin Khilji, who belonged to an Afghan tribe, wrested power from Balban's successors and established the Khilji dynasty. His nephew, Alauddin Khilji, was the next Khilji sultan. Aiming to conquer the whole of India, he launched successful expeditions against the rich kingdoms south of Delhi between 1299 and 1305 and extended the sultanate. His architectural vision was grandiose in conception, as evidenced by the unfinished Alai Minar (ambitiously begun as a gigantic rival of the Qutb Minar), the impressive Alai Darwaza, and the sizable extensions added to the Quwwat-ul-Islam Masjid built by Aibak.

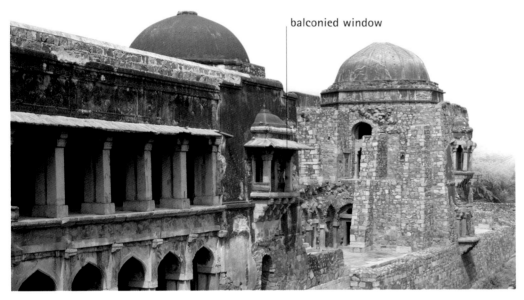

balconied window

HAUZ KHAS MADRASA

The Tughlaq sultans

The first Tughlaq sultan was Ghiyasuddin Tughlaq, who established his capital at Tughlaqabad, the third of Delhi's seven cities. There were 11 rulers of the Tughlaq dynasty, but only the first three generations were interested in architecture. Firoz Shah Tughlaq was a prolific builder who added the fourth and fifth storeys of the Qutb Minar and created his own city, Firozabad, in the north of Delhi, along the Yamuna river. He also built numerous rest houses and *madrasas* (schools). A *madrasa* and an L-shaped mosque built by him can be seen in Hauz Khas, Delhi.

The Lodis

The Sayyids contributed very little to the Qutb complex, but Sikander Lodi of the Lodi dynasty carried out repairs and restoration work of the Minar. Sikander Lodi's octagonal tomb lies in the Lodi Garden, Delhi.

Influences from Afar

The new conquerors of northern India brought their own religious and social ideas with them. In architecture, too, they introduced new techniques of design. At the same time, the local craftsmen who were set to work on monuments for the new rulers managed to introduce indigenous elements in the structures. There was an initial stage where Hindu or Jain temples were destroyed and the material used for new buildings, as in the Quwwat-ul-Islam Masjid in the Qutb complex. Later, however, monuments were built from materials sourced from nearby places. One of the architectural features the Central Asian rulers brought with them was the true or keystone arch (below), which was an arch built with wedge-shaped stone blocks. Prior to this, the local craftsmen used corbelled or "false" arches.

CORBELLED OR FALSE ARCH

keystone

TRUE ARCH WITH KEYSTONE

⚖ TWO TYPES OF ARCHES
The corbelled arch was built by laying stones horizontally and rounding the edges at the top. It could not support extra weight on it, as can be seen in the Quwwat-ul-Islam Masjid screen. The true arch was first used in Balban's Tomb, which lies some distance away from the complex.

Qutb Minar

The construction of this magnificent minaret was begun by Qutbuddin Aibak in the year 1199. When Aibak died in 1210, only the first storey of the Minar had been built. Iltutmish, Aibak's son-in-law, added three more storeys to it, and Firoz Shah Tughlaq added the fourth and fifth storeys in 1368 after a lightning strike knocked off the top of the Minar. Conceived of as a tower of victory and faith, the Minar might have also served as a look-out and as a place for the muezzin's call to prayer. But it was most likely intended as a symbol of the power of Delhi's new rulers.

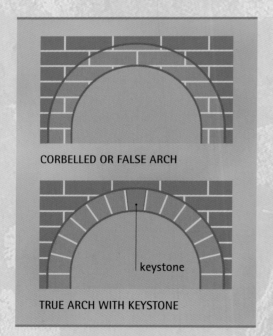

⚖ ARCHED ENTRANCE
The now-closed doorway leads to a spiral staircase with 379 steps to the top.

⚜ CALLIGRAPHIC BANDS AND FLUTINGS

The tapering shaft of the Minar is encircled by decorative bands engraved with historical information and verses from the Quran in the Naskh, or "copying", style of calligraphy. The first three storeys are fluted: alternate rounded and angular flutings (grooves) on the first storey, rounded ones on the second, and only angular flutings on the third.

Naskh lettering

rounded flutings

Aspects of the Minar

Standing 72.5m (238ft) tall, the Qutb Minar is one of the most perfect minarets ever built – and the tallest minaret in India. Its diameter at the base is 14.4m (47ft), tapering upwards to 2.75m (9ft). It was damaged by lightning in 1326, 1368, and 1503. A number of iron clamps were then added to reinforce the stone joints and to act as lightning conductors. The Minar tilts about 0.6m (2ft) towards the southwest, but this is not seen as a threat to the structure.

SMITH'S FOLLY

Major Robert Smith of the Royal Engineers added this *chhatri* (kiosk) atop the Minar in 1829 after the original cupola was struck by an earthquake. It was later removed, and came to be known as "Smith's Folly". It can be seen to the left of the main entry path.

⚜ LATER ADDITIONS

There is a marked architectural difference in the top two storeys added by Firoz Shah Tughlaq, especially evident in the liberal use of marble. The marble bands are embellished with inscriptions carved in fine calligraphy.

ornamental band

marble panelling

balcony above alcoves

BALCONIES AND ORNATE BRACKETS ⚜

The first three storeys of the Minar have projecting balconies, each opening out from the internal staircase, which are supported by elaborately carved muqarnas (stalactite brackets) above honeycomb patterned alcoves. These brackets were an architectural feature imported from the Arabic world.

Layout of the Qutb Minar complex

The Qutb Minar and complex is the crowning architectural achievement of the Delhi Sultanate. Though called a "complex", it was not planned in a cohesive way. Various rulers added structures to it over the centuries following the conquest of northern India. Among other monuments, here are the Alai Darwaza, with Imam Zamin's Tomb right next to it, and the Quwwat-ul-Islam Masjid with its spectacular sandstone screen.

❦ SKETCH OF THE COMPLEX

This illustration gives a bird's-eye view of the Qutb complex. Iltutmish's Tomb, Alauddin Khilji's Tomb and madrasa, and the Alai Minar are not shown here – their relative directions are indicated by arrows.

To Iltutmish's Tomb

Qutb Minar

Iron Pillar

Quwwat-ul-Islam Masjid

To Alai Minar

To Entrance

To Alauddin Khilji's Tomb and *madrasa*

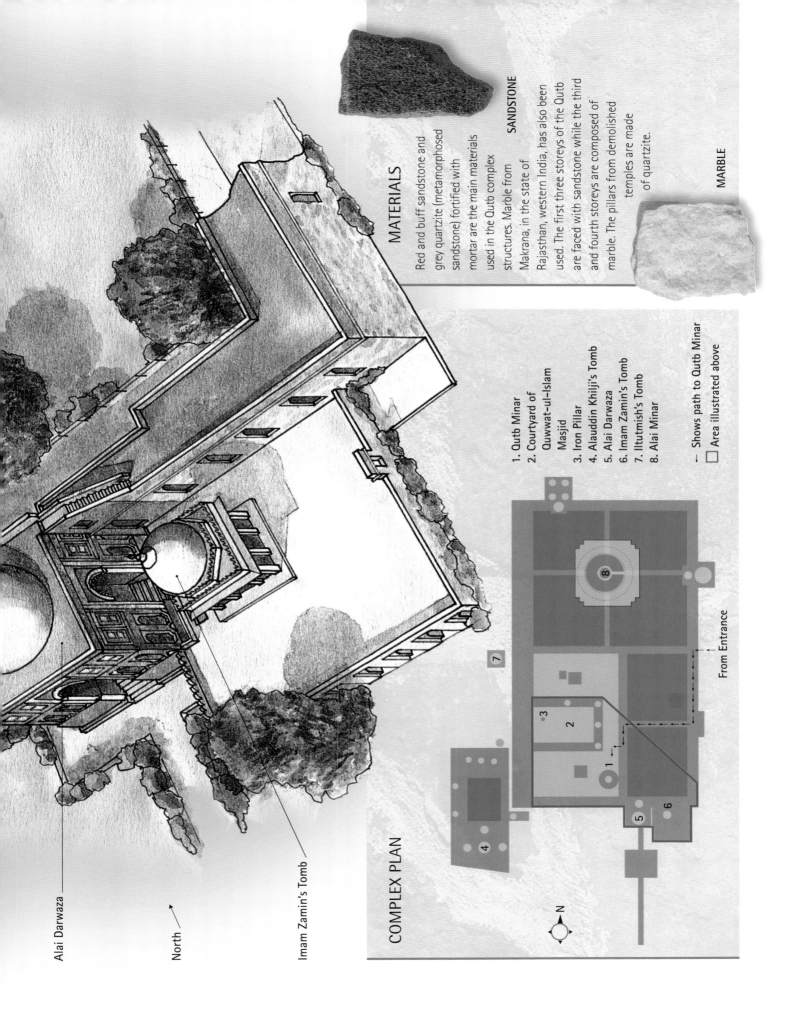

Alai Darwaza

North →

Imam Zamin's Tomb

MATERIALS

Red and buff sandstone and grey quartzite (metamorphosed sandstone) fortified with mortar are the main materials used in the Qutb complex structures. Marble from Makrana, in the state of Rajasthan, western India, has also been used. The first three storeys of the Qutb are faced with sandstone while the third and fourth storeys are composed of marble. The pillars from demolished temples are made of quartzite.

SANDSTONE

MARBLE

COMPLEX PLAN

1. Qutb Minar
2. Courtyard of Quwwat–ul–Islam Masjid
3. Iron Pillar
4. Alauddin Khilji's Tomb
5. Alai Darwaza
6. Imam Zamin's Tomb
7. Iltutmish's Tomb
8. Alai Minar

→ Shows path to Qutb Minar
☐ Area illustrated above

From Entrance

N

PILLAR AND SCREEN

The maqsura or screen of the late 12th-century Quwwat-ul-Islam Masjid forms a backdrop for the famed fourth-century Iron Pillar. The red sandstone screen is decorated with floral carvings and calligraphy. The Iron Pillar is said to have been brought to Qila Rai Pithora from central India by Anangapal, a Rajput ruler of Delhi, and placed with the group of 27 temples that stood there.

✿ CLOISTERED COURTYARD

The mosque is built on the platform (reached by steep steps on the north, east, and west sides) of an earlier temple. The central courtyard, where people gathered to pray, is rectangular and measures 43 x 33m (141 x 108ft).

Quwwat-ul-Islam Masjid

Commissioned by Qutbuddin Aibak, the Quwwat-ul-Islam (Might of Islam) Masjid was the first congregational mosque to be built in India. Constructed between 1193 and 1197, the mosque consists of a courtyard enclosed by pillared cloisters on three sides and an elaborately decorated screen.

Standing tall at 7m (2ft) in the courtyard is the Iron Pillar. It bears an inscription describing it as a flagstaff of the Hindu deity Vishnu and commemorates King Chandragupta II, which dates it to the fourth-century Gupta period.

FUSION OF STYLES

Heralding a new architectural style combining Hindu and Islamic decorative elements, the mosque is composed of material taken from 27 demolished temples. Hindu motifs on the pillars, such as *ghata-pallava* (flower-pots), lotuses, and tasselled ropes, blend with Islamic calligraphy and patterns on the sandstone screen of the mosque.

ORNAMENTAL FLOWER-POT

✿ PILLARED VERANDAH

The ornate pillars of the verandahs are square in shape, in the Hindu style.

FLORAL MOTIFS ON CEILING

THE IRON PILLAR ✿

This pillar is composed of pure iron (98 per cent). A tribute to Indian metallurgy, it has shown almost no signs of rusting over the past 16 centuries.

Sandstone screen

Once the mosque was completed in 1197, a *maqsura* (a screen demarcating an enclosed prayer space) was constructed in front of the prayer hall by Aibak in 1199. Consisting of a main central arch flanked by smaller arches, it faces towards the west, the direction of Mecca. It is said to be modelled on the screen of Prophet Muhammad's mosque in Medina. Iltutmish and later, Alauddin Khilji, extended it to enclose the Qutb Minar and the Alai Minar.

ORNATE CALLIGRAPHY

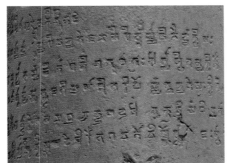

🪷 GRAND ARCHES
The ogee-shaped (pointed) arches of the maqsura are lavishly ornamented with geometric and arabesque patterns as well as Quranic inscriptions.

🪷 SANSKRIT INSCRIPTION
Engraved on the iron pillar is an inscription in Sanskrit in the Gupta-Brahmi script mentioning King Chandragupta II.

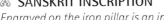

Alai Darwaza

Remarkable for its perfect proportions and ornamented façade, the Alai Darwaza, built by Alauddin Khilji in 1311, stands to the southeast of the Qutb Minar. It was the only one of four planned gateways to the Minar that was actually built because Alauddin died in 1316, before he could complete the construction. The Darwaza is square in shape and has lofty doorways that are arched openings to the four main compass points. One of the earliest buildings to use the true arch, the structure features an external relief of inscriptional panels in marble, and decorative details in red sandstone. The central arch rises to nearly the whole height of the structure, its bands embellished with arabesque, geometric, and floral patterns. It is surmounted by a dome supported by recessed corner arches. Parts of the upper wall facing have come off, the square outline of the present parapet being the result of repair work carried out in 1828 by Major Robert Smith, a British military engineer.

DETAIL

❦ WINDOW

The windows of the Darwaza feature jaalis (latticed screens) set within arches. The lotus-bud fringe on the arch is characteristic of the Khilji period.

SCREEN FROM INTERIOR

wide dome

carved marble panels

🪶 **GATEWAY TO THE MINAR**
*Inscriptions on the archways mention
Alauddin's title, and record his
extension of the Quwwat-ul-Islam
Masjid in 1311.*

A builder with visions of grandeur

Apart from constructing the impressive Alai Darwaza, Alauddin Khilji
extended the Quwwat-ul-Islam Masjid's enclosure and screen and
started the construction of the massive Alai Minar. The foundations
of Siri, the second city of Delhi (and the first to be
built by a Delhi sultan) were laid during his reign.
He also built a *madrasa* and what would eventually
be his tomb. Near Siri, he had a vast *hauz khas*
(reservoir) built to supply water to his citadel.

🪶 **CONTRAST IN COLOURS**
*On the sides of the central arch are marble
floral motifs offset by carved sandstone
lotus buds and twining stems; below is
a richly patterned band in sandstone.*

Imam Zamin's Tomb

Imam Zamin (his actual name was Muhammad Ali) was a 15th-century Sufi saint who came to Delhi from Turkestan during the reign of Sikander Lodi. He probably held a position of some importance in the Quwwat-ul-Islam Masjid. His tomb was built beside the eastern gateway of the Alai Darwaza during the reign of Mughal emperor Humayun, which makes it a later structure than the other monuments in the complex. The square building rises 16.5m (54ft) high and is decorated with marble panelling above the *chhajjas* (sloping eaves).

❦ MARBLE SLAB

An inscription in Naskh lettering above the doorway states that the saint built the tomb between1537 and1538, and died a year later.

SAINTLY AURA ❧

Marked by simplicity, this small structure bears a large dome on an octagonal base, topped by stepped battlements.

LATTICED SCREENS

The sandstone screens on three sides of the tomb filter the glare of sunshine. They stand out for their intricate geometrical patterns and star shapes.

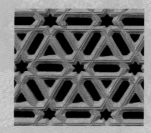

DESIGN DETAIL

INTERIOR ✎
The 12 pilasters inside Imam Zamin's tomb are connected by sandstone jaalis (latticed screens). Marble has been used for the sepulchre and for decorating the interior, particularly the richly carved mihrab (Mecca-facing prayer niche).

Alauddin's Madrasa and Tomb

The *madrasa* of Alauddin Khilji lies to the southwest of the Quwwat-ul-Islam Masjid. Built by Alauddin as a school to teach Islamic scripture, it is a complex of small chambers, some facing a quadrangular lawn. It is capped by high domes and the arches of the doorways are corbelled. To the south of the court is a large square structure, now in ruins, said to be the tomb of Alauddin; the remains of a projecting portico can be seen, but the dome that originally surmounted the tomb has vanished.

✿ **ALAUDDIN'S RESTING PLACE**
The western wall of Alauddin Khilji's tomb has a small mihrab for offering prayers.

✿ **SCHOOL AND SEPULCHRE**
The concept of a combined madrasa (below) and tomb (below left) is seen here for the first time in India.

Iltutmish's Tomb

Shamsuddin Iltutmish, the successor of Qutbuddin Aibak, built this tomb for himself in 1235. The tomb is located to the northwest of the Qutb complex, near Iltutmish's extensions to the Quwwat-ul-Islam Masjid. It was originally capped by a dome supported by "squinch arches", a type of true arch (see p.96), but this collapsed because the local artisans were unfamiliar with the technique of constructing true arches. The exterior walls are unornamented, relieved only by simple carved bands. In contrast, the interior is richly adorned with geometric and arabesque patterns as well as Quranic inscriptions in Naskh and Kufic lettering.

⚜ **UNEMBELLISHED EXTERIOR**
Each side of this tomb, a square structure with a plain façade, is 9m (29.5ft) in length. It has entrances on three sides, and was originally covered by a dome.

OPEN CHAMBER ✣
The marble cenotaph lies in the middle of the open tomb chamber. The actual kabr *or grave lies in the crypt, ringed by elaborately ornamented squinch arches.*

❧ **CENTRAL MIHRAB**
On the closed western wall are three mihrabs. The central one is made of marble, its arches, pillars, and panels decorated with geometrical and floral carvings.

squinch arch

🔖 **RICHLY ORNAMENTED ARCHES**
*A profusion of carved calligraphic inscriptions
and floral patterns cover the three arched doorways
of Iltutmish's tomb; this offsets the simplicity of the
plain exterior walls.*

Alai Minar

A short walk away from the Quwwat-ul-Islam Masjid and Alauddin's *madrasa* is the Alai Minar. This unfinished minaret (only the first storey was constructed) was built by Alauddin Khilji around the year 1315. Standing 24.5m (80ft) tall, it was intended to be twice the height and size of the Qutb Minar – a part of his grand project of extending the Quwwat-ul-Islam Masjid to twice its original size. Unlike the Qutb Minar, it stands on a platform. Work on the Minar was stopped after Alauddin's death in 1316.

🔖 **THE SECOND MINAR**
*This incomplete structure has angular flutings on
the outside, an entrance on the east, and a gently
sloping ramp on the inside. It gives an idea of how
the Qutb Minar looked when it was begun.*

incomplete base made
of sandstone rubble

Konark

King Narasimhadeva I of the 13th-century Eastern Ganga dynasty was an ambitious ruler who wanted to build a magnificent temple to display the greatness of the architecture of Kalinga (the present-day state of Orissa) and to pay homage to Surya, the sun god. The Sun Temple was built at Konark in Orissa, home to perhaps the largest concentration of temples in India. In Hinduism, it is believed that the sun begins the day as Brahma the creator, then becomes Shiva the destroyer at noon, and ends the day as Vishnu the sustainer, thus embodying the holy trinity of Hinduism's most important gods. Ancient Hindu religious texts mention Konark (or Konarak) as a centre for sun worship. On the sandy shores of the Bay of Bengal, the temple was designed as a gigantic chariot for the sun god, complete with wheels and horses ready to carry Surya on his daily journey across the sky. Its 12 pairs of wheels and seven horses represent time. The 24 wheels reflect the 24 hours of a day, in 12 pairs that perhaps denote the 12 months in a year, while the seven horses are the seven days of a week. The temple faces the east and catches the sun from dawn to dusk; the name Konark literally translates into *kona* (corner) and *arka* (sun). The Sun Temple is renowned for the superb sculptures that jostle for space on almost every surface. The many myths and legends associated with this masterpiece make it resonate with mystery, with erotic sculptures adding to its earthly allure. A UNESCO World Heritage Site, the Sun Temple is no longer a living temple, but its colossal proportions and architectural magnificence inspire awe and delight.

GLORY OF THE SUN
The Sun Temple at Konark, Orissa, lies on the eastern coast of India.

Kings of Kalinga

A formidable power in ancient India, the kingdom of Kalinga (present-day Orissa) was conquered by Mauryan emperor Ashoka. Under Ashoka, Kalinga flourished, but his rule did not last long. The Chedi kings conquered the territory, the most important of them being King Kharavela, who was a patron of architecture – the earliest surviving monuments of Orissa date from his reign. A number of obscure kings ruled till the 11th century CE. Then came the Eastern Ganga dynasty, which ruled from the 11th to the 15th century. Under its control, Kalinga enjoyed a long period of stability and became a renowned centre of art, philosophy, and temple architecture. Two of India's most famous temples – Konark's Sun Temple and the Jagannath Temple at Puri – were built under the patronage of Eastern Ganga rulers.

- ❧ c.268–231 BCE **Emperor Ashoka** rules over the Mauryan empire.

- ❧ c.261 BCE **Ashoka** conquers Kalinga.

- ❧ 1st century BCE **Kharavela** assumes power.

- ❧ 1038 CE **Trikalingadhipat,** a local chieftain, comes to power; the **Eastern Ganga dynasty** is established.

- ❧ 1078–1147 **Anantavarman Codagangadeva** rules over Kalinga.

- ❧ 1238–1264 **Narasimhadeva I** reigns.
- ❧ c.1250 **Sun Temple** at Konark.

- ❧ 1435 Ganga reign ends; **Surya dynasty** (1435–1568) rules over Kalinga.

- ❧ 1568 **Kalapahada**, a Muslim warlord, conquers Kalinga; the Sun Temple is possibly desecrated and abandoned.

A Golden Period

When Narasimhadeva I ascended the throne in 1238 CE, he faced threats from neighbouring rulers such as the Kakatiyas of the south and the sultan of Bengal. He defeated his enemies and then settled down to rule Kalinga. It was a time of peace and prosperity, and the king used it well, turning his attention to effective governance, charitable activities, and building temples. In *Ekavali*, a composition by Vidyadhara, his court poet, he is eulogized as a great builder and patron. His greatest achievement was the construction of the magnificent Sun Temple at Konark, built in homage to the sun god.

The story of Samba

The history of the Sun Temple is inextricably linked to the legend of Samba, the son of Lord Krishna. The story goes that Samba inadvertently intruded on Lord Krishna's wives in their secret bathing place. Enraged at his impropriety, Lord Krishna cursed Samba with leprosy. Later, when he realized that Samba had not gone to the spot intentionally, he took pity on his son and told him to pray to Surya, the sun god. After a long penance of 12 years, Samba was cured when Surya left a white lotus for him at Konark. In gratitude, Samba constructed a shrine on the spot to honour the god.

THE SUN GOD ❧
This statue on the north wall of the temple portrays Surya in high boots, with his hair tied in a bun. The statue is 3.38m (11ft) high and 1.8m (6ft) wide.

⚜ FRIEZE ON WALL

A procession of figures, depicting the everyday life of Kalinga, marches across this frieze on the wall of the temple.

Trade with foreign lands

Konark was once a busy port of Kalinga and had extensive maritime relations with several Asian and African countries. In the 1st century BCE, it controlled most of the trade links on the eastern coast in the Bay of Bengal. During the rule of the Ganga dynasty, trade with countries such as Burma (Myanmar) prospered. Foreigners visited the royal court bearing gifts; a relief on the top frieze on the south side of the temple's platform depicts visitors presenting an African giraffe to the king, who is mounted on a magnificent elephant (left).

KING RECEIVING VISITORS

FALL OF THE TOWER

The Sun Temple once had a lofty tower, about 70m (230ft) high. Its colossal size, as well as the temple's proximity to the sea, made it an important navigational aid for European sailors heading towards Calcutta (Kolkata) – they began to call the temple the Black Pagoda. The tower, however, caved in by the 19th century, most likely due to corrosion caused by seawinds and sand. This 1837 sketch (right) by James Fergusson, a British archaeologist, shows a portion of the tower behind the temple. This, too, was decimated by a strong gale in October 1848.

LAST REMAINS OF KONARK'S TOWER

COLOSSAL LIONS
Two magnificent statues of rearing lions stand guard at the steps leading to the dance pavilion. The lions each crush an elephant holding a human figure in its trunk.

Kalinga Temple Style

Formerly called Kalinga, Orissa is famous for its temples. The most exceptional in terms of architecture and sculpture is the magnificent Sun Temple of Konark, built by artisans who had honed their skills constructing earlier religious buildings over decades. Like many typical Hindu temples in eastern India, the complex included a *natmandir* (dance pavilion), *jagamohana* (main assembly hall), and a *rekha deul* (sanctuary). The square *jagamohana* is on a *pabhaga* (platform) where the remains of the sanctuary also stand. The *jagamohana* and the sanctuary had four sections each, which is typical of Orissan architecture, but on an exceptionally large scale. These sections are the *pabhaga*, the *bada* (main part of the structure), the *gandi* (tiered tower), and the *mastaka* (the crowning spire), each component perfectly complementing the others from the base to the top.

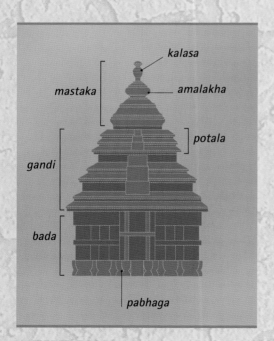

⚜ TIERED ROOF
The three potalas *(tiers) composed of projections and recesses give the roof a pagoda-like look. The* kalasha *that capped the* mastaka *no longer exists.*

Entrance from the East

The magnificent tiered roof of the Sun Temple looms large behind the now roofless dance pavilion. Both face east to greet the sun at dawn. Guarding the approach to the pavilion are two giant lions, representing the king's might. Each menacing lion crushes a cowering elephant, which in turn holds a human body in its trunk. All this, and the original tower standing 70m (230ft) high over the temple's sanctuary, would have inspired visitors with awe as they came to pay homage to Surya.

rampant lion

SHOW OF MIGHT ⟩
Perhaps the sight of a lion subduing an elephant was also meant to ward off intruders.

Ornamental dance pavilion

Also known as the *bhoga-mandapa* (hall of offerings to the deity), the pillared dance pavilion is believed to have been used by musicians and dancers for festivities in honour of the sun god. It is built on a platform and its missing roof was also probably tiered like the roof of the *jagamohana*. A number of images relating to dance and music are carved on its platform, pillars, and pilasters. The exterior of the platform is covered with sculpted figures in suspended animation, some in niches. Many depict women in various poses: with arms raised over the head, holding a flower, or caressing a child. Some of the niches near the corners have images of deities, while high up on the platform are rows showing geese, elephants, palanquin-bearers, and marching soldiers. From the open-air pavilion, the visual impact of the front of the temple is breathtaking.

❧ LEADING UP TO THE PAVILION
This flight of steps on the east, flanked by a pair of lions and elephants, leads to the platform on which dance pavilion stands.

ETERNAL RHYTHMS ❧
Figures on the face of this pillar created a serene ambience for the dancers and musicians performing in the dance pavilion.

Sculptured pillars

The majestic pillars at the centre of the pavilion are covered in fine sculptures, including rows of figures that shimmer with expression and movement. Dancers and musicians can be seen playing a variety of instruments, such as the flute, cymbals, and *dholak* (oblong drum). Carvings of sensuous, slender-waisted *alasa-kanyas* (maidens) and *mithunas* (amorous couples) also adorn the pillars. Terrifying mythical beasts stamp and roar as they rampage around the columns.

❧ MUSICIANS AND BEASTS
A musician playing a flute and a buxom female dancer flank a hybrid lion in this frieze.

Layout of the Sun Temple complex

The Sun Temple stands in a rectangular complex along with other minor temples and sculptures. Directly in front of the temple lies the dance pavilion, aligned on an east-west axis with the main assembly hall and sanctuary. The remains of a small platform for the musicians are visible between the pavilion and the assembly hall. To the south and east of the compound are the kitchen and the Mayadevi and Vaishnava temples, while the Shrine of the Nine Planets – a stone slab carved with deities of the nine planets – lies in the northeast corner. The plan illustrated below shows the temple's layout in its original state; the secondary shrines on the sides and back of the sanctuary are badly dilapidated. Though the interior of the main assembly hall is inaccessible, the walk around the temple is mesmerizing.

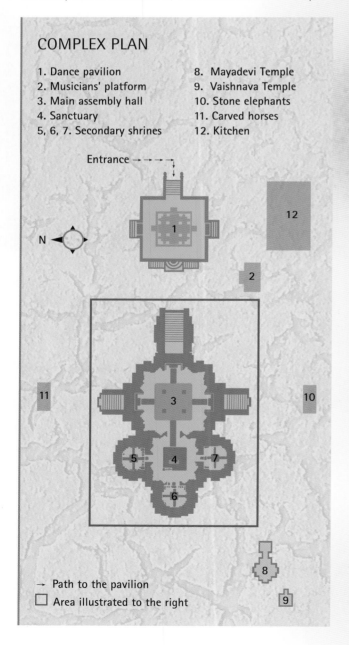

COMPLEX PLAN

1. Dance pavilion
2. Musicians' platform
3. Main assembly hall
4. Sanctuary
5, 6, 7. Secondary shrines
8. Mayadevi Temple
9. Vaishnava Temple
10. Stone elephants
11. Carved horses
12. Kitchen

Entrance → → →

N

→ Path to the pavilion
☐ Area illustrated to the right

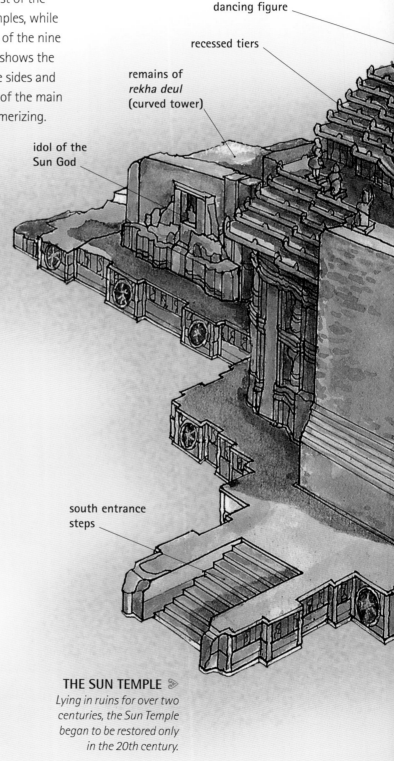

dancing figure

recessed tiers

remains of *rekha deul* (curved tower)

idol of the Sun God

south entrance steps

THE SUN TEMPLE ▷
Lying in ruins for over two centuries, the Sun Temple began to be restored only in the 20th century.

pot finial
(now missing)

amalakha
(fluted stone)

MATERIALS

Three types of metamorphic rock were used to build the temple
– khondalite, chlorite, and laterite. These were not available
locally, so they were probably brought from far-flung areas
by rafts on the river Chandrabhaga. The main material used
for contruction was khondalite, which was soft and easy to
carve but quickly corroded, leading to the collapse of some
parts of the structure. Chlorite, a greenish rock that
is hard and durable, was used mainly for the
doorframes and some sculptures, while
ochre-coloured laterite was used to
construct platforms and stairways.

CHLORITE

North

ornate *bada*
(wall below
roof)

pabhanga
(platform)

east entrance
steps

chariot wheel

doorway of *jagmohana*
(main assembly hall)

carved horse

The main temple

The architect, Bishnu Maharana, designed the temple as a gigantic chariot of Surya. To achieve this, he built the main assembly hall, the sanctuary, and two subsidiary shrines as one whole, not as separate units, on a shared platform. The assembly hall, or *jagamohana*, is the best-preserved portion of the temple. The three-tiered roof resembles a pagoda, which is why the temple was called the "Black Pagoda" by European sailors. Its height of about 39m (128ft) indicates that, in proportion, the height of the now ruined sanctuary and its tower may have been 61m (200ft). The platform on which they were built is 4m (13ft) high, with flights of steps from the east, west, and north sides. Splendid carvings on the sides of the platform depict the religious, military, social, and domestic aspects of 13th-century life.

DANCING FIGURE

amalakha
(fluted stone)

animated dancer

STEPPED ROOF ≫
The recesses between each tier are covered with sculptures, many of them free-standing dancers and musicians.

CARVINGS ON ROOF TIERS

✤ **FEMALE MUSICIAN**
*A vivacious celestial figure on
the roof dances to the rhythm
of her cylindrical drum.*

The assembly hall

The *jagamohana* has been boarded up since 1905 for conservation, so the interior is now inaccessible. Historical records indicate that it was unadorned but plastered, with a false ceiling resting on four massive pillars. These collapsed in 1848; subsequently, the hall was filled with sand to prevent further damage. The sanctuary behind the *jagamohana*, before it caved in, was connected to the hall by an internal corridor. It is said that the *garbha-griha* (sanctum) within the sanctuary once contained a consecrated idol of the sun god, but it is now empty.

Eastern doorway

Of the three doorways to the *jagamohana* of the Sun Temple, the one facing the east is the best preserved. It is made of chlorite and is divided into eight frames, each bearing exquisite carvings of motifs such as leaves on stems and the double coil of a *naga* (serpent) couple. The frames gradually recede and diminish in size with the outermost frame projecting the most. The motifs on the frames climb all the way up, but stop at the centre of the lintel to make space for another set of intricate carvings on a panel. The lowest panel shows an image of Lakshmi, the Hindu goddess of wealth, flanked by a pair of elephants.

STEPS TO THE JAGAMOHANA ✤
*Stone steps on the east lead to the
platform and doorway. Images of
deities once adorned the doorway's
lintel, which has since collapsed.*

✤ **ORNATE DOOR-FRAME**
*Fine ornamental scrollwork adorns
the surface of each frame of the
doorway; tiny figures of door-
guards stand at the base.*

The sun god's chariot

Ancient Iranian texts record the sun god crossing the heavens in his divine chariot, and it is said that Narasimhadeva I requested experts from the Magi, a sun-worshipping clan of Iran, to help his architect to design the temple. This cultural exchange of ideas is reflected in the sun god statue wearing high boots (left), which is unusual for a Hindu deity. It is one of three images of Surya that stand in niches on the south, west, and north walls of the temple. The temple, which took 12 years to complete, has always amazed visitors – Rabindranath Tagore, the 1913 Nobel Prize Laureate in Literature, remarked, "Here the language of stone surpasses the language of man".

⚘ MAJESTIC RIDER
Astride his horse, the sun god is ready to cross the skies. This statue in a niche on the south wall shows the god wearing a crown, short dhoti *(loin cloth), and high boots.*

CELESTIAL CHARIOT ⧉
This symbolic vehicle of the sun god is drawn by seven caparisoned horses, as though straining at the harness.

READY FOR FLIGHT

An allegory of time

The sun is synonymous with time, and it is believed that the 24 wheels of this chariot-temple represent the 24 hours of a day and the seven horses are the seven days of the week. The temple has suffered the ravages of time and now only one horse remains intact. The celestial chariot is also a symbolic processional vehicle that is accompanied by musicians and dancers on the roof and façade of the surviving portions of the temple and its platform. At the bottom of the platform runs a frieze of 1,700 elephants (see pp.124–25). The splendour of the temple prompted Abul Fazl, a16th-century historian at the Mughal court, to remark, "Even those whose judgement is critical and who are difficult to please stand astonished at its sight."

STATUE OF SURYA ON WEST WALL

The chariot wheel

The chariot of the sun god has 24 wheels, twelve pairs on each side of the *jagamohana's* platform. Each wheel is 3.5m (10ft) in diameter and is decorated with intricate carvings. The craftsmanship demonstrates an impressive eye for detail and accuracy, with even the axle kept in position by a pin, as in a functional wheel. Eight spokes radiate from the hub to the rim and each spoke is interspersed with a beaded rod to strengthen the wheel.

⌂ ROYAL ELEPHANT
This carving on a spoke depicts a scene from an expedition. Elephants were used for warfare, hunting, and transportation.

⌂ BATHING MAIDEN
A royal lady sits cross-legged on a stool while two handmaidens help her bathe. One helper is pouring water while the other holds her robes.

⚘ **AMOROUS FIGURES**
A number of erotic sculptures are featured on the wheels. These carvings, based on poses described in the Kamasutra, *celebrate the joys of life.*

Portraying life

The richly carved spokes of each wheel bear medallions that contain carvings of everyday scenes from royal, military, and domestic life. Another medallion decorates the face of the axle. The hub around the axle is decorated with carvings of lotus petals. The rim of the wheel is embellished with a profusion of animals intertwined with creepers. All are masterpieces in miniature.

⚘ **HUNTING SCENE**
A soldier mounted on a rearing war horse strikes a beast with a lance; held within a finely carved medallion, this composition pulsates with energy.

The language of stone

The vibrant sculptures bring to life the period in which this majestic temple was built and can be classified into five broad categories: deities and royalty; celestial musicians and dancers; animals and mythical beasts; statues of amorous couples and maidens; and decorative motifs. Apart from gods and goddesses, a large number of depictions relate to myriad facets of royal life, both within and outside the palace. There are also portrayals of half-human and half-serpent figures called *nagas*, possibly to emphasize the supernatural character of the temple. A number of animal statues – such as monkeys, tigers, deer, and peacocks – indicate the artists were influenced by Buddhist texts such as the *Jataka Tales*. These tales show the Buddha taking the form of different animals to impart moral values.

PANEL OF FIGURES
On either side of the miniature temple in this panel on the temple's platform are dancers and human-serpent nagas.

COUPLE IN A NICHE
A male and female stand together in a niche sheltered by a canopy. They are flanked by two sensuous women.

MYTHICAL BEAST
A tusked hybrid of an elephant and lion crushes a human figure. The beast is covered in jewellery and is exquisitely carved.

Sensual art

A number of sculptures adorning the walls of the Sun Temple celebrate the union between males and females, using explicit erotic imagery. Several are placed in niches shaded by leafy branches or overhanging canopies. Amorous couples in a variety of embraces or maidens in alluring poses are richly decked with jewellery such as crowns, necklaces, bracelets, and bangles. Among the most outstanding are the nymphs on the first and second tiers of main assembly hall's roof. In their original state, these statues were polished or painted in vivid colours to highlight their sensuality and may have been symbolic and erotic in equal measure. Some scholars suggest that these sculptures symbolize a union with the divine.

MÉNAGE À TROIS

EVERYDAY LIFE
This family appears on one of the few depictions that record the daily activities of ordinary subjects – Konark's sculptors were mostly preoccupied with the world of kings, gods, and goddesses.

sculpted lovers

A SYMBOL OF PROCREATION
A graceful couple stands on an ornate circular pedestal in a niche framed by vertical panels of floral motifs.

Mayadevi Temple

To the southwest of the main temple are the remains of a shrine dedicated to Mayadevi, believed to be one of the sun god's wives. According to legend, however, the shrine was built for Ramachandi, a local goddess. Built in the typical temple style of Orissa, the temple stood on a platform. Though the roof of the structure has collapsed, remnants of the temple's walls are covered with carvings that depict hunting scenes, erotic figures, and floral motifs. Low steps lead to a dais in front of the doorway; only the pillars can be seen now.

NORTH FACE
An image of Surya on horseback stands in a niche in the northern wall of the platform.

WATER SPOUT
This crocodile on the side of the platform helped to drain water from the temple interior.

Around the Sun Temple

There are several smaller structures in the rectangular complex of the Sun Temple, but these have been reduced to their plinths. To the south of the dance pavilion are the remains of the kitchen, where *bhog* (offerings of food to the deities) was cooked, with a well nearby to provide water. To the southwest of the Mayadevi Temple is a small Vaishnava shrine, which indicates that other deities besides Surya were also worshipped within the precinct. Statues of mythical beasts are on display throughout the complex, along with several large, free-standing carved animals on the ground or on small platforms. These include colossal, caparisoned elephants on the north side and horses in full battle gear on the south, impressive in their scale and power.

GARGOYLE ON GUARD ⟫
This fierce-looking monster with a gaping mouth and protruding belly was perhaps placed in the temple precinct to scare away intruders.

⚐ **WAR ELEPHANT**
A life-sized military elephant carries the body of a slain soldier in its trunk. This royal animal is adorned with a head-dress, anklets, and other ornaments.

⚐ **BATTLE HORSE**
A large horse tramples an enemy soldier during battle; its bridle, harness, and saddle are carved in fine detail.

ornate head–gear

Hampi

The Vijayanagara empire was established in 1336 by Harihara I and Bukka I, sons of Sangama, a chieftain in south India. Both were officers in the army of Muhammad-bin-Tughlaq, Sultan of Delhi, but they rebelled and won independence after a hard-fought battle. To celebrate their great victory, they called their fledgling kingdom, soon to become an impressive empire, Vijayanagara or "City of Victory". It lies in a splendid setting of massive boulders and craggy hills, with the river Tungabhadra on one side. The city was divided, for practical purposes, into three parts – the sacred centre with numerous temples, the urban area where the subjects lived, and the royal complex of buildings meant exclusively for the monarchs and their families. According to accounts by Portuguese, Italian, and Persian visitors, it seems that as the

♨ **MAGNIFICENT CAPITAL**
Hampi lies on the south bank of the Tungabhadra river, in the Bellary district of Karnataka.

kingdom grew into a formidable empire, it traded with many countries and became famous for its art and culture. Its capital city was Hampi – the name by which the ruins are popularly known today. The empire flourished for 200 years but it collapsed in 1565, after the battle at Talikota between the monarch and a league of the sultans of neighbouring states. After being defeated, Vijayanagara broke up into small fiefdoms ruled by the Nayakas. Hampi is known for its colossal granite statues and fine carvings, for its distinctive style of architecture in large rectangular temple complexes with ornate pillars, pavilions, and gateways, and for an ingenious waterworks system. A UNESCO World Heritage Site, Hampi is fittingly called the largest open-air museum in the world.

Kings of Vijayanagara

After the Sangama brothers Harihara I and Bukka I laid the foundation for the Vijayanagara empire, succeeding rulers had the difficult task of protecting and expanding it. Krishnadeva Raya of the Tuluva dynasty is thought to be one of the most outstanding rulers of medieval India. He was an accomplished poet and scholar and left an indelible cultural footprint on the empire that flourished under him. He patronized temple building and often celebrated his military victories with splendid monuments. His reign became known as the golden age of Vijayanagara. The remains at Hampi showcase some of the finest architecture of India.

⮞ 1336 The Vijayanagara empire is founded with Hampi as its capital.

⮞ 1336-1485 Rule of the **Sangamas**
1336-1356 **Harihara I**
1356-1377 **Bukka I**
1377-1404 **Harihara II** rules and builds an efficient aqueduct system.
1406-1422 **Devaraya I** rules and is successful against the kings of Orissa.

⮞ 1486-1505 Rule of the **Saluvas**
1491-1505 **Narasimha Raya II**

⮞ 1505-1542 Rule of the **Tuluvas**
1503-1509 **Viranarasimha Raya**
1509-1529 **Krishnadeva Raya**, the greatest of the Vijayanagara kings.
1529-1542 **Achyutaraya** rules and expands the empire.

⮞ 1542-1565 Reign of **Aliya Rama Raya** of the **Aravidu dynasty**

⮞ 1565 The battle of Talikota leads to the breakup of the Vijayanagara empire.

The Saga of Hampi

A mythological story explains that the name Hampi is derived from Pampa – the goddess of the river Tungabhadra. Hampi was a pilgrimage centre before the Sangama brothers established the Vijayanagara kingdom, and had been ruled by a succession of dynasties including the Kadambas and Hoysalas. Harihara I and Bukka I concentrated on using the natural environs – the river and the boulders – to protect

RIVER TUNGABHADRA

their kingdom from invaders. The Sangamas made Hampi their capital and Virupaksha (a form of Lord Shiva) their presiding deity.

❧ **PANORAMIC VIEW**
Boulders and small temples on the Hemakuta Hill overlook the northern gateway of the Virupaksha Temple.

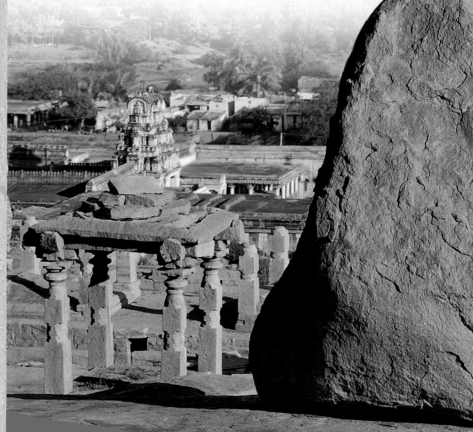

A world city

By the end of the 15th century, the Vijayanagara empire had grown very powerful and news of its wealth and might had travelled to many countries. Ships laden with goods sailed as far as Venice, as recounted by Italian traveller Niccolo Conti who visited Vijayanagara in the 15th century. Under Krishnadeva Raya, Vijayanagara reached great heights and became famous for its bazaars, where everything from precious jewels to horses and camels were traded. Textiles and spices were brought from all over the empire to the city for trade. Today only the ruins of these marketplaces remain.

⚜ FOREIGN TRADING
Robed traders (perhaps Persian) greet the king. Buying and selling horses for military purposes was a major part of Vijayanagara's commerce.

⚜ KRISHNADEVA RAYA
In this frieze, a subject greets the king, who sits elegantly with a handmaiden behind him.

Virupaksha Temple's north gate

THE RAMAYANA IN STONE

Hampi and its surroundings are considered holy ground because of temples dedicated to the gods Shiva and Vishnu. The two most sacred temples in Hampi – the Vitthala Temple and the Hazara Rama Temple – are dedicated to Vishnu and his 7th incarnation Rama. However, some areas are also believed to be part of Kishkindha, the monkey kingdom fought over by the brothers Vali and Sugriva, as narrated in the epic *Ramayana*. Several scenes from the *Ramayana* are carved on the walls of the Hazara Rama.

⚜ VALI AND SUGRIVA
This carving shows the brothers locked in a power struggle. Sugriva was finally crowned king with Rama's help.

Boulder Land

The geological history of Vijayanagara tells us that the granite boulders dominating the landscape were formed in the Archaean period (2,500–3,800 million years ago). Harihara I and Bukka I chose the site of the Vijayanagara kingdom for two reasons: the irregular granite boulders and the torrential river Tungabhadra provided natural fortification; and the granite was easily accessible for building palaces and other structures. The two brothers showed great foresight – the mighty Vijayanagara empire lasted 200 years. Although the granite was difficult to cut, skilled artisans carved exceptional pillars, monoliths, and shrines that tell their own stories. The granite monoliths, astounding in size and craftsmanship, together with the temples and boulders dotting this vast landscape, make Hampi a spectacular site.

Approach to Virupaksha

The main shrine in Hampi is the Virupaksha Temple where Shiva or Pampapati (husband of Pampa) is worshipped in the form of a *lingam* (phallic symbol). In front of its main eastern *gopuram* (entrance tower) is the Hampi Bazaar, a kilometre-long street flanked by single- and double-storeyed pavilions,

that dates back to the 16th and mid-17th centuries. The street in front of the temple is wide enough for a chariot to travel during the annual Chariot Festival that celebrates the marriage of Pampa with Shiva.

✎ MAIN GATEWAY
Each tier of this east-facing entrance – 52m (171ft) high – is ornately carved.

▲ GRANITE GIANTS
Surface erosion over millions of years and continued exposure to the elements weathered the rocks to give them their unique look.

INNER ENTRANCE

Virupaksha Temple

This complex originally had a few small Shiva shrines from the 7th century on which the present structures were built, making this one of the oldest living temples in India. A large courtyard lies beyond the east *gopuram*, from where a second courtyard can be accessed through the inner gateway. In the centre is a single-storey ornate *ranga mandapa* (temple hall) built by Krishnadeva Raya in 1510 to celebrate his coronation. A Nandi shrine faces the *ranga mandapa*. Beyond can be seen the towering north gateway.

GRANITE NANDI STATUE
Nandi the bull is the vehicle of Shiva. Statues of Nandi are a common feature in Shiva temples.

THE NORTH GATEWAY
This five-storeyed tower, also called Kangiri gopuram, *has beautiful carvings on all its tiers.*

finial atop the Nandi shrine

RANGA MANDAPA PILLARS

Layout of the Hampi complex

The abundance of granite boulders inspired the Vijayanagara builders to evolve a distinct style of architecture. The craggy landscape was not conducive to conventional building but the gradual addition of incredible structures by later monarchs places Hampi among the most unusual archaeological sites in India. The temple complexes and other structures are spread over 26km (16 miles) of this undulating landscape. The Virupaksha Temple is a good point of entry to begin the visit. This temple and the Vitthala complex are the two most interesting complexes.

MATERIALS

The architects of Vijayanagara defied the rough landscape to create masterpieces. The main material used for the construction of buildings was granite slabs. Granite was used for massive monoliths that were carved *in situ*. These were mostly coarse but impressive because of their proportions. Soapstone was readily available and was used extensively for intricately detailed carvings on pillars and tiles. Bricks plastered with mortar were used to line water tanks and channels and, at times, to create an attractive geometric pattern, which can be seen in the construction of the stepped tank in the royal enclosure.

GRANITE

Vitthala Temple

King's Balance

Achyutaraya Temple

Matanga Hill

Hampi Bazaar

River Tungabhadra

Kadalekalu Ganesh

Sasivekalu Ganesh

Virupaksha Temple

☐ Area illustrated below

VITTHALA TEMPLE ◈
One of the most ornate temple complexes in India, this architectural gem was built in the 15th century.

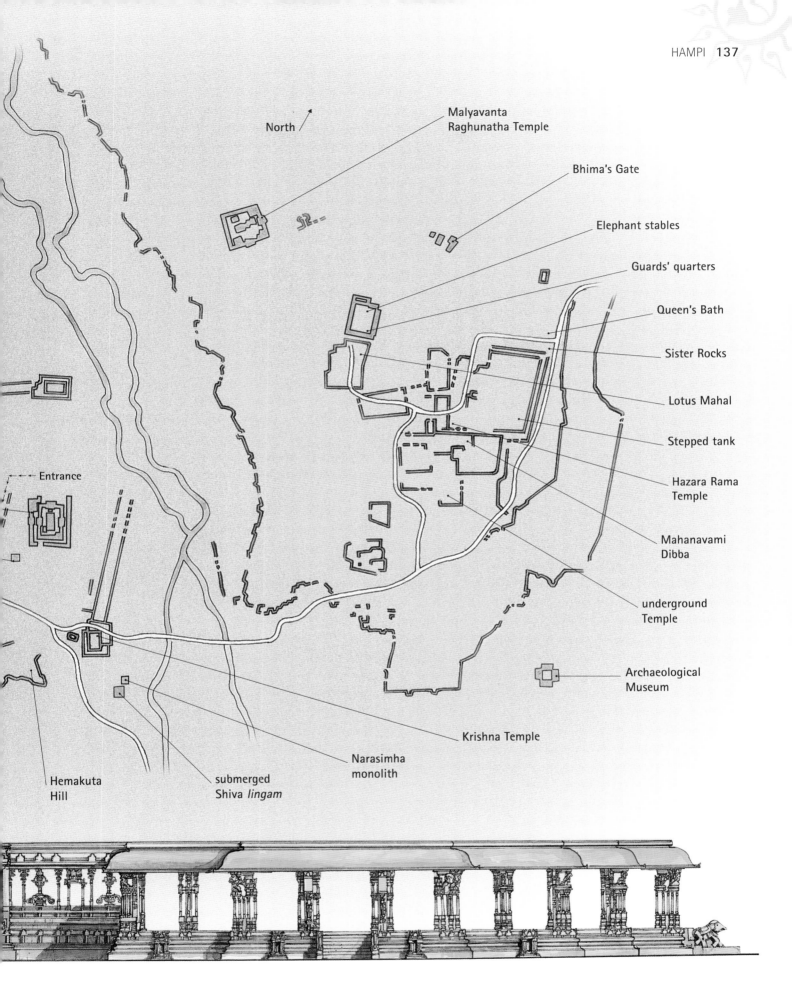

North

Malyavanta
Raghunatha Temple

Bhima's Gate

Elephant stables

Guards' quarters

Queen's Bath

Sister Rocks

Lotus Mahal

Stepped tank

Hazara Rama
Temple

Mahanavami
Dibba

underground
Temple

Archaeological
Museum

Entrance

Krishna Temple

Narasimha
monolith

Hemakuta
Hill

submerged
Shiva *lingam*

BOULDER-STREWN HILL

Hemakuta Hill

In the sacred centre, near the Virupaksha Temple, is Hemakuta Hill from where almost all of Hampi can be seen. Legend has it that Shiva stayed here while contemplating marriage to Pampa. When he finally decided to marry her, the sky miraculously rained gold on the hill – giving it the eponymous name *Hema* (gold in Sanskrit). There are a number of big and small temples, gateways, and pavilions here, with most of the shrines dedicated to Shiva. Some of these predate the Virupaksha Temple.

⚜ DOUBLE-STOREYED GATE
This gate is one of the two entrances to the hill; the other one is next to the Virupaksha Temple.

❦ A SCENIC VIEW
Small Shiva temples with tiered roofs grace the hill above the two entrance towers of Virupaksha Temple.

Sasivekalu and Kadalekalu Ganeshas

Two massive images of the elephant-headed god Ganesha are found on the slope of Hemakuta Hill. The Sasivekalu (mustard seed) Ganesha is a 2.4m (8ft) high monolith seated in an open-pillared hall, while the Kadalekalu (gram seed) Ganesha is a 4.5m (15ft) statue. The idols are thought to have been named according to the shape of their bellies. According to Hindu mythology, Ganesha removes obstacles. He is depicted with four arms and a protruding stomach that signifies the bounty of nature, and in one hand he holds a part of his broken tusk, signifying sacrifice.

KADALEKALU GANESHA

SASIVEKALU GANESHA

Krishna Temple

This temple was built by Krishnadeva Raya in 1513 to celebrate his victory over the eastern kingdom of Utkala (present-day Orissa). An inscription on a slab inside relates the story of the temple and the king's conquest. The inner sanctum, which is without the main idol, is built in such a way that natural light filters in through small cavities in the roof. The ten *avataras* (incarnations) of Vishnu – Lord Krishna is regarded as one of them – are carved on the walls and pillars of the temple.

KRISHNA ❧
This image of Krishna as a child taming a serpent is carved on a pillar in the temple.

main temple hall

❧ **ORNATE ROOFS**
The smaller prayer halls around the main temple hall have richly carved pillars and roofs.

COLOSSAL FORM OF VISHNU

Narasimha monolith

This magnificent figure of Vishnu in his Narasimha form (half-man, half-lion), the fourth incarnation of the god of preservation, is carved out of a single granite rock. Commissioned in 1528 by Krishnadeva Raya, it is an imposing statue 6.7m (22ft) high. It is also called Ugranarasimha (the terrifying Narasimha). He is shown sitting cross-legged in a yoga position on the coils of the divine serpent Adisesha, whose seven hoods majestically spread out behind the deity, sheltering him. Above the hoods is a lion head that completes this intimidating figure of Vishnu.

Achyutaraya Temple

Near the Hampi Bazaar is the Achyutaraya Temple. Though this temple was built for the deity Tiruvengalanathan, a form of Vishnu, it is better known as the Achyutaraya Temple, named for the Tuluva king in whose reign it was built. The temple plan consists of two rectangular enclosures, one inside the other, with the deity at the centre. The outer rectangle can be entered through a ruined tower, and another tower leads to the smaller rectangular complex, both towers aligned on the same axis. The walls of both courtyards are lined with pillared verandahs, though the inner ones are better preserved. Finished in 1534, this temple was perhaps the last project made on this massive scale by the Vijayanagara architects before the fall of the empire.

THREE DANCING FIGURES

PILLARED PAVILION 🐚
Pillars flank the entrance to the main hall. Intricately carved figures adorn the pillars of the temple.

Submerged Shiva lingam

Near the Narasimha is a 3m (10ft) tall Shiva *lingam* also called Badavilinga Temple. Legend has it that an impoverished woman commissioned the construction to prove her devotion to Shiva – in the local language *bada* means "poor". The *lingam* also has Shiva's three eyes carved on it, signifying his power.

🐚 **ON A BED OF WATER**
Standing in a semi-covered chamber, the lower part of the lingam *is always submerged in water. This water is channelled from the river Tungabhadra.*

MATANGA HILL

Close to the Achyutaraya Temple is the Matanga Hill, which is is the highest point in Hampi and lies at its centre. From this vantage point one can get a breathtaking view of Hampi – a sight that inspired Abdul Razzak, the Persian ambassador who visited Vijayanagara in 1443, to remark, "The city is such that the pupil of the eye has never seen a place like it, and the ear of intelligence has never been informed that there existed anything to equal it in the world."

King's Balance

This unusual structure was used by the kings to weigh themselves against gold or grain that was then distributed to the poor and to the priests. It is approximately 5m (16ft) high and is also known as Tula Bhara (weighing scales full of goods) or Tula Purushadana (weighing scales used for charity). It stands tall like a gateway just before the Vitthala Temple.

MAIN HALL
The monolithic pillars of this hall in the Achyutaraya Temple have beautifully carved scenes from Hindu mythology.

CHARITY OF KINGS
A pair of weighing scales was hung from the three loops on the stone beam.

Vitthala Temple

A couple of kilometres east of the Hampi Bazaar lies the grand Vitthala Temple complex. Its construction was started by Krishnadeva Raya in 1513 and continued by his successor, Achyutaraya. According to local legend, the temple was built as an abode for Vitthala or Vishnu on earth but when it was ready the deity refused to live in it because it was too ostentatious. The rectangular complex is 152m (500 ft) long and 94m (310 ft) wide. It has three entrance towers – in the east, south, and north. Though the main sanctuary still exists, it no longer contains a consecrated idol of Vishnu, the second god in the Hindu trinity.

☙ ENTRANCE TOWER
Like most gopurams, the entrance tower is capped by two stone cow horns, indicating the cow is sacred to Hindus.

☙ MUSICAL PILLARS
These hollow granite pillars at the assembly hall below produce musical notes of different pitches when tapped lightly.

RAGHUNATHA TEMPLE

Close to the Vitthala Temple complex is the Malyavanta Hill with the beautiful Raghunatha Temple. A narrow, slightly steep, but paved path leads to the top. It is believed that Rama and his brother Lakshmana lived on this hill while waiting for the monsoon season to end before marching to Lanka to rescue Rama's wife, Sita, who had been abducted by Ravana, king of Lanka.

TEMPLE ON THE HILL

STONE CHARIOT ☙
This shrine, shaped as a chariot, stands in front of the temple; it is dedicated to Garuda, the eagle mount of Vishnu.

Temple layout

The Vitthala Temple is 8m (25ft) high and 70m (230ft) long, and displays the remarkable level of expertise that the architects and artisans of Vijayanagara had reached. The complex showcases three basic structures typical of Vijayanagara temple architecture – *an ardha-mandapa* (open hall with pillars), a *mandapa* (closed assembly hall), and the *garbha-griha* (inner sanctum for the idol). Facing the temple is the famous stone chariot with wheels so realistic they look as if they could actually work. The steps to the chariot are guarded by stone elephants.

OPEN HALLS WITH RICHLY CARVED PILLARS

ORNAMENTAL BALUSTRADE

⊗ AMAZING REPLICA
The hub and lotus-shaped spokes of this chariot wheel have the exact proportions of a real wheel.

LEAPING YALLIS ⊗
Several pillars of the temple are carved out of a single stone. The carved forms represent yallis, mythical beasts.

HIGH ARCHES
Patterned arches chiselled out of stone frame the front of the quarters. The architecture blends harmoniously with the other buildings in the royal complex.

Guards' quarters

The Guards' quarters in the royal area are built close to the Elephant stables, indicating that they were, perhaps, used as a residence for guards and mahouts. Many buildings in this area showcase the cosmopolitan culture of the Vijayanagara rulers, who borrowed architectural ideas from the neighbouring Deccan sultanate to create an interesting blend of Islamic and Hindu architecture. This mix is seen in the use of pointed arches – a typical Islamic feature – adorned with Hindu floral motifs in the Guards' quarters. This building now houses an archaeological sculpture gallery.

Elephant stables

The stables are built in perfect symmetry with 11 high vaulted chambers to house the royal elephants. According to Abdul Razzak, the Persian ambassador, each elephant had a separate stall and the ceiling was made of strong wooden beams. Each stall has metal rings hanging from the ceiling, which were used to tie the elephants. The Islamic-style domes above the stables are made of brick and mortar and have an alternating tiered and ribbed pattern. They flank the central projection that resembles a Hindu temple roof.

ACCESS FOR THE MAHOUT ≫
Small arched openings on either side of each stall allowed the mahout to enter and exit.

Lotus Palace

This double-storeyed palace in the royal enclosure was built in the 16th century as a summer retreat for the queens of Vijayanagara – its high ceilings and many archways cooled the palace in the hot months. The building stands on a platform carved out of granite slabs. The high recessed arches are an example of Islamic design and are adorned with intricate lotus motifs that are typical of Hindu architecture, displaying a rich synthesis of Hindu-Islamic architecture. The tiered domes of this summer palace – it has eight pyramidal roofs surrounding a higher central roof – resemble the petals of the lotus flower and give the building its name. In contrast to the ornate façade, the interior of the palace is unadorned. The second storey has many balconies and arched windows that are decorated with intricate floral motifs. Near the palace are three watch towers that were built to provide the royal families with security.

WATCH TOWER

RECESSED ARCHES

TWO-STOREYED PALACE
The exterior shows the symmetrical plan of the building. The high arches are embellished with intricate floral carvings.

inverted lotus carving

over–hanging canopy

Underground Shiva Temple

Close to the royal complex is this temple built by the Tuluva king Krishnadeva Raya. An inscription in the temple tells us that it was constructed on his coronation. There is a gateway at ground level from where one can descend into the temple complex. This temple was probably built for the royal family to pray privately to Prasanna Virupaksha (Gracious Shiva), the state deity. Near the main hall is a small temple dedicated to Shiva's consort, Pampa.

DANCING SHIVA ON PILLAR

THE SUNKEN TEMPLE
This temple, also known as Prasanna Virupaksha Temple, lies several metres below ground level.

MAIN HALL ✎
The large main hall of the temple has cubical pillars supporting the roof.

FLOODED INTERIOR
Water is always present inside this low-lying temple, making it difficult to gain access to the sanctum.

Sister Rocks

Near the Underground Temple are the Sister Rocks. These are two massive boulders leaning into each other. Legend has it that two sisters insulted the goddess Pampa and she turned them into stone in revenge. They are also known as Akka-tangi-gundu or "Sister Boulders".

🔺 NATURAL ARCH
The unusual formation of these two rocks forms a gateway. The boulders of Hampi were part of enormous monoliths that cracked due to erosion over centuries

AQUEDUCT SYSTEM

A well-developed waterworks system carried water from the river Tungabhadra to the numerous tanks and temples of Hampi. The 24km (15m)-long stone ducting runs mainly along the ground except in some places where it was raised on granite pillars to give it structural stability. The system was put in place in the 14th century by Harihara II of the Sangama dynasty and a large part of it is still intact and functioning efficiently today. The water was used for domestic and irrigation purposes as well as temple rituals. Hampi's ingenious aqueduct system reflects the exceptional workmanship of the engineers and stonemasons of the Vijayanagara empire.

WATER CANAL IN THE UNDERGROUND TEMPLE

Hazara Rama Temple

This temple in the royal enclosure was built in the 15th century by Sangama king Devaraya II and used as a private place of worship for the rulers and their families. One legend states that it is called the Hazara (thousand) Rama because its walls have more than a thousand scenes from the epic *Ramayana* carved on its walls and pillars. Another legend claims that the temple gets its name from the local word *hazaramu*, which means "hall". The inscriptions at the site indicate that this temple was built to pay homage to Rama. The walls of the temple are built on a moulded platform. To the south of the main entrance are two gateways leading to the rest of the royal centre.

FISH-HEADED SPOUT

⚜ **WATER OUTLET**
This ornate fountain is fed by the stone aqueduct that brought water from the river Tungabhadra to the temple.

🍃 **RICH EXTERIOR**
The tiered roof has sculptures of deities in niches and the space between each is filled with rows of attendants.

TEMPLE HALL
There are four cubical pillars at the centre of the closed hall.

Mythology in granite

Though not a big temple complex by Vijayanagara standards, the Hazara Rama site is significant for the scenes from the *Ramayana* carved on its walls and pillars. The panels tell the story of Rama in chronological order. There are also several finely carved sculptures of Vishnu and his other incarnations, including his rarely depicted form as the Buddha. There is an empty pedestal in the sanctum where the consecrated idols of Rama and his wife, Sita, may have been.

SCENE FROM THE RAMAYANA

CARVING IN SOAPSTONE

sloping canopy over the porch

PROFUSION OF IMAGES
Carvings depict a procession of horses and elephants, from one of the episodes of the Ramayana, *in friezes engraved on the exterior walls of the temple.*

Mahanavami Dibba

A distinctive feature in the royal enclosure is the *Dibba* (platform), which sits on a natural elevation and is 12m (40ft) high. The platform is thought to have been built in stages and was completed in the 16th century to celebrate Krishnadeva Raya's victory over Orissa. The king sat on top of this dais, which faces east, and watched the celebration of the Mahanavami or Dashehra festival that took place over nine days at the end of the monsoon, after which the king planned his military strategy. Each of the three ascending tiers of the platform has carved scenes in panels. In 1520, Domingo Paes, a Portuguese visitor, called this a "House of Victory".

⚙ ROYAL STEPS
The king walked up these steps to reach the dais. There are stairways on the south and west sides.

PANEL DETAIL ⫸
Enemy soldiers attack a royal elephant during the battle between Krishnadeva Raya and the king of Orissa.

Stepped tank

This recently excavated tank is an architectural feat of perfect symmetry. Constructed out of slabs of chlorite schist (a type of metamorphic rock not available locally) and lined with brick, it is 22m (72ft) square and almost 7m (23ft) deep. It is remarkable for the workmanship of the steps and landings, which are placed in a flawless geometrical pattern of five tiers that descend to the bottom of the tank on all four sides. The tank was built for storing and supplying water brought here from the river Tungabhadra via the aqueduct system.

FEAT OF ARCHITECTURE ⫸
The tank was fed through a spout projecting from a raised water channel supported by strong granite pillars.

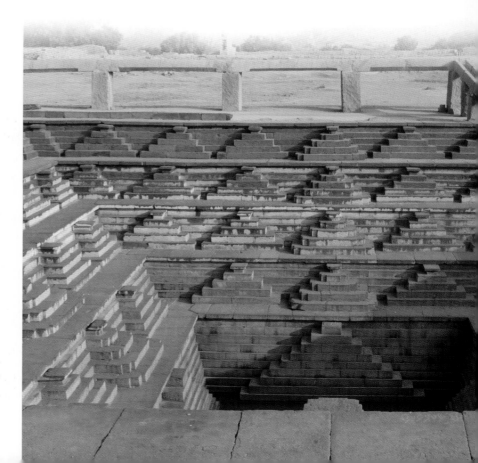

Queen's Bath

This exquisite 15th-century rectangular building in the royal enclosure is built using Hindu and Islamic styles of architecture. Though the façade is simple, the interior is rich in floral Hindu motifs and geometric Islamic designs. The bathing pavilion, meant only for the royal family, has 24 rooms with arches that are roofed with high domes made in the Islamic style around the square uncovered bath. An aqueduct brought water to it from the river Tungabhadra via Hampi's waterworks system (see p.147).

The bath is 15m (50ft) long and 2m (6ft) deep and is reached by climbing down steps that are in one corner. The pavilion's exterior is surrounded by a large moat-like depression, perhaps made to store and drain water or to keep intruders out.

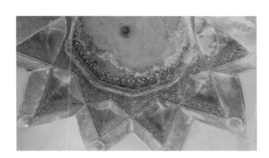

ARCHED WINDOW   **GEOMETRIC PATTERN ON CEILING**

☞ **BALCONIES OVER THE BATH**
Eight balconies with windows project over the basin. The pointed arches of the windows are built in Islamic style.

Stone gateway

This well-constructed archway, built in the 15th century stands approximately 17m (56ft) high. It is called Bhima's Gate because it contains a well-preserved bas-relief carving of Bhima – a character of legendary power who was one of the five Pandava brothers from the epic *Mahabharata*. The gateway complex is to the southeast of the royal enclosure and is an excellent example of Vijayanagara military architecture. It is designed with walls in a zigzag pattern that would make it virtually impossible for an invading army on elephants to enter and manoeuvre through.

☞ **BHIMA BAS-RELIEF**
The detailed carving shows Bhima with a club in one hand and a celestial lotus in the other.

BHIMA'S GATE

Humayun's Tomb

A tranquil oasis in a bustling city, Humayun's Tomb – a UNESCO World Heritage Site – is one of the best-preserved examples of Mughal architecture in Delhi. It was built between 1562 and 1571 under the supervision of Mirak Mirza Ghiyas, a Persian architect. Humayun's senior wife, Haji Begum, commissioned him to design the mausoleum, six years after her husband's death in 1556. Some attribute its construction to Humayun's son, Akbar, considered to be the greatest Mughal ruler. The tombs of members of the royal family, including Humayun's wives, are also in the mausoleum. Built by Persian and Indian craftsmen at a cost of 1.5 million rupees, it is a spectacular example of the synthesis of Persian and pre-Mughal Indo-Islamic architectural traditions. Its central octagonal chamber is surrounded by four corner chambers and imposing central arches on four sides – these features, together with the majestic double dome, reflect a strong Persian influence. On the other hand, the elevation of the tomb on an arcaded plinth, the beautifully finished red sandstone with marble inlay work, and the graceful silhouette of pavilions and cupolas are pre-Mughal in style. Its grand scale, ornamental details, and garden setting became a hallmark of subsequent Mughal architecture, which reached its zenith 70 years later in Shah Jahan's Taj Mahal. Also within the tomb complex are several other 16th-century structures, such as Afsarwala's Mosque and Tomb, Isa Khan's Mosque and Tomb, and Nai ka Gumbad (Barber's Tomb).

⚭ HISTORIC CITY
Delhi has been the centre of power for many kingdoms down the ages.

The Mughal Empire

Founded by Babur, a Central Asian chieftain and descendant of Chenghiz Khan and of Tamerlaine, the Mughal empire remained a dominant force in India for almost 200 years. Under Akbar, the empire extended from Afghanistan in the northwest to Bengal in the east, and from Kashmir in the north to the Deccan in the south. Connoisseurs of literature, the arts, and architecture, which flourished under their patronage, the Mughals played a pivotal role in creating a rich pluralistic culture that blended the best of Islamic and Hindu traditions.

- 1526 **Babur** defeats Ibrahim Lodi, the last sultan of Delhi, marking the foundation of Mughal rule in India.

- 1530 **Humayun** ascends the throne, but loses it to Sher Shah Suri, an Afghan warlord from Bihar, in 1540.

- 1540–1555 **Sher Shah Suri** rules over north India from his base at Purana Qila (Old Fort) in Delhi. **Humayun** becomes a fugitive in western India; flees to Persia.

- 1555 **Humayun** regains lost territories.

- 1556 Humayun dies. **Akbar** succeeds him; expands the Mughal empire.

- 1605 Akbar dies. His eldest son, Salim, assumes control of the empire, taking the name **Jahangir** (World Conqueror).

- 1627 **Shah Jahan** is crowned emperor after Jahangir's death.

- 1658 **Aurangzeb** succeeds Shah Jahan. The Mughal empire begins to crumble after his death in 1707.

A Chequered Life

Born in 1508, Nasiruddin Muhammad Humayun ("Humayun" means "fortunate") was perhaps the most unfortunate of the Mughal rulers. After Babur's death in 1530, he succeeded to the throne, but his reign was marked by political strife, even with his own brothers. Lacking his father's military acumen, he was defeated by Sher Shah Suri. Forced into exile for 15 years, he was a homeless wanderer until the Shah of Persia gave him refuge and an army of 12,000 soldiers. He then reclaimed his territories, but died shortly afterwards.

Pleasure and superstition

Affable and cultured, Humayun was not an able commander, although he was courageous. An easygoing ruler, he did not make the effort to consolidate his victories despite successful campaigns against Malwa and Gujarat. A skilled mathematician and astronomer, he preferred to spend most of his time in esoteric pursuits. He was unusually superstitious, to such an extent that he organized the administration of his kingdom on astrological lines and even wore clothes of the colour appropriate to the planet of the day.

EMPEROR HUMAYUN
Humayun's fascination with Persian high culture began at the court of Shah Tahmasp, where he had sought refuge after being exiled.

❧ **SHER MANDAL**
Situated in the Purana Qila, this double-storeyed octagonal pavilion is thought to have served as Humayun's library.

Sher Shah Suri

The founder of the Suri dynasty, Sher Shah Suri defeated Humayun to emerge as the undisputed ruler of north India. A wise administrator, he initiated several reforms to improve revenue collection, besides building roads, caravanserais, and military posts. He died in 1545, after an artillery rocket exploded near him, and was buried in a beautiful mausoleum at Sasaram, Bihar.

WARRIOR AND STATESMAN ❧
Renowned for his triumphs on the battlefield, Sher Shah Suri was also an able and exemplary ruler.

❧ **PURANA QILA**
Oblong in plan, the fort has walls of rubble, studded with arches.

Dinpanah and Purana Qila

Soon after his accession in 1530, Humayun begun building a new city on the banks of the river Yamuna, which he named Dinpanah (Refuge of the Faithful). After his defeat, the victorious Sher Shah used the same site to establish his own city, called Shergarh (Tiger's Fort). The ruins of the inner citadel of the city still survive, now known as Purana Qila (Old Fort). Among the few buildings within the fort, two are particularly noteworthy – the Qala-i-Kuhna mosque and the Sher Mandal, both built by Sher Shah.

QALA-I-KUHNA MOSQUE ❧
This single-domed sandstone mosque has five arched doorways adorned with black and white marble.

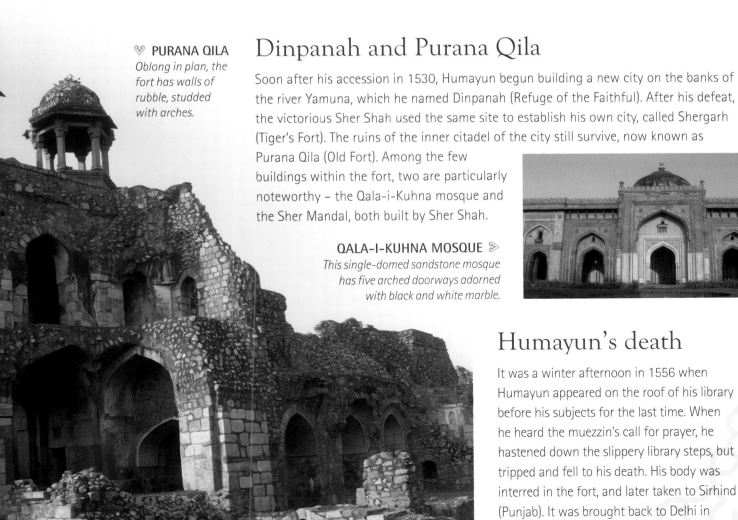

Humayun's death

It was a winter afternoon in 1556 when Humayun appeared on the roof of his library before his subjects for the last time. When he heard the muezzin's call for prayer, he hastened down the slippery library steps, but tripped and fell to his death. His body was interred in the fort, and later taken to Sirhind (Punjab). It was brought back to Delhi in 1568 when his tomb was completed.

Synthesis of Styles

Mughal rulers admired the Persian architectural tradition, adopting its grandeur and sophisticated geometrical proportions. The fusion of Persian and indigenous styles in Mughal architecture is best exemplified in Humayun's Tomb. The mausoleum is based on Persian prototypes, its architect, Mirak Mirza Ghiyas, being a Persian from Bukhara. Haji Begum, who had lived with Humayun during his exile in Persia, seems to have been influenced by the architecture she saw there. Persian features include the three great arches on each side, the high double dome (used in Persia since the 13th century), landscaping of the gardens in the *charbagh* style, arch-netting in the vaults, and geometrically arranged coloured tiles. These features are combined with pre-Mughal elements such as marble inlay work, lotus-bud fringed arches, *jaali* (lattice work) screens, *chhatris* (pavilions with umbrella-shaped domes), and wide *chhajjas* (overhanging eaves).

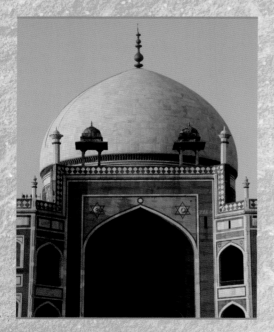

ARCHITECTURAL HARMONY
The pre-Mughal-style chhatris *blend perfectly with the dome and arches of Persian design.*

Gateways

Two impressive gateways – on the west and the south – pierce the wall enclosing the mausoleum and its gardens. Built of rubble masonry and mortar, the wall is 5.8m (20ft) high, with arched recesses facing the gardens and merlons strengthening the wall on the outside. Within the site are smaller gateways: the northern entrance to the Arab Sarai, a caravanserai said to have been built by Haji Begum, has a central arch flanked by projecting balconies that are supported by carved brackets.

GATEWAY OF THE BU HALIMA GARDEN

The first entrance

Leading to the west gate is the double-storeyed, rectangular gateway between the garden of Bu Halima and the path to Humayun's Tomb. Made of rubble and plastered masonry, it has an imposing central arch on the side facing the west gate. The arch bears traces of the original enamelled tiles in vivid colours.

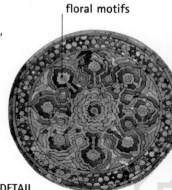

floral motifs

TILE INLAY DETAIL

West gate

Now the main entrance for visitors to the tomb, the west gate is two storeys high. Deeply recessed bays punctuate the sandstone façade, which bears marble ornamentation, such as six-pointed stars on the spandrels (right-angled spaces above an arch) of the central arch. At the centre of the gateway is a large square hall, with a dome-shaped ceiling and arches on the east and west sides.

GRACEFUL DOMES ❧
The parapet is flanked by marble-domed, pillared chhatris.

WEST GATE

FIRST GLIMPSE OF THE TOMB

South gate

Standing on a podium reached by five steps, the south or "Royal" gate is 15.5m (52ft) high. Its walls have arched recesses, while slender turrets, each capped with a marble lotus, stand at the corners. On the ground floor is an octagonal central hall. Once the main entrance to the tomb, this gate is now closed.

PLEASING PROPORTIONS ❧
The placement of the arches on the gate display the typical symmetry of Persian architecture.

Layout of the tomb complex

The plan of the site of Humayun's Tomb is geometrical, with the mausoleum set in the centre of an enclosed *charbagh*, a garden divided into four quadrants. The tomb itself, essentially square in shape – 45m (148ft) on each side – has chamferred (flat-surfaced) corners, giving it an irregular octagonal shape. The four projections are interspersed with *iwans* (arched recesses), which form the main access points to the central hall. The east, west, and north sides of the façade are nearly identical. Inside, on the ground floor, is the octagonal central chamber, which contains the cenotaph and opens out to four octagonal chambers at the diagonals. A gallery on the second floor overlooks the cenotaph.

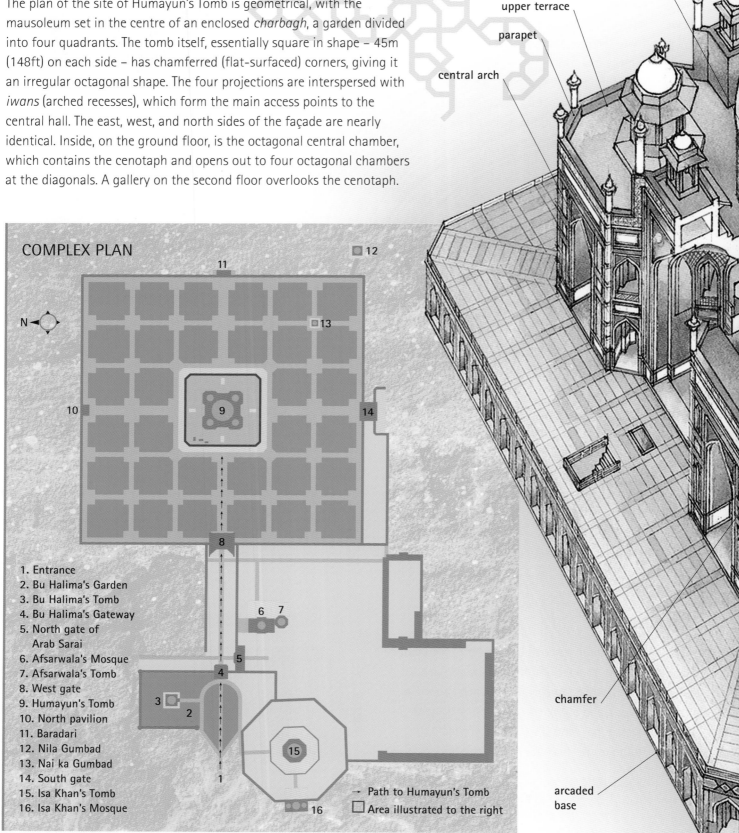

COMPLEX PLAN

N

1. Entrance
2. Bu Halima's Garden
3. Bu Halima's Tomb
4. Bu Halima's Gateway
5. North gate of Arab Sarai
6. Afsarwala's Mosque
7. Afsarwala's Tomb
8. West gate
9. Humayun's Tomb
10. North pavilion
11. Baradari
12. Nila Gumbad
13. Nai ka Gumbad
14. South gate
15. Isa Khan's Tomb
16. Isa Khan's Mosque

→ Path to Humayun's Tomb
□ Area illustrated to the right

outer dome
upper terrace
parapet
central arch
chamfer
arcaded base

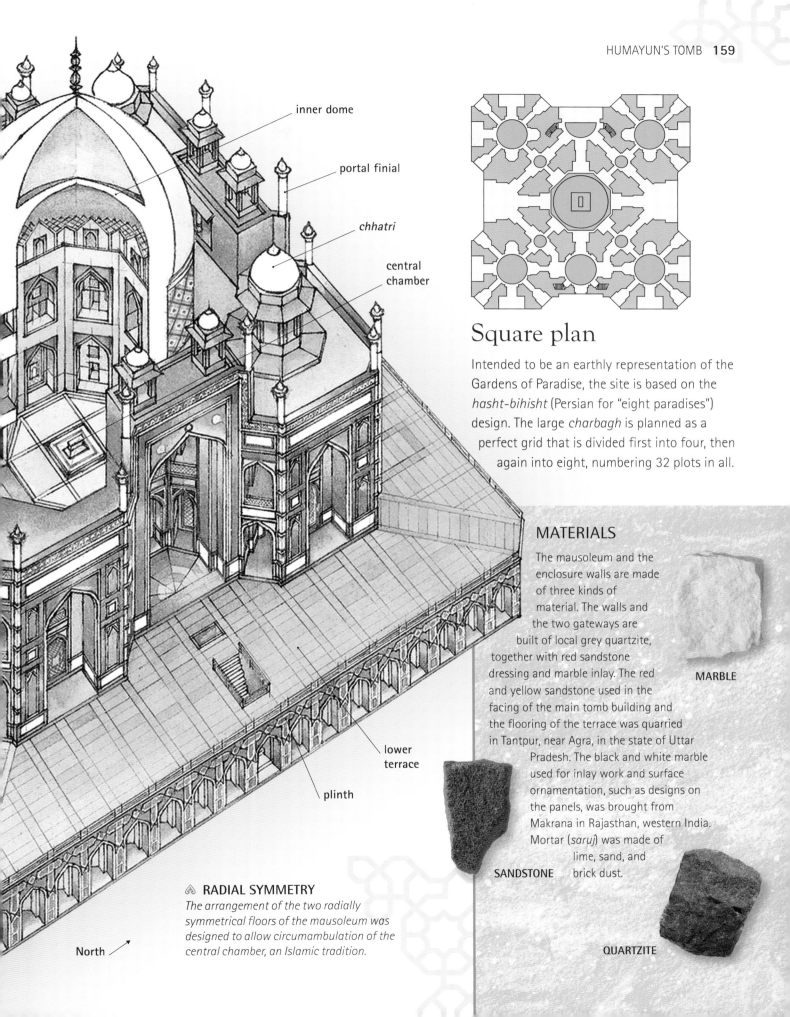

inner dome

portal finial

chhatri

central chamber

lower terrace

plinth

North

⚜ RADIAL SYMMETRY

The arrangement of the two radially symmetrical floors of the mausoleum was designed to allow circumambulation of the central chamber, an Islamic tradition.

Square plan

Intended to be an earthly representation of the Gardens of Paradise, the site is based on the *hasht-bihisht* (Persian for "eight paradises") design. The large *charbagh* is planned as a perfect grid that is divided first into four, then again into eight, numbering 32 plots in all.

MATERIALS

The mausoleum and the enclosure walls are made of three kinds of material. The walls and the two gateways are built of local grey quartzite, together with red sandstone dressing and marble inlay. The red and yellow sandstone used in the facing of the main tomb building and the flooring of the terrace was quarried in Tantpur, near Agra, in the state of Uttar Pradesh. The black and white marble used for inlay work and surface ornamentation, such as designs on the panels, was brought from Makrana in Rajasthan, western India. Mortar (*saruj*) was made of lime, sand, and brick dust.

MARBLE

SANDSTONE

QUARTZITE

The charbagh

The *charbagh* (*char* means four; *bagh* means garden) was created as a sacred space lined with canals (signifying the rivers of Paradise), *khiyabans* (pathways), and flowering trees. Now, after more than 400 years of neglect, trees have been re-planted and water channels repaired to restore flowing water in a major project carried out by the Aga Khan Trust for Culture and the Archaeological Survey of India.

carved base

SANDSTONE FOUNTAIN

⚜ **QUADRILATERAL GARDENS**
Lining the square gardens with geometric precision are paved khiyabans *and water channels, radiating from a central pool.*

✎ **REFLECTED DOME**
Water now flows in the newly restored channels.

The garden tomb

The centrepiece of the *charbagh*, Humayun's mausoleum was the first imperial garden tomb in India and the inspiration for other such tombs, especially Shah Jahan's Taj Mahal. High rubble walls enclose the garden on three sides, while the fourth side stretches by what was once the bank of the river Yamuna. The finely proportioned mausoleum, a massive structure built around a rubble core, is a spectacular composition of a double dome, arches, *chhatris*, turrets, marble inlay, and *jaali* screens.

◈ CHAMFERRED CORNER
The sides of the tomb meet at chamferred corners, each with an arch, lending depth to the structure.

The plinth

lofty central arch

Studded with arched alcoves, 17 on each side, the imposing plinth on which the tomb stands is 7m (23ft) high and 99m (325ft) wide. Composed of rubble masonry finished with red sandstone and marble, it sits on a podium built of quartzite. The plinth consists of multiple (56) chambers containing more than 100 gravestones, a departure from the single chamber of earlier tombs. The central arch on each side opens to a staircase that leads up to the terrace.

◈ ARCADED PODIUM
Deeply recessed alcoves, each framed by a Persian-style pointed arch, run on the sides of the plinth.

octagonal star

WHITE AND RED ◈
Geometric patterns, such as this eight-pointed star, are set in sandstone and marble.

◈ MAIN ENTRANCE
This imposing arch leads to the main cenotaph; the jaali balustrade encloses a sunken staircase.

latticed screen

stars and hexagons

GEOMETRIC PATTERNS

MIHRAB ON SCREEN

The terraces

Vast terraces, on the lower and upper levels, surround the mausoleum, offering spectacular views of the *charbagh* and the other monuments nearby. Finely worked *jaali* sandstone screens, later a signature element in Mughal architecture, can be seen on all sides of the lower terrace. Sunlight flows through them into the mausoleum, illuminating the *mihrab* (Mecca-facing prayer niche) set in the centre of a screen. The red sandstone walls and floors are offset by black and white marble inlay, creating an austere yet elegant effect.

◈ MARBLE GRAVES
Several graves, thought to be of Humayun's descendants, lie here.

WESTERN FAÇADE ◈
Facing the stairs to the terrace are these deeply recessed arches.

DOUBLE DOME

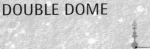

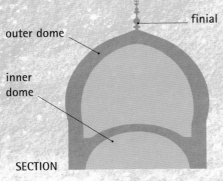

SECTION

Composed of two shells, with a gap in between, a double dome balances the dome's height. The inner shell provides a vaulted ceiling in proportion to the central chamber's dimensions, while the outer one complements the dome's silhouette.

OUTLINE AGAINST THE SKY ❧
Encircling the dome are chhatris, *each crowned with a cupola, echoing the contours of the dome.*

Dome and finial

Rising in splendour from the elongated sandstone drum, the marble-covered dome is 38m (125ft) high. It is a double dome (see box, left), the first such structure in India. A typical Persian architectural feature, the dome was first used in India when the Delhi Sultanate rulers of the 13th century introduced it, first as the half-dome (roughly semicircular in shape). The dome of Humayun's mausoleum is surmounted by a copper brass finial capped by a crescent in the Persian style. It is 5.5m (18ft) high – equal to a double-storeyed house!

⚜ FINE CRAFTSMANSHIP
*The ornate ceiling of the entrance
to the tomb chamber exemplifies
the Persian attention to detail.*

❧ STONE SCREEN
*Among the pre-
Mughal decorative
features of Humayun's
Tomb are intricately
patterned* jaalis *that
filter in light, gently
illuminating the
gravestone.*

Humayun's cenotaph

Entered from the arched doorways of the southern façade,
the double-storeyed, octagonal central chamber contains
Humayun's cenotaph. It has three levels, the middle one being
a gallery. Each level has latticed screens and arched niches. The
low ceiling, built in proportion to the interior height, is carried
on squinches, which bear interlaced patterns on the spandrels.
The central chamber is connected to secondary chambers and
arched lobbies, but the
openings are closed
with screens.

⚜ MIHRAB
*A mihrab inscribed on the western
wall indicates the direction to which
worshippers turned for prayers.*

THE SARCOPHAGUS ❧
*The unadorned white marble
sarcophagus stands on a simple black
and white marble platform. The grave
itself lies below it.*

✥ NORTHWEST CHAMBER
It is said that Humayun's two wives, Haji Begum and Hamida Banu, and Shah Jahan's son, Dara Shikoh, are interred in this tomb-chamber.

Secondary tombs

Several tombs of lesser-known Mughals are housed in the four smaller, octagonal chambers radiating diagonally from the central chamber. Although it is not possible to identify individual graves since they are uninscribed, several later Mughal emperors, such as Jahandar Shah, Farukkhsiyar, and Alamgir II are believed to be buried here.

floral motifs ___

geometric patterns ___

WALL PANEL

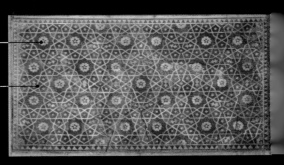

✥ SOUTHEAST CHAMBER
Traditional funerary symbols – a penstand (for men) and a writing tablet (for women) – were used to mark the graves.

Nai ka Gumbad

Around Humayun's mausoleum are other tombs and buildings of interest. To its southeast lies the Nai ka Gumbad (Barber's Tomb), said to have been built for Humayun's favourite barber. A square structure, it stands on a platform that is 2.44m (8.1ft) high, with seven steps leading up to it. A double dome rises above the central recessed arches. A *chhatri*, bearing traces of blue, green, and yellow tile inlay, stands on each corner of the roof, adding to the elegance of the tomb.

⚜ **RIBBED CEILING**
Intersecting arched ribs meet at the circular flower-patterned centre.

❦ **TOMB-CHAMBER**
Sunlight flows through the jaali *screen, illuminating the graves inside.*

THE BARBER'S TOMB

intricate carving

⚜ **LATTICED SCREEN**
Finely worked geometric patterns embellish this sandstone screen.

North pavilion

Near the wall to the north of the tomb enclosure is a square pavilion, which stands on a platform that is 3m (10ft) high. It was thought to be a *hammam* (bath-house), but was probably the hub of an ingenious water supply system used to irrigate the *charbagh*. At its centre is an octagonal water tank, 1m (3.3ft) deep, with a channel leading to a chute. A deep well behind the pavilion was the source of water, which flowed into the tank (pumped with water-drawing mechanisms, such as the Persian wheel) down the chute to the pool outside and, through stone channels, to the garden.

SANDSTONE SCREEN

— water chute

✥ ZIGZAG DESIGN
A sloping sandstone chute, with chevron patterns, leads to an octagonal pool.

BLUE-TILED DOME ✥
Traces of the original tiles still glitter on the dome.

✥ SUPPLY OF WATER
This square structure was the centre of the irrigation system that watered the gardens of the tomb enclosure.

Baradari

At the centre of the enclosure's eastern wall is the Baradari (open-sided pavilion), from where the river Yamuna could be seen flowing by. Rectangular in shape, it has six red sandstone columns, each intricately carved. The central chamber, its eastern side facing the riverfront, has arched recesses on both sides.

Nila Gumbad

Outside the wall of the main tomb enclosure, to the east, is the imposing Nila Gumbad (Blue-domed Tomb). Said to be the tomb of Fahim Khan, the attendant of Abdul Rahim Khan-i-Khanan, an eminent Mughal general (whose own mausoleum is nearby), it is an octagonal structure with recessed arches on the sides. The dome rises from a low-arched drum and is crowned by a finial in the shape of an inverted lotus.

Afsarwala's Tomb and Mosque

To the southwest of Humayun's Tomb is Afsarwala's Tomb and Mosque (*afsar* means "officer", although no one knows who this person was). Both structures date to the early Mughal period. The tomb is octagonal, with deeply recessed arches. The mosque is a three-arched structure conforming to the triple *iwans* (arched recesses) of Persia. It has a prayer hall with three bays and is capped by a dome.

SHARED PLINTH
The tomb (left) and the mosque (right) stand on the same rubble platform.

ARCADED HALL
The mosque is built of grey quartzite faced with red sandstone.

DOORWAY
This corbelled arch with marble inlay, leads to the tomb chamber.

CALLIGRAPHY DETAIL

Garden of Bu Halima

Enclosed by a rubble wall, with square *chhatris* at its corners, is the well-laid out garden of Bu Halima, named after a lady about whom little is known. An unmarked grave, believed to be hers, lies in a ruined structure – one of the earliest Mughal tombs in Delhi – near the northeast entrance to Humayun's Tomb.

Isa Khan's Mosque

Built in 1547, thus pre-dating Humayun's Tomb, this mosque stands near the tomb of Isa Khan, an influential nobleman in the court of Sher Shah Suri and his son, Islam Shah. Capped by a large central dome and octagonal *chhatris*, it has arches decorated with brightly coloured tiles. The prayer hall has three bays.

COMBINATION OF MATERIALS ≫
The central bay and the parapets are built in red sandstone, harmonizing with the dressed stone masonry of the walls.

TILE INLAY DETAIL

Isa Khan's Tomb

One of the finest examples of Mughal architecture, this tomb stands in a garden to the south of Bu Halima's Garden. Built in 1547, it is said to have been influenced by the tomb of Sikander Lodi, built about 100 years earlier (in the modern Lodi Garden). Octagonal in plan, it is encircled by a verandah with three arches on each side, the spandrels decorated with patterns in blue, green, and yellow enamelled tiles. Inside the tomb chamber are six graves, the largest one being Isa Khan's. The square doorways are enclosed with fine *jaalis*.

DOMED PAVILION ≫
The eight terrace pavilions are adorned with coloured tiles.

♥ **STRENGTH AND GRACE**
The deep octagonal chhajja *above the arcaded verandah, parapets, and turrets lend an air of solidity to the tomb.*

rounded turret

dome on a 16-sided drum

Fatehpur Sikri

A nondescript little village, Sikri's sole claim to fame was that it was the home of the Sufi mystic, Sheikh Salim Chishti. Then, in 1568, its fortunes changed dramatically. The Mughal emperor Akbar came to visit the saint. At that time, Akbar was at the peak of his glory – he had a powerful and stable empire, the royal treasury was comfortably full, and there was peace in the land. But Akbar himself was not at peace – his kingdom had no male heir. The anguished father went on a pilgrimage to the humble lodging of Salim Chishti, making one last desperate appeal for a son to inherit his empire. Akbar's prayers were answered. The saint prophesied that he would have three sons. On 30 August 1569, the first of these was born to Akbar's queen, Harkha. The grateful emperor named him Salim, after the Sufi saint, and decided to build a new imperial capital at Sikri as a tribute to the mystic. And so the rocky, barren ridge was transformed over the next few years into a magnificent citadel with a separate sacred complex specially constructed for the saint. From here Akbar marched out to conquer Gujarat and on his return, he renamed the city as Fatehpur (City of Victory). This was the first planned city of the Mughal empire and the monuments in sandstone exemplified Mughal architecture at its finest. But the splendour of this citadel was shortlived – it was abandoned in 1585, possibly due to shortage of water. Today, Fatehpur Sikri is a ghost town with palaces, mosques, and pavilions that offer a mere glimpse of their former grandeur – and a more sombre reminder of the hubris of kings.

CITY OF VICTORY
Fatehpur Sikri lies 40km (25 miles) from the city of Agra, in the state of Uttar Pradesh.

The Mughal Dynasty

One of the greatest medieval dynasties in the world, the Mughals established their rule in India after Zahiruddin Babur entered India from Central Asia in 1526. His descendants expanded and strengthened the empire. For more than a century afterwards, the splendour of the Mughal court was well-documented. In fact, the word "mogul", denoting a powerful personage, is derived from "Mughal". After the death of Aurangzeb, the last great Mughal, the empire declined. It came to an end when Bahadur Shah Zafar was dethroned by the British in 1857.

- 🪶 1526 **Babur** defeats Ibrahim Lodi and establishes the Mughal dynasty with **Agra** as the chief city.

- 🪶 1530 Babur dies, and his son **Humayun** accedes to the throne.

- 🪶 1556 Humayun dies, succeeded by his son **Akbar**.

- 🪶 1571 **Akbar moves his capital** from Agra to a newly built city near Sikri named **Fatehpur**.

- 🪶 1585 **Akbar transfers his capital** from Fatehpur Sikri to Lahore.

- 🪶 1605 Akbar dies, succeeded by his son **Jahangir**.

- 🪶 1627 Jahangir dies, war of succession follows. **Shah Jahan** accedes to the throne in 1628.

- 🪶 1658 Shah Jahan deposed by his son **Aurangzeb**. Shah Jahan dies in 1666.

- 🪶 1707 **Aurangzeb** dies and the **empire gradually declines.**

Akbar

AKBAR THE GREAT

Known as Akbar the Great, Jalaluddin Muhammad Akbar became emperor when he was only 13 years old after his father, Humayun, died. With the help of his guardian Bairam Khan, he extended control over northern India. After he came of age in 1560, Akbar achieved a series of military successes, his empire stretching from Kashmir in the north and Afghanistan in the west to Bengal in the east and the Deccan in the south. His reign was marked by an efficient centralized government administered by *mansabdars* (warrior-aristocrats). He followed a policy of religious tolerance, reducing the influence of the *ulema* (Islamic scholars) and abolishing *jizya* (taxes imposed on non-Muslim residents), which helped to unify the empire.

AGRA FORT 🪶
This fort was rebuilt in red sandstone by Akbar at his first capital.

Realizing an imperial vision

The vast stretches of India ruled over by Akbar witnessed the creation of impressive buildings like the palace forts at Agra, Allahabad, Ajmer, and Lahore (now in Pakistan), that symbolized his might as an empire-builder. Agra was his capital at first and it is here that he built the Agra Fort between 1565 and 1573. Forming a crescent along the Yamuna riverfront with imposing sandstone ramparts, it encompassed an enormous range of courtly buildings. Akbar then built a new capital called Fatehpur, a fine example of a Mughal city, constructed between 1571 and 1585. This capital was abandoned when Akbar went on to Lahore, where he had already demolished a 3000-year-old mud fort to build the Lahore Fort in 1566. He also designed and started the construction of his own tomb at Sikandra, near Agra.

COINS FROM AKBAR'S ERA
Gold coins were struck in Fatehpur Sikri, but the metal was refined in mints elsewhere in the empire.

GRAND CAPITAL
Built atop a sandstone ridge, Fatehpur Sikri was planned as the magnificent new capital of Akbar, with superbly crafted buildings.

NINE GEMS

A connoisseur of fine arts, Akbar attracted the best talents to his court. Known as the *navratnas* or nine gems, this elite group comprised Abul Fazl, chronicler of Akbar's rule; his brother Faizi, poet; Tansen, classical singer and disciple of Swami Haridas; Birbal, minister and court jester;

TANSEN
Dressed as a commoner, Akbar visits Swami Haridas at Vrindavan; Tansen is seated in the centre.

BIRBAL

Raja Todar Mal, who overhauled the empire's revenue system; Raja Man Singh of Amber; Abdul Rahim Khan-i-Khan, poet, linguist, and general; and Mullah do Piaza and Fakir Azia-ud-din, advisors to the emperor.

COURTYARD OF THE DAULAT KHANA
Silhouetted against the sky are the graceful Panch Mahal and the Diwan-i-Khas, which overlook the Anoop Talao in the courtyard.

Sandstone Splendour

Stretching across the top of a ridge overlooking a now dried up lake, is Fatehpur Sikri, once the imperial capital of Akbar. It encompasses about 6km (3.7miles), with a high, battlemented wall running on three sides and the fourth opening out to the lake. It is from the highest terrace of Panch Mahal, the five-storeyed pavilion at the centre, that a panoramic view of the palaces, pavilions, shrines, and gateways casts its spell on a visitor, conjuring up images of the days gone by. These architectural gems have been constructed in a fusion of Central Asian and Rajasthani styles, with intricate *jaalis* (filigreed stone screens), *chhajjas* (sloping eaves), *chhatris* (pavilions with umbrella-shaped domes), sumptuous carving, and surface ornamentation, such as those on spandrels (triangular spaces above an arch). The gateways include the Badshahi and Buland Darwazas that lead to the sacred complex.

⚜ GRAND GATEWAY
The Buland Darwaza is the greatest monumental structure created in Akbar's reign.

Entering Fatehpur Sikri

Standing sentinel, one after the other, a series of Darwazas (gateways) lead into Fatehpur Sikri. These gateways once formed effective barriers on the road to the royal complex. They included the Delhi, Lal (Red), Akbarabad or Agra, Suraj (Sun) or Bir, Chandar (Moon), and Gwalior Darwazas, as well as the Terha (Crooked), and Ajmeri Darwazas. The final gateway at the main entrance was the Naubat Khana (Drum House).

DOMED PAVILIONS

♥ NAUBAT KHANA
A roll of drums from this triple-arched gateway announced the emperor's entry.

chhajja

HATHI POL (ELEPHANT GATEWAY)
The remnants of two stone elephants flank this gateway leading to the harem palaces.

AGRA GATEWAY
The road from Agra enters through the pointed arches of this gateway to the royal complex of Fatehpur Sikri.

chhatri in Rajasthani style

TANSEN'S BARADARI

Gracing the eastern edge of the Fatehpur ridge, this single-storeyed, rectangular building called a *baradari* (pavilion) is named after the legendary musician, Mian Tansen.

STAR PATTERNS
The verandah walls bear inlay work in sandstone and marble.

PILLARED VERANDAH
The pillars of the verandah are crowned with ornate brackets.

Layout of the Fatehpur Sikri complex

Symbolizing an all-powerful monarchy, the Fatehpur Sikri complex is based on a large-scale, yet carefully envisaged plan. Approached from the dry bed of the lake, the Hiran Minar (Deer Tower) is visible, axially aligned to the Hathi Pol (Elephant Gateway). The rich array of buildings can roughly be divided into two parts – the imperial and the sacred complex. The former comprises the private quarters of the emperor, known as the Daulat Khana (Abode of Fortune), and includes the palaces of the queens. Here too are the halls for public and private audiences, and the treasuries. The Buland Darwaza (Lofty Gateway) leads to the sacred quadrangle, which includes Sheikh Salim Chishti's *dargah* (shrine and tomb).

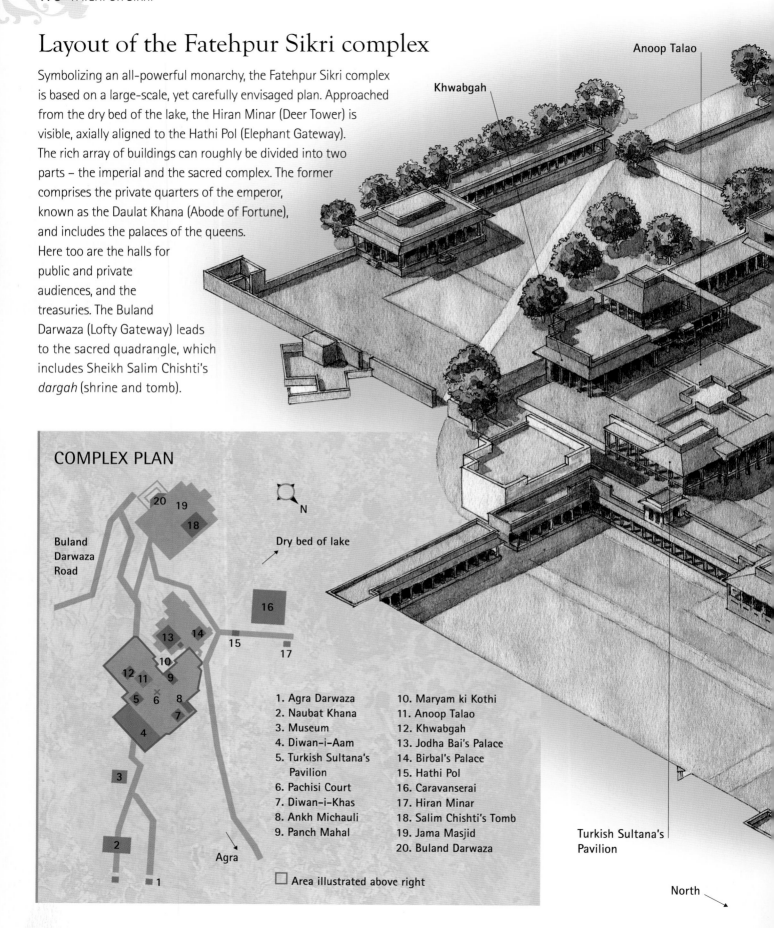

Anoop Talao

Khwabgah

Turkish Sultana's Pavilion

North

COMPLEX PLAN

Buland Darwaza Road

Dry bed of lake

N

Agra

1. Agra Darwaza
2. Naubat Khana
3. Museum
4. Diwan-i-Aam
5. Turkish Sultana's Pavilion
6. Pachisi Court
7. Diwan-i-Khas
8. Ankh Michauli
9. Panch Mahal
10. Maryam ki Kothi
11. Anoop Talao
12. Khwabgah
13. Jodha Bai's Palace
14. Birbal's Palace
15. Hathi Pol
16. Caravanserai
17. Hiran Minar
18. Salim Chishti's Tomb
19. Jama Masjid
20. Buland Darwaza

☐ Area illustrated above right

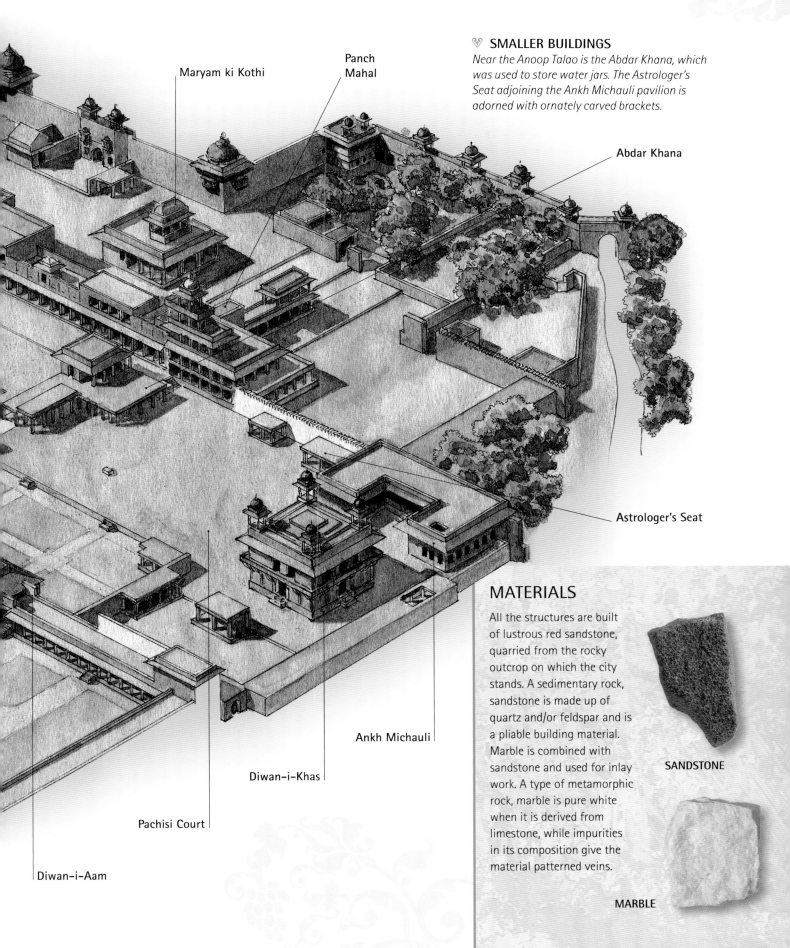

Maryam ki Kothi

Panch Mahal

✿ SMALLER BUILDINGS

Near the Anoop Talao is the Abdar Khana, which was used to store water jars. The Astrologer's Seat adjoining the Ankh Michauli pavilion is adorned with ornately carved brackets.

Abdar Khana

Astrologer's Seat

Ankh Michauli

MATERIALS

All the structures are built of lustrous red sandstone, quarried from the rocky outcrop on which the city stands. A sedimentary rock, sandstone is made up of quartz and/or feldspar and is a pliable building material. Marble is combined with sandstone and used for inlay work. A type of metamorphic rock, marble is pure white when it is derived from limestone, while impurities in its composition give the material patterned veins.

SANDSTONE

Diwan-i-Khas

Pachisi Court

Diwan-i-Aam

MARBLE

Diwan-i-Aam

Built along the sandstone ridge are the imperial buildings with three main areas – the official section, the *mardana* (men's quarters), and the *zenana* (women's quarters). Concentric terraces separate the public spaces, which include the Diwan-i-Aam (Hall for Public Audiences), Diwan-i-Khas (Hall for Private Audiences), and the Pachisi Court, from the Daulat Khana, the private royal quarters. The Hathi Pol (Elephant Gateway) leads to the spacious courtyard, surrounded by a colonnade of 111 bays, of the Diwan-i-Aam. Akbar sat in the hall every morning, three hours after sunrise, to dispense justice, and petitioners and courtiers gathered to listen to his address from the royal pavilion, which was draped with rich tapestries. The emperor's seat, on a carved platform within the central bay, is cordoned off by perforated screens. Opposite the pavilion, on the right of the path that leads to the courtyard, is a heavy stone ring embedded in the ground. It was perhaps used to tether the state elephant, which reportedly crushed the condemned to death.

❧ PACHISI COURT
The court's paving is set in squares, like a giant chessboard, where Pachisi, a dice game, was played (pachisi means "twenty-fiver", the highest score at a throw).

❧ INTRICATE DESIGNS
Finely carved in geometrical patterns, sandstone screens line the sides of the emperor's platform; it was from here that he entered the Daulat Khana.

marble cupola

❧ DIWAN-I-AAM
The pavilion is a graceful composition of a pitched stone roof, five arched openings, pillars crowned by ornate brackets, and chhajjas.

HALL FOR PRIVATE AUDIENCES

❦ ORNATE CAPITAL
The central axis of the hall is supported by a circular arrangement of 36 brackets that seem to branch out infinitely, the pattern inspired by the Gujarati style.

❦ CENTRAL PILLAR
The massive Lotus Throne pillar with carved brackets supported Akbar's throne on top.

platform where Akbar's throne was placed

Diwan-i-Khas

Blending different architectural styles, the Diwan-i-Khas stands in the northeast corner of the royal complex. Symbolic of the emperor's supreme power, Akbar's throne was placed on a circular platform resting on an imposing, richly carved pillar in the centre, while ministers and nobles were seated in the galleries radiating from it.

inverted lotus on finial

DIN-I-ILAHI

Akbar also held private audiences for religious leaders and sages of all faiths, the venue being the Ibadat Khana (House of Worship), which no longer stands. He created a new faith called Din-i-Ilahi (Divine Faith) based on the teachings of various religions. In this miniature painting (right), he is shown holding discussions with religious leaders (Jesuit priests are in black) in the Ibadat Khana.

AKBAR IN COURT

⚜ **STONE STRUTS**
Mythical makars or guardian beasts are carved on the struts supported by corbels (grooves) on the walls.

⚜ **ROYAL HALLS**
Two halls are placed at right angles to the central connecting chamber in this thick-walled structure.

Ankh Michauli

It is said that the ladies of the harem played *ankh michauli* (blind man's buff) in this labyrinthine building, but its secret alcoves and deep wall recesses suggest that it may have been part of the imperial treasury.

Anoop Talao

Northeast of the Diwan-i-Khas is the Anoop Talao (Peerless Pool) in the courtyard of the Daulat Khana. Serenely beautiful, this square water tank extends to 30m (98ft) on each side. Abul Fazl records that in April 1578, the emperor ordered the tank to be filled with gold, silver, and copper coins so that people could collect the "sublime bounty".

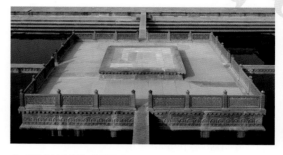

⚜ **TRANQUIL CENTRE**
A sandstone island, enclosed by an ornate balustrade, lies at the centre of the Anoop Talao, with four bridges leading to it.

Khwabgah

Within the Khwabgah (Chamber of Dreams) lie the private sleeping-quarters of the emperor, with an ingenious ventilating shaft. A secret room behind the Kitab Khana or library (that according to Abul Fazl housed 25,000 manuscripts), as well as the emperor's chamber, still bear traces of painted murals in yellow and blue that once covered the walls.

⚜ **ARCHED PASSAGE**
This covered corridor leads to the personal sleeping-chamber of the emperor.

Panch Mahal

This five-storeyed palace is also known as Badgir (Windcatcher) because its structure, with the storeys rising in decreasing sizes, is designed to cool the interiors. The building is remarkable for the varied designs of the columns, with motifs ranging from the *fleur-de-lis* (stylized flower) to the bell and chain. The ground floor contains 84 pillars, which incidentally, is an auspicious number for Hindus. The Panch Mahal is topped by a graceful *chhatri*, and was probably enclosed by perforated stone screens to veil the ladies of the court from public view.

MOTIF VARIETY
Carved columns have unique designs such as the fleur-de-lis.

LATTICE WORK
The fourth floor is surrounded by beautiful latticed balustrades.

PILLARED SPLENDOUR
The second floor of the Panch Mahal has 56 pillars, with a row of six pillars in a north to south direction and another row of four pillars running east to west. The carved pillars differ in shape, some being octagonal, others circular.

chhatri

latticed balustrades

Harem Sara

A maze of interconnected buildings, the Harem Sara (Imperial Harem Complex) includes Jodha Bai's Palace, Panch Mahal, Maryam ki Kothi, and Hawa Mahal. The heart of the complex, where the high-ranking women lived, was screened to the east from the Daulat Khana. A vast pillared structure near the palaces may have been an enclosure for elephants, horses, or camels, but was probably used as servants' quarters.

♥ COLONNADED ENCLOSURE
The stone rings in the bays are said to have been used to tether animals.

⚜ PALACE ENTRANCE
This double-storeyed doorway was guarded by eunuchs.

low, perforated
stone railing

Jodha Bai's Palace

The most conspicuous building in the Harem Sara is Jodha Bai's Palace. It is conjectured that Jodha Bai was Akbar's Hindu queen, but the palace was actually the residence of several of the emperor's wives. Built in a fusion of Hindu and Islamic styles, it features graceful pavilions and enclosed balconies.

Rajasthani-style *chhatri*

chhajja

♥ INNER COURTYARD
The palace consists of apartments linked by colonnaded corridors to an enormous, secluded courtyard.

NATURAL LIGHT
Sunlight filtering through the delicately filigreed arch casts a glow on the interior.

Maryam ki Kothi

Probably the residence of Hamida Banu Begum, Akbar's mother (known as Maryam Makani, or "equal to Mary"), this two-storeyed *kothi* (house) was covered with frescoes, representing scenes from the Persian epic *Hamza Nama*, and gilt work, which is why it is also called the Sunehra Makan (Golden House). Stone eaves supported by heavy brackets encircle the palace, with carvings inspired by Hindu imagery from the *Ramayana*.

Turkish Sultana's Pavilion

This pavilion overlooking the Anoop Talao may have been used by Akbar's Turkish queens. It is also known as "Superb Jewel Casket" for its intricately carved verandah pillars with arabesque designs. The brackets are decorated with bell-shaped, floral, and herringbone carvings and display fine filigree workmanship.

STONE ROOF
The pavilion is topped with an unusual stone and imitation clay-tiled roof.

filigreed railing

HERRINGBONE CARVINGS

Birbal's House

To the north of the harem complex is Birbal's House (a misnomer, since Birbal, Akbar's favourite minister, did not live here). It was probably occupied by Akbar's senior queens, Ruqayya Sultana Begum and Salima Sultana Begum, or by Birbal's daughter, who was one of Akbar's wives. A two-storeyed structure, it stands on a massive platform, with a pyramidal roof capping the porch. The interior is divided into three bays, separated by ornate pilasters that bear a variety of arabesque and floral designs.

CUSPED NICHE
Rosettes adorn the spandrels above this cusped niche flanked by richly carved panels.

arabesque patterns on brackets

ornate pillars

LOFTY DOMES OF BIRBAL'S HOUSE
Rising from an octagonal base are two domes capped by finials on an inverted lotus base.

FINE MOTIFS
This intricate design of lotus petals is bordered by geometric patterns.

BRACKETS
The brackets and pillars in the house are elaborately carved.

FLORAL PATTERNS

Sangin Burj

Unique for its monumental outer arch, which proclaims the might of its builder by its size, the Sangin Burj (Massive Bastion) is a structure that, together with the Hathi Pol, forms the grand gateway to the harem complex. Made of red and buff sandstone covered with semi-circular patterns, the Burj is in an octagonal form. Combined with its arches, the whole effect is one of strength blended with elegance.

POINTED ARCHES OF THE NAGINA MASJID

Nagina Masjid

A private mosque for the ladies of the imperial harem, the Nagina (or Jewel) Masjid stands at the north of the harem complex. Divided into three bays by square pillars, it has niches ornamented with finely carved rosettes on the spandrels above the arches.

Hawa Mahal

To the right of Jodha Bai's palace is the Hawa Mahal, the Palace of Winds. A pavilion designed to catch the breeze, it is enclosed by square columns and exquisite stone screens that ensured privacy for the ladies of the harem. It overlooks a garden laid out in the *charbagh* (quadrilateral garden) style, divided by channels.

WATER SUPPLY

Down the road from the Hathi Pol is an octagonal platform with a deep *baoli* (step-well) at its centre. Huge windlasses beneath the platform were turned by men all day and night to pump up water, which flowed through aqueducts to the palace *hammams* (Turkish baths). Seen below is part of the pulley system used to supply the Hakim's Hammam, probably the royal baths, with water.

stone pillars

HAKIM'S HAMMAM
Ropes and buckets were attached to stone pillars on the terrace of this hammam to pull up water.

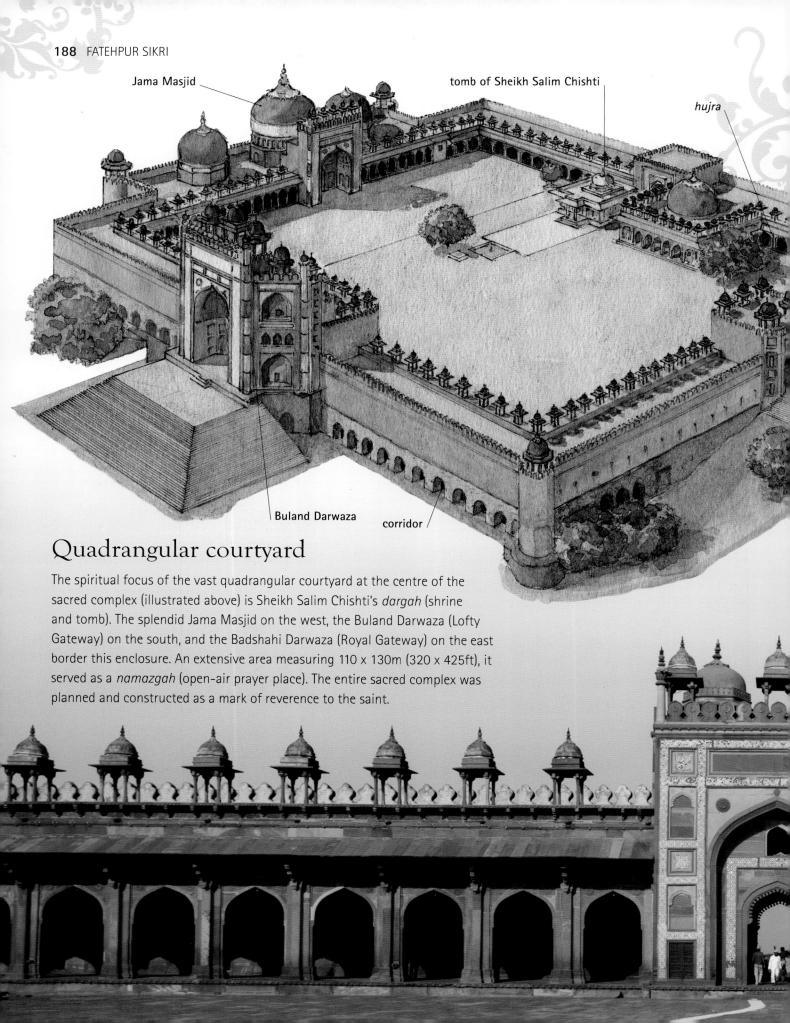

Jama Masjid

tomb of Sheikh Salim Chishti

hujra

Buland Darwaza

corridor

Quadrangular courtyard

The spiritual focus of the vast quadrangular courtyard at the centre of the
sacred complex (illustrated above) is Sheikh Salim Chishti's *dargah* (shrine
and tomb). The splendid Jama Masjid on the west, the Buland Darwaza (Lofty
Gateway) on the south, and the Badshahi Darwaza (Royal Gateway) on the east
border this enclosure. An extensive area measuring 110 x 130m (320 x 425ft), it
served as a *namazgah* (open-air prayer place). The entire sacred complex was
planned and constructed as a mark of reverence to the saint.

MONUMENTAL ENTRANCE ❧
The Jama Masjid is entered through this magnificent recessed central archway flanked by domes; each of the marble spandrels is ornamented by a single sandstone rosette.

Badshahi Darwaza

🜂 **ARCADED PRAYER HALLS**
Hujras *with flat-roofed pillared galleries run on the left and right of the courtyard of the mosque.*

Jama Masjid

A grand open mosque, the Jama Masjid towers over Fatehpur Sikri, situated as it is on a high point of the ridge on which the citadel is built. The congregational quadrangle is flanked by *hujras* (cloistered prayer halls). The mosque contains three chambers, capped by domes. The white central dome has floral patterns painted in deep blues and brown-red and the *mihrabs* (Mecca-facing prayer niches) are richly carved with inlaid geometrical designs, coloured tiles, and calligraphic inscriptions.

Badshahi Darwaza

It was from the steep steps of this Royal Gateway that Emperor Akbar entered the Jama Masjid to join congregational prayers. Adorned with bands of buff sandstone carved in geometrical designs, it has two arches, one above the other. From here, a view of the immense courtyard is overwhelming. The smaller entrance arch is cusped and decorated with stylized pomegranates, the tip of each arch ending in a carved lotus bud.

♥ **ARCHED OPENINGS**
Crowning the rows of rooms, built to accommodate mullahs *(religious teachers), are a series of* chhatris *flanking the central archway.*

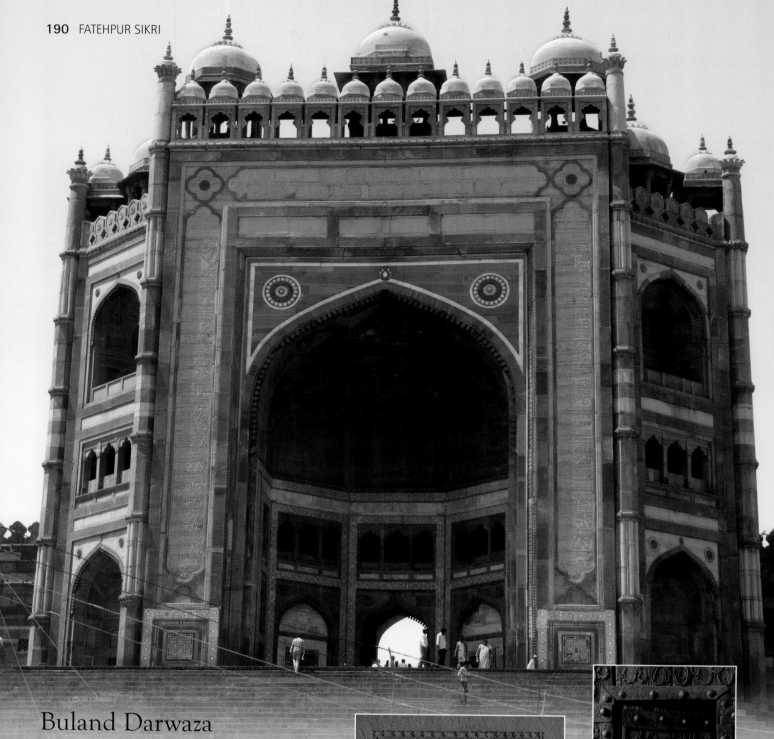

Buland Darwaza

Erected by Akbar to mark his conquest over Gujarat in 1573, the 54m (177ft) Buland Darwaza (Lofty Gateway) dominates the sacred complex. It is reached by a great flight of 42 steps. The main arch of this magnificent gateway stands in the centre of three projecting sides of an octagon centred on the apex of the dome, and a row of *chhatris* crowns the parapet. The red spandrels are framed by bands of yellow-buff sandstone, below which are panels of marble inlay in geometric patterns.

⚜ SACRED VERSES
Calligraphic inscriptions from the Quran, cut in bold letters of the Naskh script, highlight the façade of the gateway.

⚜ WOODEN DOOR
Horseshoes cover the upper part of the door, hammered in by peasants for luck.

Salim Chishti's Tomb

The tomb of Sheikh Salim Chishti, the Sufi saint revered by Akbar, was originally made of sandstone and later sheathed in exquisitely carved white marble. The verandah of the domed cenotaph is enclosed by fine screens with chiselled hexagons and interlacing patterns. The cenotaph stands on a platform decorated with a mosaic of black and yellow marble, while stylized peacocks' tails adorn the bases of the porch columns. A richly carved doorway leads to the inner tomb that has a canopy delicately inlaid with mother-of-pearl.

FLORAL DOORKNOB

♥ SERPENTINE BRACKETS

Carved out of a single marble block, each bracket in the porch is shaped into a graceful stylized snake.

MAKING A WISH

Visitors tie cotton threads on the marble screen surrounding the tomb in the belief that any wish they make will come true, just as Akbar was blessed by the saint and had three sons.

Jamat Khana

Enclosed by an elegant stone screen and an arcaded verandah, this square structure was once an assembly hall for Salim Chishti's disciples and later, the tomb of his descendants. The doors have intricate relief carvings.

DOMED SPLENDOUR ⬙
Rising above the sandstone roof is a grand dome surrounded by the cupolas of 36 small, graceful chhatris.

♥ LIGHTING THE WAY
Lamps were probably suspended from the "tusks" to guide visitors by akash deep (heavenly light) at night.

Hiran Minar

Studded with stone projections resembling elephants' tusks, the Hiran Minar (Deer Tower) is believed to be a memorial to Akbar's favourite elephant, also called Hiran. It is a 22m (73ft) high tower, with rosettes ornamenting the spandrels of the arched doorway. Bordered by a stone panel and flanked by blind arches, the door leads to 53 steps that wind up to the top of the tower. Here, a panoramic vista stretches before the viewer.

Stone Cutters' Mosque

The oldest place of worship at Fatehpur Sikri, the Stone Cutters' Mosque stands on the left of the Jama Masjid. Built in deep red sandstone by local quarrymen to honour Sheikh Salim Chishti, it shows slightly rough workmanship. Of the five bays, the central one has a richly cusped arch, where the saint would meditate, and behind it is an ornamented *mihrab*.

STYLIZED SNAKE BRACKETS

Caravanserai

Building shelters for travellers passing through was considered the moral duty of a Muslim ruler, and caravanserais number in the thousands in India. Standing as a fortified enclosure with octagonal bastions at its corners, the Fatehpur Sikri caravanserai is very well preserved. The quadrangle is divided by a low terrace, in front of which is a water tank.

SHELTERED ROOMS 🔖
Screened by arches, rectangular openings lead into rooms; each corner has three rooms arranged around a courtyard.

Rang Mahal

This palace, now dilapidated, was constructed in 1569, before Akbar decided to shift his capital to Sikri. It is said that Akbar built it for his favourite queen Harkha, the mother of Prince Salim, who was born here. The eastern gate's wide archway displays cusps emerging from the mouths of small elephants. In one of the courtyards is a pair of tall twelve-sided columns with remarkable double capitals, the beautiful brackets shaped like the heads of horses. Stylized peacocks' tails adorn other columns of the palace.

ARCHED NICHE 🔖
Rosettes decorate the spandrels of this red sandstone niche, the arch rising above the doorway.

🔖 **FLORAL BANDS**
Framing the recessed wall on three sides are ornamental bands with flower motifs.

Amber Fort

Historically, Rajasthan was never unified as a single state. Instead, over the centuries, the region was divided into a number of kingdoms presided over by Rajput warrior families, who fought with each other for supremacy, but also united against such common enemies as the neighbouring sultans of Delhi. This more or less continuous state of warfare also characterized the Rajput relationship with the Mughals in the 16th and 17th centuries, despite marriage alliances between the Rajputs and Mughal emperors. It explains why Rajput forts and palaces were conceived as formidable citadels, elevated on hilltops that overlooked the cities below. Among the most imposing of these forts in Rajasthan is that at Amber, headquarters of the Kachhwaha rulers from the beginning of the 16th century until their

⚑ RAJPUT CITADEL
Amber was the seat of the Rajputs before the capital shifted to Jaipur.

move in 1727 to the newly planned city of Jaipur, a short distance away. The Amber Fort is built as a series of courtyards ascending a steep hill that overlooks a strategic pass, through which the highway to Delhi runs. It was developed by two Kachhwaha rulers, Man Singh (r.1590–1615) and Mirza Jai Singh (r.1621–1667), into a showpiece of Rajput strength and magnificence. The fort has sumptuous halls, apartments, and pavilions facing paved courtyards and formal gardens with pools, water channels, and fountains. The carved marble panels, inlaid mirrorwork, and vivid murals imitate the decoration of Mughal palaces. This is not surprising, since Man Singh and Mirza Jai Singh were commanders in the army of the Mughal emperors, at a time when Mughal influence was strong.

The Rajputs of Amber

Rajputs are believed to have a long genealogy; some of the warrior clans are of the Sun dynasty, others of the Moon. The Kachhwahas are *suryavanshi* (of the Sun dynasty), tracing their descent from Kush, son of Lord Rama. They came into prominence in the tenth century as the rulers of Gwalior in central India, but in 986, Ishwar Das, the king of Gwalior, abdicated to lead a life of renunciation in the Himalayas. His sons moved to the west (present-day Rajasthan), after being forced to flee from Gwalior by their uncle. One of them, Sodh Rai, defeated the Meenas, the tribal chiefs of Dausa (near modern Jaipur) and set up a principality there. In 1037, his son and grandson, Dhola Rai and Kakil Dev, occupied the Meena stronghold at Amber and made it the capital of the Kachhwahas. The clan ruled for centuries, gaining in strength in the 16th century when they formed alliances with the Mughal emperors. Listed below are some of the rulers of Amber:

- **1036–1038 Kakil Dev**
  Conquers Amber with his father. Builds a fort there.

- **1548–1574 Bharmal Singh**
  Gains power for Amber by entering into a political alliance with the Mughals.

- **1590–1615 Man Singh I**
  Begins building the Amber Fort in 1592 on the ruins of Kakil Dev's fort.

- **1622–1668 Jai Singh I**
  Completes construction of the Amber Fort.

- **1700–1744 Jai Singh II**
  Moves the capital from Amber to Jainagara (present-day Jaipur) in 1727.

Fort on a Hill

The picturesque Amber Fort stretches across a rocky hill overlooking a gorge, in which the Maota Lake nestles. The town of Amber was founded by the Meena chief, Raja Alan Singh, and was dedicated to Amba, the Mother Goddess, from whom it gets its name. By 967, Amber was a flourishing settlement. In 1037, it was conquered by the Kachhwaha Rajputs, who ruled till 1727. The present citadel was built in 1592, but most of its splendid palaces, pavilions, and gardens were created by Jai Singh I.

Raja Man Singh I

A warrior and wise administrator, Raja Man Singh I was one of the *navratnas* (nine gems) in the court of Mughal emperor Akbar. Commander-in-chief in the Mughal army, he fought in many Mughal campaigns, often emerging victorious. With varied interests, such as art, crafts, literature, and the performing arts, he was a multi-faceted personality. For his kingdom, he was an absentee ruler, carrying out his duties in the army and as governor of the provinces of Kabul, Bihar, and Bengal, but the Kachhwaha principality expanded during his rule.

THE TOWN OF AMBER ⊱
This historic town lies on the site (the foothills below the Amber Fort) of the early capital of the Kachhwaha kings.

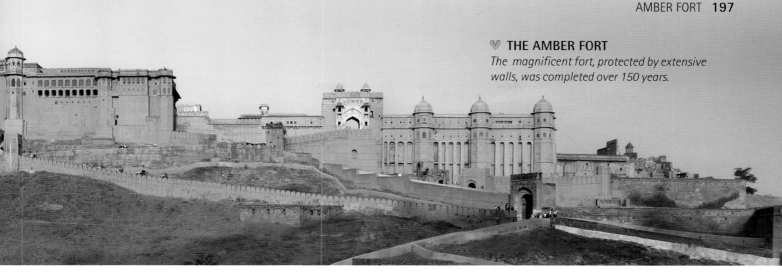

♥ THE AMBER FORT
The magnificent fort, protected by extensive walls, was completed over 150 years.

Raja Jai Singh I and II

The title of honour "Mirza" was conferred on Raja Jai Singh I by Shah Jahan, in recognition of his bravery in battles during the Mughal military campaigns (he served under three Mughal emperors – Jahangir, Shah Jahan, and Aurangzeb). His namesake, Raja Jai Singh II, would later build Jaipur – he was given the title of "Sawai" (one and a quarter times superior to everyone) by Aurangzeb. The two Jai Singhs were the greatest builders among the Kachhwahas, exhibiting a talent for architectural design.

⚜ RAJA JAI SINGH II
The Raja shifted the capital to Jaipur in 1727 and built several splendid palaces there.

CHANDRA MAHAL ⚜
This grand palace of Raja Jai Singh II in Jaipur is now home to the royal family of Jaipur.

CONNECTING WITH THE MUGHALS

The Kachhwahas recognized the expediency of aligning themselves with the powerful Mughal emperors. The astute diplomatic move of Raja Bharmal, who gave his daughter in marriage to the Mughal emperor Akbar, resulted in the Amber royal family's prominence, as did Raja Man Singh and Raja Jai Singh I's feats of valour in the Mughal army. The Rajas also adopted Mughal craft skills, such as *meenakari* (enamel work) in jewellery.

⚜ MEENAKARI
Fine meenakari *work introduced by Mughal craftsmen is now part of Rajput tradition.*

Forts and Palaces

The Rajputs have always been great patrons of art and architecture. Since they were essentially warriors, forts have always been the focal point of their settlements. Constructed as inner citadels, surrounded by a town and enclosed by a fortified wall, they were usually built on hills for natural protection, and surrounded by wide moats to make them impregnable. Opulent palaces were built within the forts in a sophisticated architectural style – with distinctive indigenous features (see below) that were influenced by Persian and Mughal architecture, particularly in the use of domes and arches. Some of the finest Rajput forts and palaces can be seen in cities such as Jaisalmer, Jodhpur, Udaipur, and Jaipur.

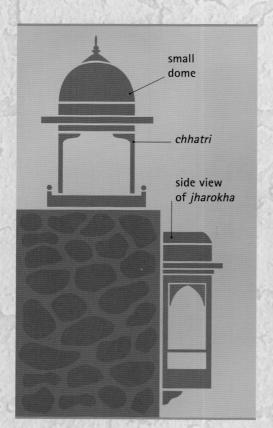

small dome

chhatri

side view of *jharokha*

⌂ ARCHITECTURAL FEATURES
The chhatri (kiosk) and jharokha (protruding balcony) are typical elements of the Rajput style.

The Entrance

Winding up the hillside, the cobbled road leads to the Suraj Pol (Sun Gate), the main entrance gate. It is so called because it faces the direction of the rising sun, the Kachhwaha family emblem. A royal way to reach the Suraj

Pol is to ride up on one of the colourfully caparisoned elephants waiting at the foothill, just as the kings did. This gate opens into the Jaleb Chowk, the courtyard where elephants and horses used to be tethered.

⌐ SURAJ POL
Sturdy parapets surmount the arches of this imposing gateway, balanced by graceful chhatris.

Chand Pol

Across the Jaleb Chowk, opposite the Suraj Pol, is the Chand Pol (Moon Gate), which was the main entrance for commoners. The upper storey, from where kettle drums and other musical instruments were played, is the Naubat Khana (Music Gallery). Next to the gate are the quarters for the elephants and horses. A stone path through Chand Pol leads to the ancient temples and other remains of the old town outside the fort.

jharokha

♨ JALEB CHOWK
This vast courtyard was the parade ground where the royal army would assemble; it is lined with barracks.

⚜ SINGH POL
A jharokha sits atop the arch of this gate.

FRESCO IN NICHE

Singh Pol

A broad flight of steps towards the corner of Jaleb Chowk leads to the double gateway of the Singh Pol (Lion Gate). Built by Raja Ram Singh I, son of Raja Jai Singh I, this gateway has two arches and is decorated with frescoes. Crowned with a *jharokha* in true Rajput style, it is flanked by two *chhatris*. Next to this gateway stands the temple of the family deity of the Kachhwahas, which is called the Shila Devi Temple. The interiors of this temple are decorated with exquisite marble work. The Singh Pol leads to the imperial quarters of the fort.

THE SHILA DEVI LEGEND

The Shila Devi Temple is an impressive shrine featuring silver doors with deities displayed in raised relief work. The temple is named after Shila Devi ("Shila" means stone slab and "Devi" means goddess). According to legend, Raja Man Singh I prayed to the goddess, seeking victory over the rulers of Bengal. She appeared in his dream and asked him to recover her statue submerged in the sea near Jessore (now in Bangladesh) and install it in a temple. The Raja recovered the statue after subjugating his enemies and had this temple constructed.

relief carving

SILVER DOOR

Layout of the Amber Fort complex

The massive ramparts of the Amber Fort follow the contours of the hill on which it stands. The fort is a splendid complex of gateways, courts, stairways, pillared pavilions, and palaces that recall the glory and wealth of Amber's former rulers. The imperial section consists of private palaces for men, apartments for the royal women and their attendants, and landscaped gardens with water channels and stone-trimmed flowerbeds. The gardens surround the Maota Lake.

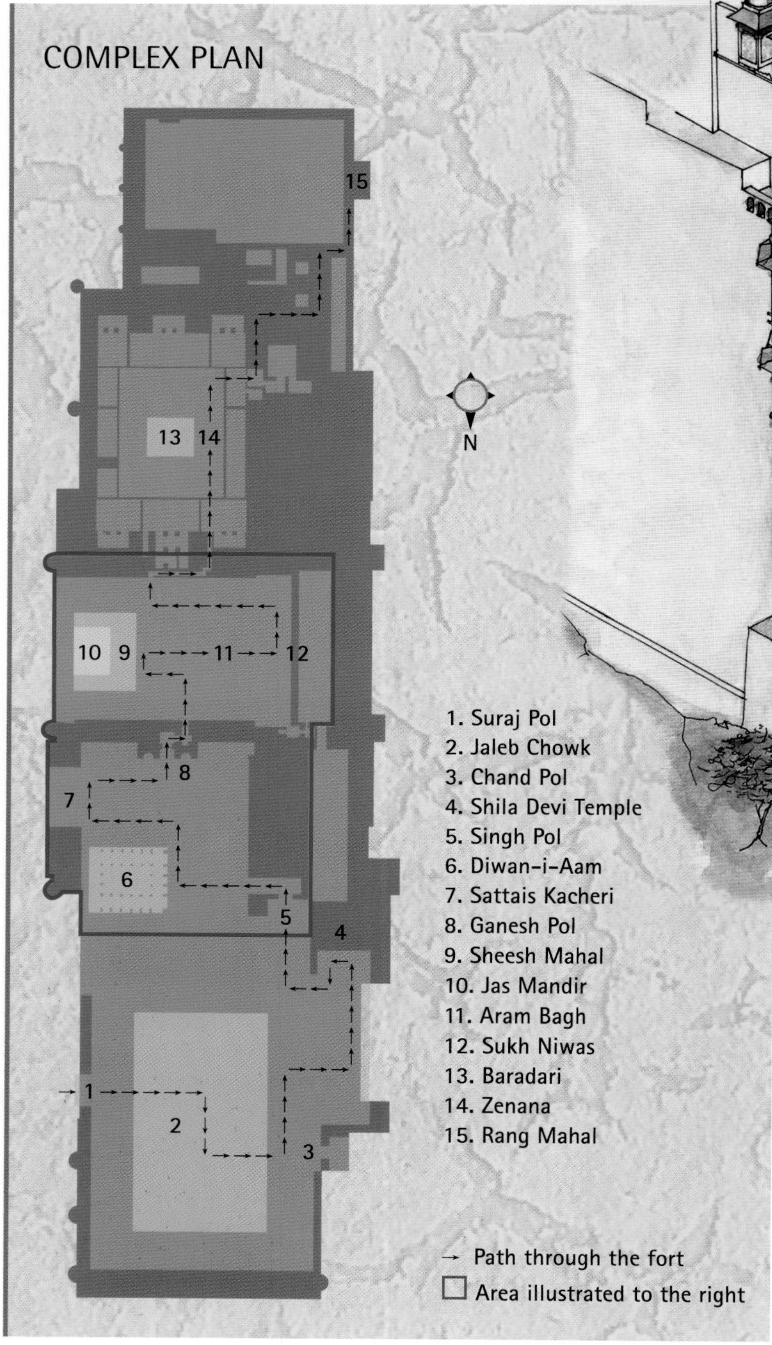

COMPLEX PLAN

N

1. Suraj Pol
2. Jaleb Chowk
3. Chand Pol
4. Shila Devi Temple
5. Singh Pol
6. Diwan-i-Aam
7. Sattais Kacheri
8. Ganesh Pol
9. Sheesh Mahal
10. Jas Mandir
11. Aram Bagh
12. Sukh Niwas
13. Baradari
14. Zenana
15. Rang Mahal

→ Path through the fort
☐ Area illustrated to the right

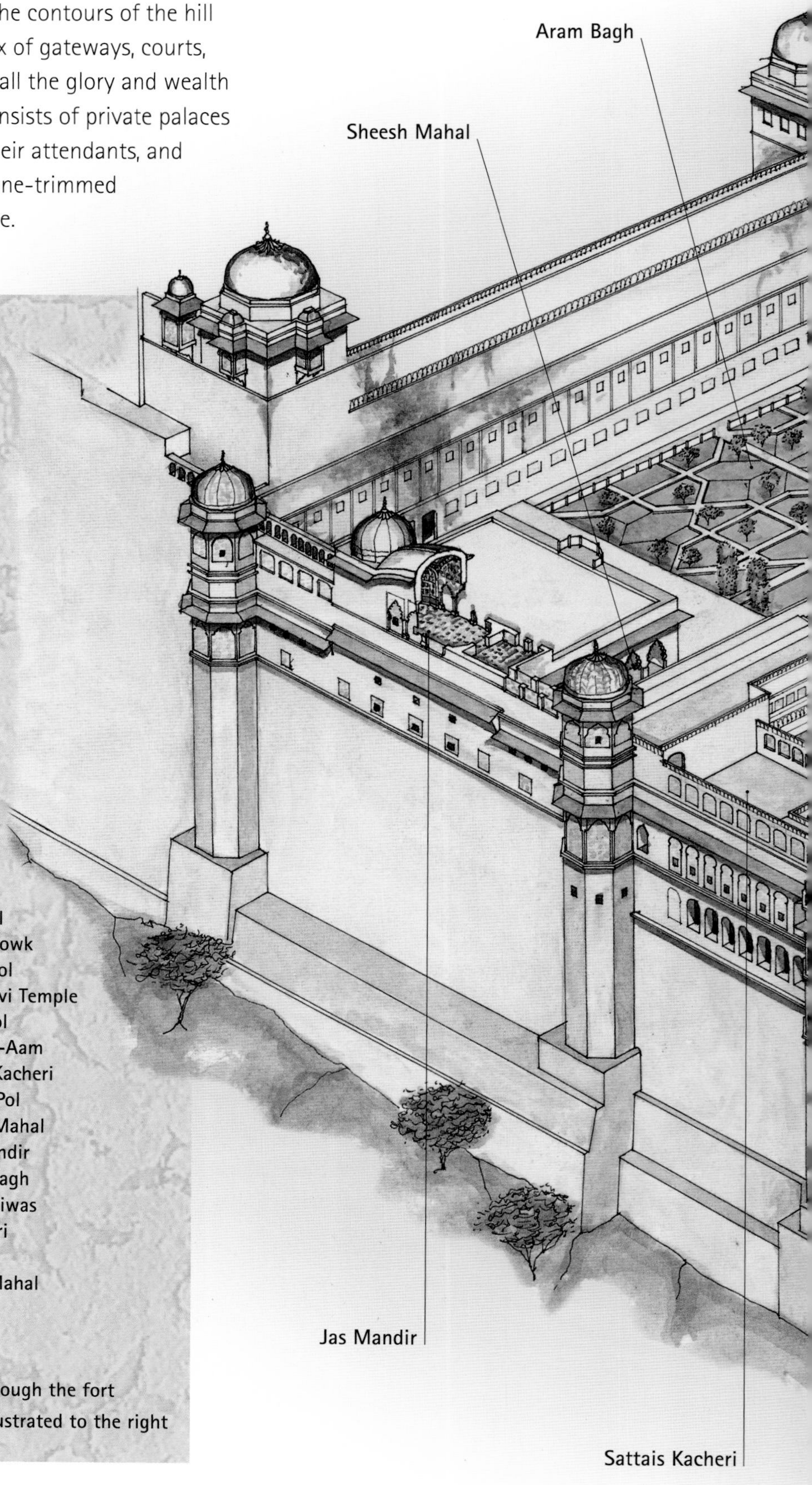

Aram Bagh

Sheesh Mahal

Jas Mandir

Sattais Kacheri

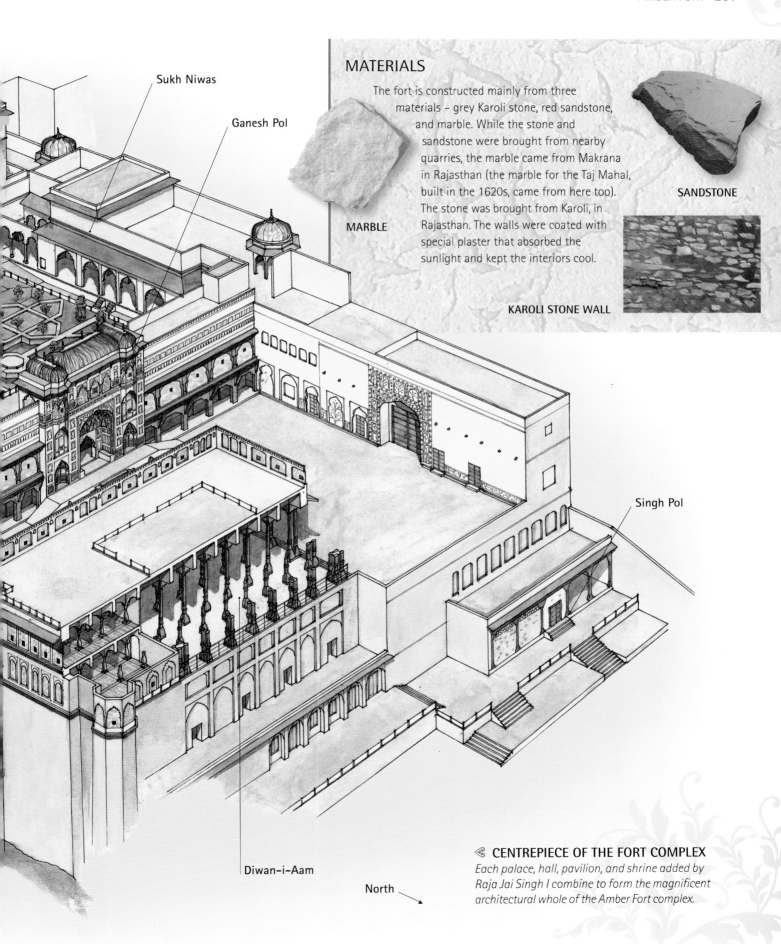

Sukh Niwas

Ganesh Pol

MATERIALS

The fort is constructed mainly from three materials – grey Karoli stone, red sandstone, and marble. While the stone and sandstone were brought from nearby quarries, the marble came from Makrana in Rajasthan (the marble for the Taj Mahal, built in the 1620s, came from here too). The stone was brought from Karoli, in Rajasthan. The walls were coated with special plaster that absorbed the sunlight and kept the interiors cool.

SANDSTONE

MARBLE

KAROLI STONE WALL

Singh Pol

Diwan-i-Aam

North

◈ CENTREPIECE OF THE FORT COMPLEX

Each palace, hall, pavilion, and shrine added by Raja Jai Singh I combine to form the magnificent architectural whole of the Amber Fort complex.

Diwan-i-Aam

A pavilion open on three sides, the Diwan-i-Aam (Hall for Public Audiences) stands on a platform. This is where the rulers received the people and heard their complaints and petitions. It consists of rows of 40 columns that are capped by carved brackets in different shapes. The outer columns are made of red sandstone while the inner ones are made of whitish grey marble. The ceiling rises towards a central rectangle, producing a canopy-like effect.

ORNATE BRACKETS

Red sandstone and white marble brackets top the columns in the Diwan-i-Aam. Elaborately carved, they display a variety of Rajput motifs, such as lotus buds, elephants, or heads of aquatic monsters with curling snouts.

✦ MAIN HALL
A chandelier and hand-controlled pulleys for fans were suspended from the hooks on the vaulted ceiling.

♥ DIWAN-I-AAM
This imposing hall was built by Raja Jai Singh I.

MOTIFS IN SANDSTONE AND MARBLE

latticed screens

carved brackets

Sattais Kacheri

Next to the Diwan-i-Aam is the administrative court called Sattais Kacheri (*sattais* means 27 and *kacheri* means court), its name derived from the fact that 27 superintendents would spend hours here supervising the governance of the kingdom. This is where the scribes would sit to record revenue petitions and present them to the rulers. The fluted columns and cusped arches are characteristic of Rajput architecture. To the right of the Sattais Kacheri lie the *hammams* (royal baths), while a row of *jharokhas* overlook the courtyard below. From the other side of this hall is a beautiful view of the Maota Lake and the gardens.

✑ DECORATED COLONNADES
The columns are made of plaster of lime and marble dust burnished to a gloss, to give it a marble-like finish.

JHAROKHA ✑
Small jharokhas *line the second storey of the Sattais Kacheri, with tiny arched openings to look out from.*

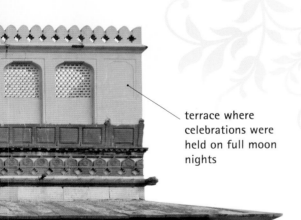

terrace where celebrations were held on full moon nights

✑ OPEN HALL
The arched hall opens out to the courtyard and gardens.

Ganesh Pol wall

IMAGE OF LORD GANESHA
Above the doorway is a painting of a seated figure of Ganesha – the elephant-headed god after whom the Ganesh Pol is named.

VAULTED CEILING
The arched vaults of the ceiling are painted with elaborate, colourful floral and leaf motifs.

Ganesh Pol

At the heart of the Amber Fort stands the magnificent Ganesh Pol. A three-storeyed gateway, it was constructed in 1640 by Raja Jai Singh I as a ceremonial gate for royal processions. The Ganesh Pol is the most ornate gateway in the Fort. Lavishly painted in the vibrant hues of natural dyes, it is decorated in a remarkable fusion of styles, featuring typical Rajasthani motifs, such as gods and goddesses, and Mughal designs, such as geometric patterns and stylized flowers encircled with foliage. The gateway leads into a courtyard, where the royal apartments are arranged around a beautiful garden.

GATEWAY WALLS
Covered with fine frescoes and mosaic work, the walls are pierced by arched windows and doorways.

gilded finial

SCREEN DETAIL

floral motif

Suhag Mandir

Suhag Mandir

The uppermost portion of the Ganesh Pol is called the Suhag Mandir (*suhag* means "good fortune", *mandir* means "temple"). It is a small hall with projecting balconies screened by delicately carved marble *jaalis* from where women, while remaining unseen, could watch royal processions in the courtyard below. It has octagonal rooms on each side that open out into the balconies.

ARCHED OPENINGS
Windows in the screens are cut out of the jaalis.

painted ceiling

CEILING OF SUHAG MANDIR

THE POL

At a time when every kingdom was considered vulnerable to attack or invasion, fortification was a prime concern. In the Rajput forts and palaces, the *pol* served just such a purpose. The word *pol* is derived from the Sanskrit word *pratoli*, meaning "gateway" or "entrance to an enclosed area". A *pol* guarded the town, which had only one or two such gateways, the other entrances being kept secret from outsiders. The *pols* often display intricately carved façades and fresco work on the walls.

INTERIOR OF SHEESH MAHAL
The arabesque designs and floral motifs on the ceiling are inlaid with mirror slivers.

ROYAL CHAMBERS ✎
Arched doorways and halls lead to the private apartments of the king.

Sheesh Mahal

Tiny, glittering shards of mirror cover the ceiling and walls of this palace, giving it the name Sheesh Mahal (*sheesh* means "mirror" and *mahal* means "palace"). It is also known as Diwan-i-Khas (Hall for Private Audiences) as the king met high-ranking nobles and merchants in the central hall, which is surrounded by a verandah. Since the Sheesh Mahal was built during Raja Jai Singh's time, it is also referred to as Jai Mandir. The inner rooms comprised the winter palace of Raja Jai Singh – thick velvet drapes and mirrors reflecting the light and heat of the oil lamps kept these rooms warm.

MIRROR WORK ✎
The flowers seem to end in scorpions' tails, a typical Rajasthani motif.

✎ MARBLE RELIEF
Mughal floral designs are combined with butterflies, another Rajasthani motif.

⚜ SHEESH MAHAL VERANDAH
*The stately verandah of the Sheesh Mahal, embellished
with marble panels and mirror work, formed part of
the personal apartments of the ruler.*

Jas Mandir

Above the Sheesh Mahal is the Jas Mandir, the summer palace of Raja Jai
Singh. Crowned by a curved roof and *chhatris*, its ceiling is decorated with
elegant alabaster relief work and glass inlay. It has fine marble screens
overlooking the Maota Lake. Here, cool breeze from the lake would waft
in through screens lined with *khus* (fragrant grass), scenting the air.

⚜ CAPITAL
*Stylized petal
shapes arranged
in tiers decorate
the capitals of the
double columns.
These columns
support the arches
of the Sheesh
Mahal's verandah.*

ARABESQUE MOTIF

⚜ CURVED CEILING
*Geometric designs give way to floral
patterns where the ceiling curves up
in the main hall of the Sheesh Mahal.*

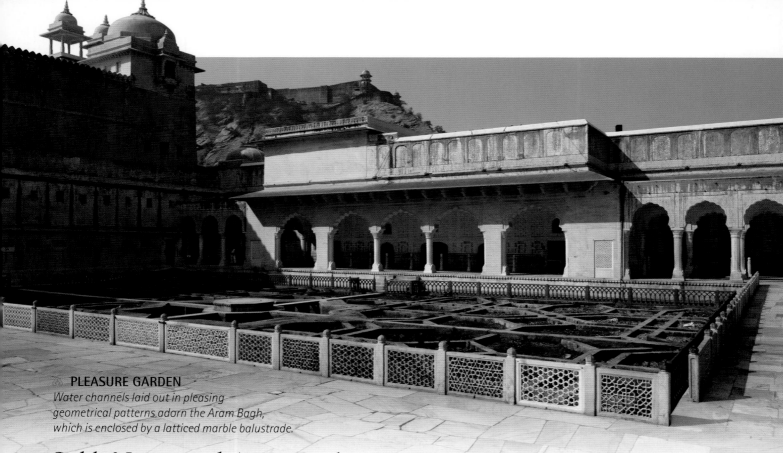

PLEASURE GARDEN
Water channels laid out in pleasing geometrical patterns adorn the Aram Bagh, which is enclosed by a latticed marble balustrade.

Sukh Niwas and Aram Bagh

The Sukh Niwas (*sukh* means "peace" and *niwas* means "house") is set on the opposite side of the Sheesh Mahal. It consists of a central chamber with rooms for the queens on either side. The doors of the rooms are carved from fragrant sandalwood, inlaid with ivory. In front of the Sukh Niwas lies a formal Mughal-style garden called the Aram Bagh (Garden of Leisure). The queens would spend many hours in these gardens, which were decorated with fountains and pools filled with coloured water.

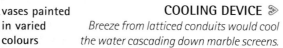
vases painted in varied colours

COOLING DEVICE ❧
Breeze from latticed conduits would cool the water cascading down marble screens.

✿ ENGRAVINGS ON WALLS
The vases, unlike similar Mughal-style motifs, are engraved without handles.

ARAM BAGH ❧
This garden, divided into quadrants by geometric paths and waterways, follows the same plan as Mughal gardens.

Maota Lake and the gardens

Perched on a high hill, the Amber Fort overlooks the Maota Lake, which was the main source of water for the palaces within the fort and also served to protect the kingdom from intruders. It has three well-planned gardens, with flowerbeds laid out in geometrical patterns. The Kesar Kyari Bagh, with its star-shaped *kyaris* (flowerbeds) where *kesar* (saffron) and other exotic plants and herbs were grown, is one of them. These floating gardens (they were hollowed beneath to keep the gardens cool in summer), were the venues for entertainment. Now, the breathtaking and very informative *Son-et-Lumiere* (Sound and Light) show takes place here, using the fort as a backdrop.

SAFFRON – THE SPICE OF LIFE

For centuries, fragrant, delicate orange saffron, extracted from the saffron crocus (*Crocus sativus*) flower, has been the spice of life in many parts of India, gracing the feasts of kings and wealthy nobles. The flower has three orange stigmas and a yellow style. These are handpicked, dried, and used to colour and flavour food. It is the most expensive spice in the world.

PULLEY SYSTEM
Water stored in underground tanks was pumped up by pulleys to irrigate the gardens.

FLOWERBEDS
Rare plants were grown in aesthetically laid out, symmetrical rows of hexagonal, stone-bordered flowerbeds.

⚜ **TWELVE PILLARS**
The Baradari is named after its 12 pillars (bara means 12) and the 12 rooms that surround it.

Baradari

A high wall separates the palace of Raja Man Singh I from Jai Singh's palace. The *zenana* (women's quarters) of Man Singh's palace is the oldest part of the palace complex. The Baradari, a colonnaded pavilion, sits in the spacious courtyard surrounded by the *zenana* and it was here that the queens would enjoy performances of music and dance.

THE MUGHAL INFLUENCE

The layout of a typical Rajput palace shows similarities with those of the Mughals based on their shared views of the nature of kingship, courtly life, and the status of women. Elements like domes and arches, and features like quadrilateral gardens, *zenana* apartments, audience chambers such as the Diwan-i-Aam, are Mughal concepts of architecture that have been absorbed by the Rajputs and blended with their own style.

DIWAN-I-AAM, RED FORT

⚜ **ARCHED COLONNADE**
Graceful pillars support the cusped arches of the Baradari; flowing curtains were draped here as screens for the queens.

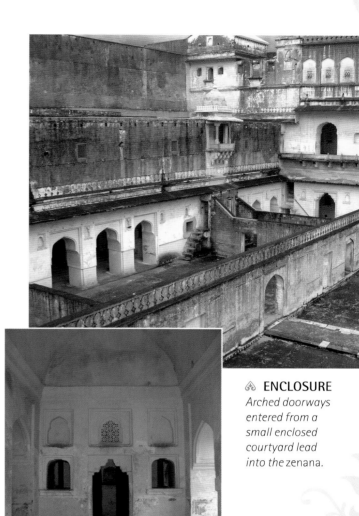

⚗ ENCLOSURE
Arched doorways entered from a small enclosed courtyard lead into the zenana.

The zenana

The *zenana* apartments, where Raja Man Singh's 12 wives and concubines lived, line all four sides of the courtyard. The guards were eunuchs as no man except the king himself could enter this area. Bearing the distinct stamp of Mughal *zenana* architecture, it consists of high walls, long galleries, as well as covered balconies and screened areas from where the royal ladies could watch cultural activities held in the courtyard. The (now faded) murals on the walls depict scenes from the life of Lord Krishna.

⚗ APARTMENT
A hall in the private chambers of the royal ladies.

⚗ ROYAL CHAMBER
Man Singh's room is situated beside the zenana apartments.

RANG MAHAL ⚗
The exquisite Rang Mahal was used by Man Singh for festivities.

Red Fort

The Red Fort (Lal Qila) in Delhi is the paramount symbol of Mughal grandeur. Made of red sandstone, this fort, now a UNESCO World Heritage Site, epitomizes the ingenuity and creativity of Mughal architecture. Located between the river Yamuna and Shahjahanabad (the seventh city of Delhi), the fort contains an array of palaces and pavilions, set in ornamental gardens. Emperor Shah Jahan commissioned the construction of the fort in the early 17th century. Under the supervision of master-architect Makramat Khan, it was completed in nine years. It is said that the construction of the fort cost over ten million rupees. In 1648, the emperor and his entourage entered the fort amidst ceremonial drumbeats and celebrations. Shahjahanabad replaced Agra as the imperial capital.

⚜ **CENTRE OF POWER**
Delhi was the administrative centre of the Mughals from 1648–1857.

Reflecting the Mughal love of opulence, brocades, curtains, carpets, cushions, and gem-encrusted walls beautified the palaces and pavilions, flowers bloomed in the gardens, and water from the river Yamuna fed the many fountains and channels.

The river flowed along the eastern wall of the fort. The decline of the Mughals coincided with attacks on the city and the vandalizing of the palaces. After 1857, British forces demolished many buildings within the fort and then occupied it. In 1947, the Red Fort was chosen as the site of a momentous event – the first hoisting of independent India's flag. This historic fort has been a spectator to an India in the making, resonating with event-filled chapters in the history of the nation.

The Mughal Emperors

The conquest of north India by Babur heralded the establishment of the Mughal dynasty. One of the greatest empires in the history of the Indian subcontinent, the Mughals ruled over 100 million subjects at the zenith of their power. Their government was based on a centralized administrative system. After two centuries of stability, the Mughal empire began to decline during the early 18th century.

- 1526 The Mughal empire is founded by **Babur**, with Agra as its chief city.

- 1530 **Humayun** accedes to the throne.

- 1555–1605 Reign of **Akbar**.

- 1605–1627 Reign of **Jahangir**.

- 1628 **Shah Jahan** accedes to the throne.

- 1648 Shah Jahan moves his capital from Agra to **Shahjahanabad**. Construction of **Red Fort** completed.

- 1658–1707 Reign of **Aurangzeb**.

- 1739 **Nadir Shah** of Persia (modern-day Iran) invades Delhi.

- 1838 **Bahadur Shah Zafar**, the last Mughal emperor, comes to the throne.

- 1857 **First War of Independence** is fought. The British East India Company quells the uprising and its army occupies Red Fort.

- 1858 The British forces exile Bahadur Shah Zafar to Myanmar, **ending Mughal rule**.

A Fort's History

The Red Fort, a testimony to the power of the Mughals, was a miniature city, east of the city of Shahjahanabad. During Emperor Shah Jahan's reign, the fort was known as Qila-i-Mubarak (Auspicious Citadel). Later, it was called the Lal Qila (Red Fort). After the Mughals, the fort was occupied by the British and, till 2003, by the Indian army.

The age of great architecture

When Prince Khurram became emperor, he took the title of Shah Jahan (King of the World). Shah Jahan, much like his grandfather Akbar, was a patron of the arts and his reign witnessed the golden age of Mughal architecture. Besides the Red Fort, his legacy includes the grand Jama Masjid in Delhi; the Shah Jahan Mosque in Sind, Pakistan; and the Moti Masjid (Pearl Mosque), Wazir Khan Mosque, sections of the Lahore Fort, and the Shalimar Gardens in Lahore, Pakistan. In Agra, he built sizeable parts of the Agra Fort as well as the magnificent Taj Mahal.

TAJ MAHAL
Considered one of the Seven Wonders of the World, the Taj Mahal was built under Shah Jahan's patronage. This exquisite memorial for his wife, Mumtaz Mahal, is faced with marble and is perfectly symmetric.

JAMA MASJID
Built in 1656 by Emperor Shah Jahan, the three-domed Jama Masjid in Delhi is one of the finest mosques in India.

INVASIONS AND PLUNDER

Marauders from regions near Delhi took advantage of Mughal vulnerability in the 18th century. In 1739, Emperor Nadir Shah of Persia reached Delhi. It is said that, angered by a rumour of his death, he ordered the slaughter of the local people. Thousands were killed, parts of the city were set on fire, and the Red Fort was pillaged. The Peacock Throne, the royal treasury, and precious jewels and manuscripts were plundered. These events were repeated when the Afghan chief, Ahmed Shah Durrani, attacked Delhi.

SHAH JAHAN
This 17th-century painting shows Emperor Shah Jahan holding court.

Modern times

After the First War of Independence in 1857, British forces stormed the city and the fort, killing hundreds of people. They demolished buildings in the fort and built huge barracks. Five decades later, the freedom movement gathered strength. In 1945, three members of the INA (Indian National Army) were tried by a British court in the fort and were eventually released. Independent India was born on 15 August 1947.

INDEPENDENT INDIA
In August 1947, Jawaharlal Nehru, India's first prime minister, hoisted the national flag at the Red Fort ramparts. This has since become a tradition for every Independence Day.

SUNEHRI MASJID
Legend has it that Nadir Shah sat on the roof of the Sunehri Masjid (Golden Mosque) in Chandni Chowk, watching the destruction of the city.

SOOTHING AMBIENCE
The fading rays of the sun fall on the interior of the Rang Mahal, bathing the palace in a mellow light.

Monumental Harmony

Established in the 16th century, the Mughal empire grew rapidly to cover most of the Indian subcontinent. This was paralleled by the development of Mughal architecture, born out of a cohesive blend of Central Asian architectural styles with indigenous forms. Mughal architecture is exemplified by Islamic elements such as calligraphy, intricately carved niches, domes, and pointed arches. The use of *chhajjas* (projecting eaves) reflects influences from Rajasthani architecture, while the curved roofs indicate a Bengali origin. Intricate inlay work and *jaalis* (perforated screens or latticed tracery) are common in Mughal buildings. The *charbagh* (quadrilateral garden layout further divided into four parts) originated in Persia. Shah Jahan's architectural style was typified by an increased use of marble and a gradual refinement in the ornamentation of buildings, such as inlaid semi-precious stones; cusped arches and foliated plinths were also extensively employed.

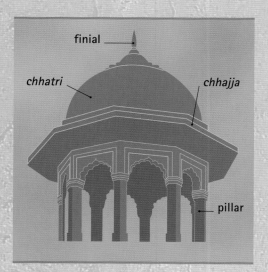

finial

chhatri

chhajja

pillar

⚜ CHHATRI
The chhatri *(umbrella-shaped pavilion), adopted from Rajasthani architecture, is a common rooftop feature in Mughal buildings.*

Gateways

The structure of the gateways and their strategic location provided major defensive advantages. The occupants of the fort could regulate entry by lifting the drawbridges, and

defend themselves against enemies while hiding behind the parapets with large merlons (upward-projecting parts of a battlement). The giant bastions also strengthened the defence. Of the five existing gates, the two major ones are the massive Lahore and Delhi Gates.

⚜ ADDITIONAL DEFENCE
In order to guard the Lahore Gate, Emperor Aurangzeb had a barbican (fortified outpost) built to the west side of the gate.

merlon on parapet

barbican of Lahore Gate

Delhi Gate

This gate, which forms part of the southern wall of the fort, faces the direction of the settlements that predated the Red Fort. Emperor Shah Jahan is said to have used this gate when he visited the Jama Masjid for Friday prayers. The Delhi Gate is protected by a barbican, while a pair of large stone elephants stand guard inside the gate.

BARBICAN OF DELHI GATE

Lahore Gate

So called because it faces Lahore (now in Pakistan), the Lahore Gate is a three-storeyed gateway set into the western wall of the Red Fort, and the fort's primary entrance. The pointed arch in the entrance is nested within another similar arch, which in turn forms a recessed sandstone façade. *Kanguras* (ornamental merlons) line the parapet above. Octagonal towers stand on the sides, capped with sandstone domes and marble finials. A series of indented niches adorn these towers.

marble domes on *chhatris*

red stone pinnacle

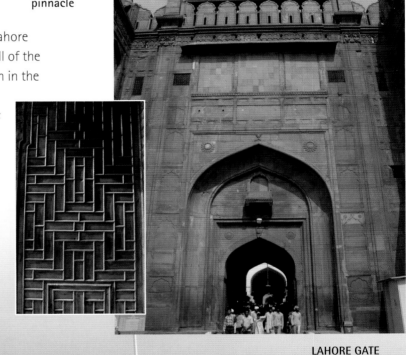

BRASS DESIGN ▧
Brass sheets were embossed onto the inner wooden doors to strengthen them.

LAHORE GATE

Layout of the Red Fort complex

Constructed on the western bank of the river Yamuna, the Red Fort is a massive fort-palace complex that marks the northeastern corner of the medieval city of Shahjahanabad. Bastions at regular intervals further strengthen the outer wall and ramparts. *Chattris* and turrets line the wall. The fort is surrounded by a now dry moat. Public entry is through the Lahore Gate on the western side of the fort. The length of the fort is about 900m (2,953ft) from north to south and 550m (1,804ft) from east to west. The outer rampart walls traverse a perimeter of 2.41km (1.5 miles). The plan below highlights the areas of historical interest in the section accessible to the public.

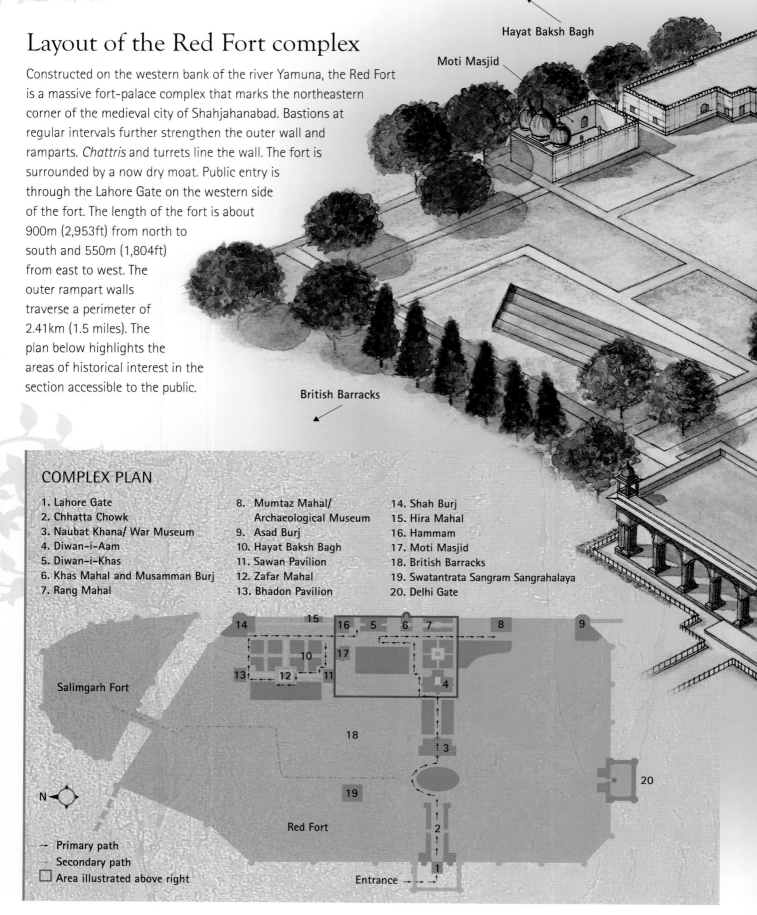

Hayat Baksh Bagh

Moti Masjid

British Barracks

COMPLEX PLAN

1. Lahore Gate
2. Chhatta Chowk
3. Naubat Khana/ War Museum
4. Diwan-i-Aam
5. Diwan-i-Khas
6. Khas Mahal and Musamman Burj
7. Rang Mahal
8. Mumtaz Mahal/ Archaeological Museum
9. Asad Burj
10. Hayat Baksh Bagh
11. Sawan Pavilion
12. Zafar Mahal
13. Bhadon Pavilion
14. Shah Burj
15. Hira Mahal
16. Hammam
17. Moti Masjid
18. British Barracks
19. Swatantrata Sangram Sangrahalaya
20. Delhi Gate

Salimgarh Fort

Red Fort

N

→ Primary path
- Secondary path
□ Area illustrated above right

Entrance →

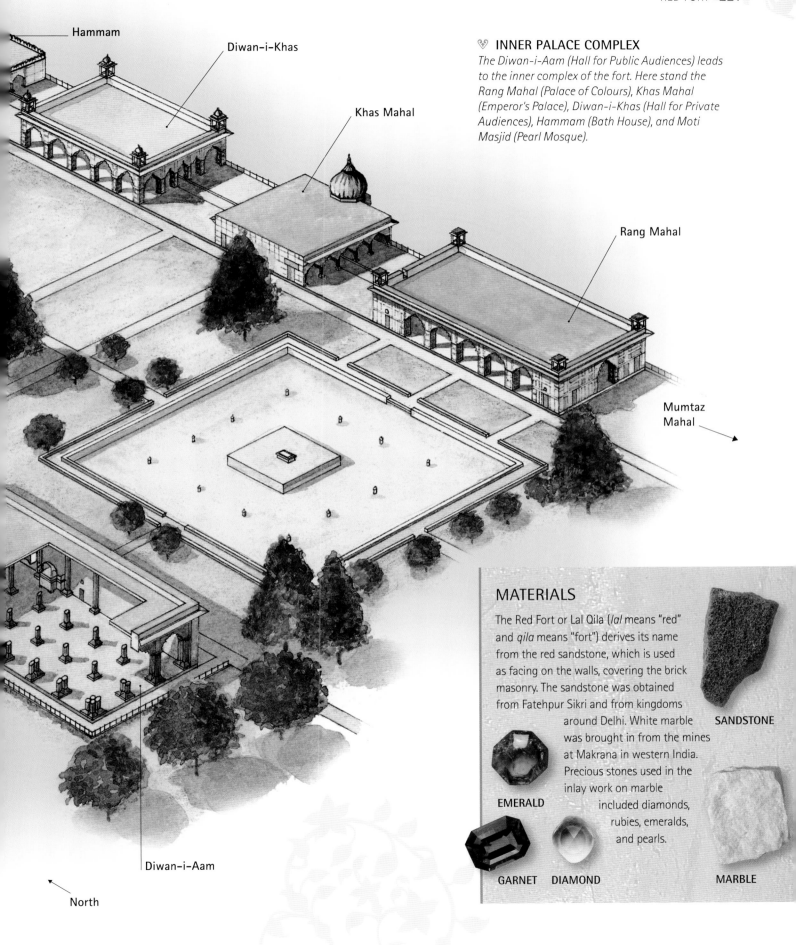

Hammam

Diwan-i-Khas

Khas Mahal

Rang Mahal

Mumtaz Mahal

Diwan-i-Aam

North

❦ INNER PALACE COMPLEX

The Diwan-i-Aam (Hall for Public Audiences) leads to the inner complex of the fort. Here stand the Rang Mahal (Palace of Colours), Khas Mahal (Emperor's Palace), Diwan-i-Khas (Hall for Private Audiences), Hammam (Bath House), and Moti Masjid (Pearl Mosque).

MATERIALS

The Red Fort or Lal Qila (*lal* means "red" and *qila* means "fort") derives its name from the red sandstone, which is used as facing on the walls, covering the brick masonry. The sandstone was obtained from Fatehpur Sikri and from kingdoms around Delhi. White marble was brought in from the mines at Makrana in western India. Precious stones used in the inlay work on marble included diamonds, rubies, emeralds, and pearls.

SANDSTONE

EMERALD

GARNET   DIAMOND

MARBLE

Chhatta Chowk

The Lahore Gate leads to a vaulted arcade called the Chhatta Chowk (Roofed Arcade), which houses one of the covered bazaars of the 17th century. Divided into two parts by an octagonal courtyard in the middle, this two-storeyed arcade has 32 bays with cusped arches. There are shops on the ground floor, as in the Mughal times. The upper floor sections are now barricaded.

❤ IMPOSING ARCHWAY
The vaulted ceiling of Chhatta Chowk is supported by broad arches bearing patterns in stucco; these were once painted and gilded.

◈ ARABESQUE DESIGN
A series of geometric designs covers the ceiling, creating a pattern. It is a common element in Mughal architecture.

MEENA BAZAAR ◈
During the Mughal period, the shops in the marketplace used to sell brocades, velvets, silverware, spices, precious stones, and weapons. Today, the shops sell handicrafts, jewellery, textiles, antiques, and other goods.

≪ **HATHI POL**
It is said that only princes on their elephants were allowed to pass through the majestic Hathi Pol (Elephant Gate).

MOTIFS ON WALL

Naubat Khana

Further on from the bazaar is a three-storeyed sandstone building called the Naubat Khana (Music Gallery). It is also referred to as the Naqqar Khana (Drum House) because this is where musicians played their instruments to announce prayers, on special occasions, and to herald the arrival of royalty. The instruments included drums, cymbals, trumpets, and the *shehnai* (an oboe-like woodwind instrument).

cusped window

recessed niche

🔊 **INDIAN WAR MEMORIAL MUSEUM**
The museum (on the second floor) contains exhibits of war-related objects such as body armour and weapons like swords, daggers, and shields. These are mainly from the Mughal era.

🔊 **TRACERY WORK**
A stone arch set into the wall on the ground floor displays tracery work incorporating calligraphic inscriptions from Persian texts.

⚜ HALL FOR PUBLIC AUDIENCES
The Diwan-i-Aam stands to the east of the Naubat Khana. The original courtyard in front has been replaced by lawns.

Diwan-i-Aam

Standing at the edge of the inner palace complex, the Diwan-i-Aam (Hall for Public Audiences) was the venue for the emperor's interactions with his subjects, who would fill the hall and the adjoining courtyard. It is said that the emperor routinely resolved disputes on the spot and inspected parades of soldiers and animals. The pillars and ceiling of the hall were originally overlaid with gilded lime stucco, traces of which are still visible. The majestic façade comprises a nine-arched arcade supported by double columns made of sandstone.

underside
of arch
was gilded

cusp

♥ CARVINGS ON PLINTH
These fine carvings on sandstone are a testament to the skill of the artisans of the Mughal age.

⚜ ASSEMBLY HALL
The roof of the main hall is supported by three parallel rows of columns that hold up a series of symmetrical, cusped arches.

Marble pavilion

Profusely carved and embellished with precious stones, the marble pavilion (Nashiman-i-Zill-Ilahi or Seat of the Shadow of God) housed the emperor's throne, and is the focal point of the great hall. The inlay work on the wall behind the pavilion is attributed by some to the French jeweller, Austin de Bordeaux. Certain panels were removed after the First War of Independence, and were later restored. Steel rails bordering the pavilion have replaced the original ones, which were made of silver.

⚜ CURVED ROOF ON PAVILION
Set in a niche in the wall at the centre of the front hall, the pavilion has a roof in the form of a curvilinear cornice; this is an adaptation of the sloping roof characteristic of Bengali architecture.

FLORAL RELIEF ⚜
Flower clusters are set within intricate borders on the relief carvings that adorn the pavilion's platform. Makrana marble, sourced from the Nagaur district in present-day Rajasthan, was used to build the pavilion.

PIETRA DURA

The wall of the central recessed arch behind the pavilion is ornamented with pietra dura or inlay work. The marble panels were decorated with multi-coloured precious and semi-precious stones to enhance the naturalism in the rendering of birds, fruits, and floral motifs.

Greek god Orpheus playing the lute

PATTERNS ON MARBLE

floral inlay work on marble

⚜ WAZIR'S DAIS
A marble dais supported by pillars stands in front of the pavilion. It was used by the wazir (prime minister) to submit public petitions to the emperor.

Diwan-i-Khas

Faced with polished marble, the Diwan-i-Khas (Hall for Private Audiences) stands atop a plinth. The scalloped arches are supported by a set of 32 columns with square shafts. Inscribed on the arches of the northern and southern walls of the Diwan-i-Khas is the famous Persian couplet: "*Agar Firdaus baru-i-zamin ast, hamin ast, hamin ast, hamin ast*" ("If there is paradise on Earth, it is this, it is this, it is this"). The Nahr-i-Bahisht (Canal of Paradise) was a channel of water that once flowed under this pavilion. The *Son-et-Lumière* (Sound and Light) show is held regularly in the grounds in front of the hall and brings the history of Delhi and the Red Fort to life.

⚜ OPULENT INTERIOR
The ceiling and walls of the chamber were embellished with silver, gold, and precious stones, before being plundered in the 18th and 19th centuries.

❦ HALL FOR PRIVATE AUDIENCES
The Diwan-i-Khas is where the emperor received important guests like kings and ambassadors in private. The Khas Mahal (Emperor's Palace) adjoins the building.

chhatri

engrailed arch

⚜ GILDED CAPITAL
The upper parts of the piers enclosing the central chamber, and the foliated arches topping the piers were originally painted in gold.

FLORAL ARTISTRY ❧
Shah Jahan's artisans used precious and semi-precious stones to adorn the floral inlay work that can be seen all over the hall.

⚜ **THRONE PEDESTAL**
The marble pedestal on which the Takht-i-Taus was placed originally stood at the centre of the hall. It is presently placed near the eastern wall.

Takht-i-Taus

More commonly known as the Peacock Throne (so called because of figures of two peacocks carved on the back of the throne), the Takht-i-Taus was placed in the central chamber of the Diwan-i-Khas and was used by the emperor on important state occasions. The throne was made of gold and studded with sapphires, emeralds, diamonds, pearls, and rubies. It was taken away by Nadir Shah of Persia when he plundered the fort in 1739. After his death, the throne was broken up. Some fragments were used in the throne that can currently be seen in the Golestan Palace in Iran.

Khas Mahal

marble platform

⚜ **PLANTS ON MARBLE**
Pietra dura work in the form of inlaid representations of foliage and flowers can be seen on the lower surface of the marble pillars.

KOH-I-NOOR

The most famous of the many precious stones in the Takht-i-Taus is a diamond called the *Koh-i-Noor* (Mountain of Light), which was embedded in the canopy of the throne. After many adventures, it is today a part of the British Crown jewels.

KOH-I-NOOR

marble-clad dome

Khas Mahal

A platform connects the Diwan-i-Khas with the Khas Mahal (Emperor's Palace or Special Palace), which contained the emperor's personal living quarters and is a composite structure consisting of three sections. The Tasbih Khana (Chamber for Prayer) and the Tosha Khana (Robe Chamber) flank the central room called the Khwabgah (Chamber of Dreams), which has marble screens on the northern and southern walls.

THE EMPEROR'S PALACE

MIZAN-I-INSAF 🦚
Resting within a crescent on the outer surface of the northern wall of the Khwabgah is the bas-relief called Mizan-i-Insaf (Scales of Justice), which was part of the emperor's insignia.

🦚 TASBIH KHANA
The first chamber is made of three rooms and a triple-arched opening facing the Diwan-i-Khas. The plain lower surface of the walls contrasts with the upper half, which is ornamented with inlay work in indented niches.

🦚 ELEPHANT HEAD
The doors on the wall flanking the Tasbih Khana are made of metal and are embellished with elephant-head brackets.

TOSHA KHANA
Also called the Baithak (Meeting Hall), this oblong hall faces south, standing adjacent to the Rang Mahal; its façade has five arches.

⚜ **CEILING OF TOSHA KHANA**
Traditional Mughal motifs seen on the ceiling were once adorned with silver and gold.

Musamman Burj

The Musamman Burj (Octagonal Tower) or the Burj-i-Tila (Golden Tower) is connected with the eastern wall of the Khwabgah in the Khas Mahal. The emperor used to appear at the window every morning, to be seen by his subjects standing below on the river-banks. A marble dome has replaced the original gilded copper dome.

MUSAMMAN BURJ

Rang Mahal

This palace lies next to the Khas Mahal and was used as a residence by the queens and their hand-maidens. The women watched elephant matches of strength on the sandy banks of the Yamuna below from the grilled openings on the eastern wall. A lavishly decorated pillared structure, the palace has a central hall with small chambers opening out from its fifteen bays. The Rang Mahal is constructed in marble and red sandstone, and the interior is adorned with delicate floral and foliage inlay work. Continuing from under the Khas Mahal, the water channel known as the Nahr-i-Bahisht flowed through the Rang Mahal into a lotus-shaped, marble fountain basin in the centre of the palace. Reflections of the inlay work would shimmer in the water of the channel and basin, heightening the beauty of the palace.

⚜ PALACE OF COLOURS
The Rang Mahal derives its name from the original coloured ornamentation in the interior.

⚜ COOLING DEVICES
Small jaalis (lattice-work) on the wall functioned as natural ventilators, filtering in air to cool the interior of the palace.

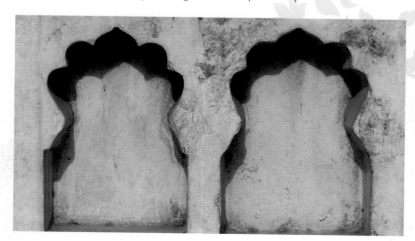

MARBLE NICHES

⚜ SHEESH MAHAL
Four chambers on the northern and southern sides of the Rang Mahal have ceilings decorated with embossed glass mirrors, which is why each of these is called a Sheesh Mahal (Palace of Mirrors).

⚜ CENTRAL ARCHWAY
The northern end of the palace opens to a triple arch with marble columns and jaali *or tracery work on top.*

Mumtaz Mahal

Princesses lived in this palace named Mumtaz Mahal (Beautiful Palace). Cusped arches framing *jaalis* line the outer walls on the sides, and floral carvings are visible at the base of the walls. Marble pillars support arches in the hall within. The Rang Mahal and the Mumtaz Mahal formed the *zenana* (women's quarters). The Asad Burj, a tower at the southeastern end of the fort, can be seen from here.

CARVINGS ON MARBLE

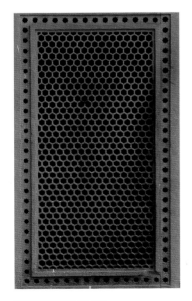

SANDSTONE JAALI

⚜ ARCHAEOLOGICAL MUSEUM
The palace is presently used by the ASI (Archaeological Survey of India) as a museum to display objects primarily from the Mughal era.

Hayat Baksh Bagh

A carefully planned garden complex, the Hayat Baksh Bagh (Life-Bestowing Garden) was made in the *charbagh* style (*char* means "four" and *bagh* means "garden"), a quadrilateral garden layout that originated in ancient Persia. This fourfold form comprised a garden intersected by a pair of channels or waterways. The point of intersection at the centre would usually be highlighted with a central pool, often with an accompanying pavilion.

BAHADUR SHAH ZAFAR'S PALACE

BRITISH BARRACKS

The barracks were built by the British after the First War of Independence (when Indian sepoys arose in rebellion against the British forces) in 1857. Large portions of the Red Fort were destroyed at the time. Some sections of the barracks were constructed in the space that was once the Mehtab Bagh (Garden of Moonlight), and these overlook the Hayat Baksh Bagh complex.

Zafar Mahal

The Zafar Mahal (Zafar's Palace) is a sandstone pavilion built by Bahadur Shah Zafar, the last Mughal emperor. It is situated in the middle of the large tank at the centre of the Hayat Baksh Bagh. The palace has a courtyard in the centre with square rooms at the four corners. The plain architectural style contrasts with Shah Jahan's, which was much more ornamental.

⚜ **SANDSTONE ARCH**
The Bhadon pavilion can be seen through an arched opening in the Zafar Mahal.

barracks

⚜ THE WATER SYSTEM
The pavilions are identical in design and formed part of the garden water system. Cascades of water flowed out from them and into the canal network, causing a cooling effect.

DETAIL ON PILLAR CAPITAL

Sawan and Bhadon pavilions

The Sawan pavilion is located at the southern end of the Hayat Baksh Bagh, while the Bhadon pavilion stands at the northern end. Sawan (derived from the Hindi word, *shravan*) and Bhadon denote the first two months of the rainy season, according to the Hindu calendar.

⚜ NICHES FOR CANDLES
Candles would burn in these niches, behind a sheet of falling water. The niches are set in the bases of the pavilions, facing the garden.

⚜ HAYAT BAKSH BAGH
The Hayat Baksh Bagh adjoins the inner palace complex. The original canals converged at the central tank.

⚜ CARVED PILLARS
The 16 marble pillars in each of the pavilions are cylindrical in shape and have moulded bases.

MARBLE PAVILION
The pavilion in front of the Shah Burj is capped by a curved roof typical of Bengali architecture.

Shah Burj

The Shah Burj (Royal Tower) is located at the northeastern corner of the Red Fort. This was used by the emperor for his private meetings with his council, which included courtiers, princes, and the *wazir* (prime minister). Water from the Yamuna would be drawn into the tower and then distributed to the rest of the fort. The pavilion in the foreground is believed to have been built by Emperor Aurangzeb.

INLAY WORK

marble incline leading to basin

NAHR-I-BAHISHT
The basin in front of the pavilion was where the canal called Nahr-i-Bahisht (Canal of Paradise) originated; it ran under the palaces and pavilions, parallel to the eastern wall of the fort.

Hira Mahal

An elevated sandstone terrace runs along the eastern wall of the fort between the Shah Burj and the Hammam (Bath House). It was on this terrace that Bahadur Shah Zafar built the pavilion called the Hira Mahal (Diamond Palace). Cusped arches and a plain marble parapet can be seen on the minimally decorated sides.

DIAMOND PALACE

Moti Masjid

Named after the pearly gloss of its marble, the Moti Masjid (Pearl Mosque) has high walls with embattled parapets. These surround the courtyard and can be seen through the latticed screen in the northern wall. Niches have been carved into the west wall. The floor inside is decorated with black marble outlines of *musallas* (prayer mats).

pinnacle

MARBLE DOMES

COPPER-PLATED DOOR

❧ BASINS FOR BATHS
Basins and tanks were provided for hot, cold, rose water, and vapour baths.

⚜ PEARL MOSQUE
The Moti Masjid was built in white marble by Emperor Aurangzeb and stands next to the Hayat Baksh Bagh.

Hammam

The Ghusal Khana (*ghusal* means "wash" and *khana* means "room") or the Hammam stands opposite the Moti Masjid. A series of pipes and tanks embedded in the walls and the ground supplied hot or cold water to the Hammam. The floor and walls of the chambers were decorated with gems and inlay work.

❧ SOUTHERN FAÇADE
Three cusped arches on the southern side face the Diwan-i-Khas. The central chamber is flanked by two smaller chambers; the channel where the Nahr-i-Bahisht flowed is visible at the centre.

spandrel

Taj Mahal

The mesmerizing beauty of the Taj Mahal has captivated people for centuries. In 1983, the Taj Mahal was declared a UNESCO World Heritage Site and cited as "one of the universally admired masterpieces of the world's heritage." Acknowledged as one of the Seven Wonders of the modern World, this exquisite marble tomb was built in the 17th century by Mughal emperor Shah Jahan in memory of his favourite wife, Mumtaz Mahal. Construction of the tomb began in 1632, employing more than 20,000 labourers for 20 years. Architects, calligraphers, and stone masons were appointed from all over the country and also from places as far as Persia. A great builder, Shah Jahan himself was involved in the planning and architecture of this breathtaking structure. During the reign of Shah Jahan, the mausoleum was known simply as the *rauza* (the tomb) and was only later called the Taj Mahal. The mausoleum is located on the bank of the Yamuna at a point where the river takes a sharp turn and flows eastwards. The Taj Mahal sits on a platform surrounded by four minarets. It is flanked by two (almost) identical structures – a Masjid (mosque) to the west and a Mehman Khana (guest house) to the east. A visit to the Agra Fort, Itmad-ud-Daulah's tomb, the nearby citadel of Fatehpur Sikri, and Akbar's tomb at Sikandra completes the historical experience that Agra has to offer.

⌂ IMPERIAL CAPITAL
The city of Agra lies in the state of Uttar Pradesh, in northern India.

The Great Mughals

One of the most powerful states of the 17th century, the Mughal Empire had a complex administrative system that enabled it to rule over more than 100 million people across most of the Indian subcontinent. After an initial period of expansion and consolidation, the empire remained a stable entity for about 180 years (1526–1707). The splendour and sophistication of its court was world famous. The slow decline of the empire ended with the deposition of Bahadur Shah Zafar, the last Mughal emperor, by the British in 1857.

- ❧ 1526 **Babur** establishes the Mughal dynasty with Agra as its chief city.

- ❧ 1530–1556 Reign of **Humayun**

- ❧ 1556–1605 Reign of **Akbar**

- ❧ 1605–1627 Reign of **Jahangir**

- ❧ 1612 **Shah Jahan**, Jahangir's son, marries **Mumtaz Mahal**.

- ❧ 1627 Jahangir dies, war of succession follows. Shah Jahan accedes to the throne in 1628.

- ❧ 1631–1632 Mumtaz Mahal dies. Shah Jahan begins construction of **Taj Mahal**.

- ❧ 1654 Taj Mahal construction completed in Agra.

- ❧ 1658 Shah Jahan deposed by his son **Aurangzeb** and imprisoned at Agra Fort.

- ❧ 1666 Shah Jahan dies and is buried in the Taj Mahal.

The Reign of Shah Jahan

Born in 1592, Prince Khurram ascended the throne as Shah Jahan (King of the World) in 1628, succeeding his father Jahangir. Shah Jahan was the fifth emperor of the Mughal dynasty. He was a visionary leader who, during his 30-year reign, extended his empire to the Deccan region of south India. Like his grandfather Akbar, Shah Jahan had a great passion for architecture and was a prolific builder. He was also a connoisseur of fine art and jewellery.

Abiding love

Shah Jahan fell in love with Arjumand Banu Begum at first sight, when he was in his teens. Five years later, at the age of 19, he married her and gave her the title of "Mumtaz Mahal" (Jewel of the Palace). She became his inseparable companion, and accompanied him even on military campaigns. After she died while giving birth to their 14th child in 1631, Shah Jahan undertook the work of building one of the world's most beautiful monuments in her memory – the Taj Mahal, a symbol of their eternal love.

ENTOMBED FOREVER

SHAH JAHAN IN HIS COURT ❧
This 17th-century painting shows Shah Jahan among his nobles, who are grouped in strict hierarchical order around His Majesty's throne.

The golden period of architecture

During his rule, Shah Jahan contributed architectural treasures that attract tourists even today – the Taj Mahal in Agra, and the Red Fort and the Jama Masjid at his grand new capital called Shahjahanabad. With the lavish use of white marble and precious and semi-precious stones, these majestic structures were symbols of Mughal wealth. Elegance and symmetry characterized the architectural wonders of Shah Jahan. In his buildings, Hindu and Islamic influences were synthesized with finesse.

DIWAN-I-AAM 🖎
The hall for Shah Jahan's public audiences at Red Fort, Delhi.

marble-clad dome

JAMA MASJID, DELHI

The emperor's last days

With his old age and poor health, Shah Jahan was reduced to being a helpless spectator to the rising animosity among his sons, who were rivals for the throne. He spent the last eight years of his life in the Agra Fort, near the Taj Mahal, where he was imprisoned by his son Aurangzeb. He was looked after by his eldest daughter Jahanara. Shah Jahan died in 1666 at the age of 74, and was buried in the funerary chamber at the Taj beside his beloved queen, Mumtaz Mahal.

IMMORTAL LOVE 🖎
According to legend, when Shah Jahan was on his death-bed, he kept his eyes fixed on the Taj Mahal, which was clearly visible from his place of confinement.

view from Agra fort

Mughal Architecture

Developed by the Mughal emperors in India in the 16th and 17th centuries, the architecture of this period combined local and foreign influences, giving rise to a unique Indo-Persian architectural style that reached its pinnacle with the creation of the Taj Mahal. Minarets and domes are distinctive features of this style. Notice the *chhatris* (pavilions with umbrella-shaped domes) that crown the gateway and the *chhajjas* (projecting eaves), which are characteristic of Rajput architecture. The *pishtaq* (portal projecting from the façade of the building) is typical of Islamic and specifically, Iranian architecture. Do stop and catch your first glimpse of the Taj – the ultimate example of a Mughal garden tomb – framed in the arch of the gateway, as Shah Jahan himself would have wished. When you enter, the lush greenery of the *charbagh* (Persian-style quadrilateral garden), provides a fitting contrast to the pristine purity of the Taj Mahal.

chhatri

chhajja

pillar

marble dome

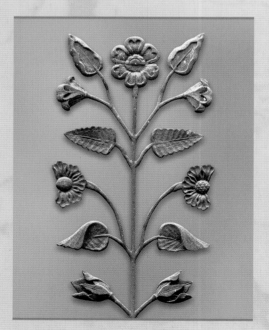

⚜ RELIEF CARVINGS
The profusion of floral motifs carved on the Taj reflects the Mughal love for gardens and flowers.

The Entrance

The original entrance to the Taj, the *darwaza-i-rauza*, is a detached gateway, a distinct feature of Islamic architecture. Rising to three storeys, it is a four-walled, red sandstone forecourt. On either side of the gateway are several rooms and halls, with the ceilings and walls decorated with elaborate geometric designs. The arabesque inlay work on the arches echoes the detailing on the façade of the Taj.

ATTACHED MINARETS ≫
At the corners of the forecourt are four minarets, each capped by a marble-domed sandstone chhatri.

pilaster

pishtaq

Alignment and symmetry

Shah Jahan's fascination for symmetry is evident in the construction of the Taj. The *darwaza-i-rauza* is aligned with the main mausoleum in such a manner that it provides a picture-perfect view of the mausoleum and its four minarets. The Taj Mahal also displays "line symmetry", which means that the mausoleum and minarets are perfectly reflected in the lotus pool in front of it. The four *chhatris* that flank the central dome serve to balance the height of the dome. It is said that Shah Jahan wanted to build a replica of the Taj in black marble for himself across the river Yamuna and connect the two structures with a bridge.

❦ DETAILING
A series of eleven small arches in red sandstone, crowned by eleven marble domes, rises above the massive arch of the central pishtaq.

FIRST GLIMPSE ❧
The arch on the main entrance frames the view of the main structure – the charbagh, *the marble mausoleum of Mumtaz Mahal, and the minarets.*

DIVINE IMPRINTS ❧
The central arch of the gateway is surrounded by a frame containing the Daybreak Sura (Sura al-Fajr) from the Quran. Throughout the complex, passages from the Quran are etched in ornate calligraphy. Interestingly, the panels on the top are written in a slightly larger size to make the script look uniform in size when viewed from below.

calligraphic inscription

Naubat Khana

On entering the complex, two Naubat Khanas (Music Galleries) can be seen on the right and left, merging into the outer garden walls. In 1982, the Naubat Khana on the left was converted into a museum with three galleries. On display are Mughal miniature paintings, manuscripts, government decrees, and specimens of calligraphy, utensils, and arms.

Layout of the Taj Mahal complex

The Taj Mahal complex is located along the bank of the river Yamuna. The mausoleum is approached through a gate that leads to the grand *darwaza-i-rauza* (the main entrance). Unlike other tombs, the Taj stands beyond the lotus pool, at the end of the *charbagh* (quadrilateral garden) instead of at the centre, with the rear elevation facing the river. Extensive calligraphic inscriptions, pietra dura (jewelled inlay work), and relief carvings in marble and sandstone adorn its exteriors and interiors. The highly ornamented cenotaphs of Mumtaz Mahal and Shah Jahan lie in the centre of the mausoleum. The Masjid (mosque) and the Mehman Khana (guest house) stand on either side of the mausoleum on the red sandstone base.

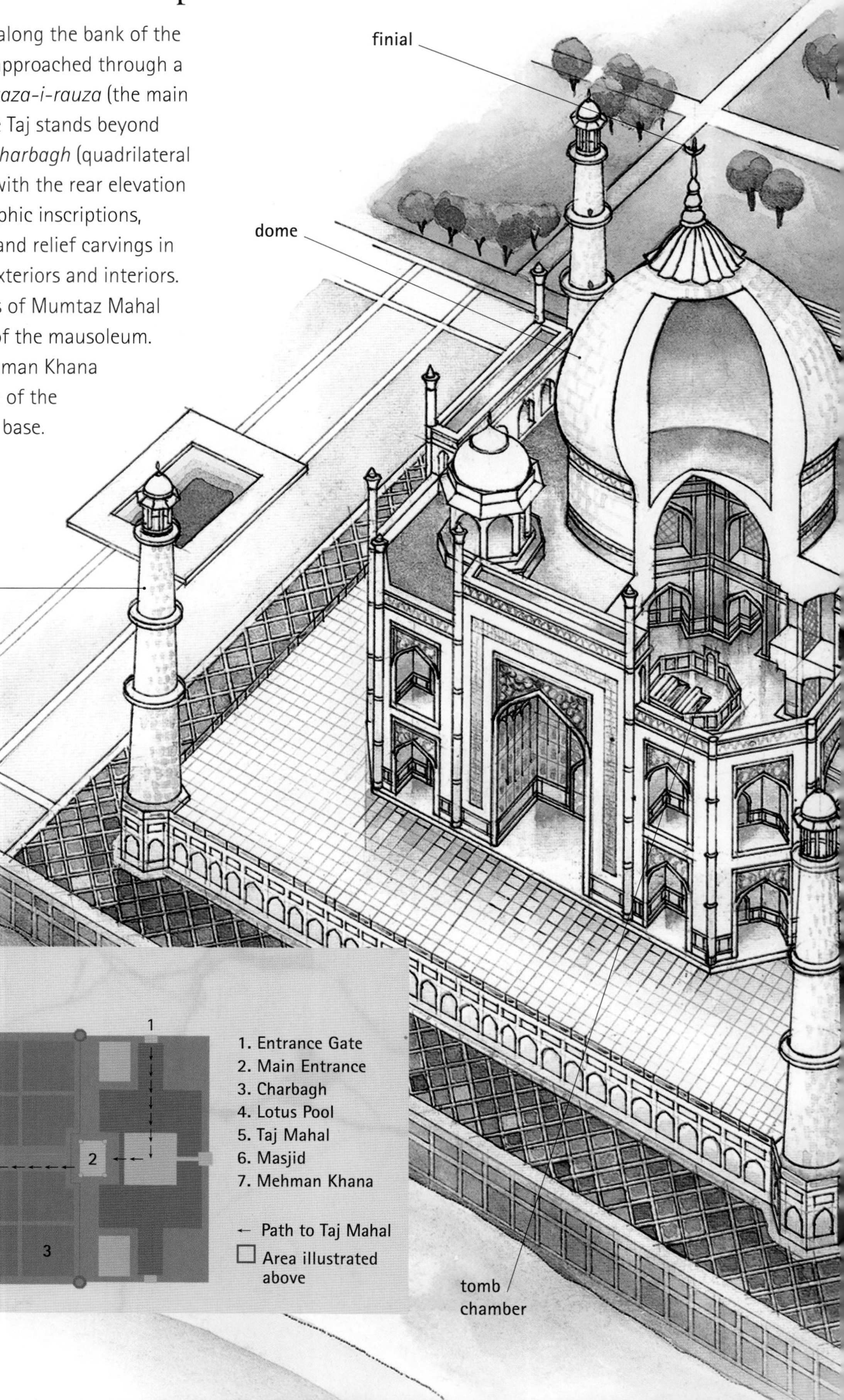

finial

dome

minaret

tomb chamber

COMPLEX PLAN

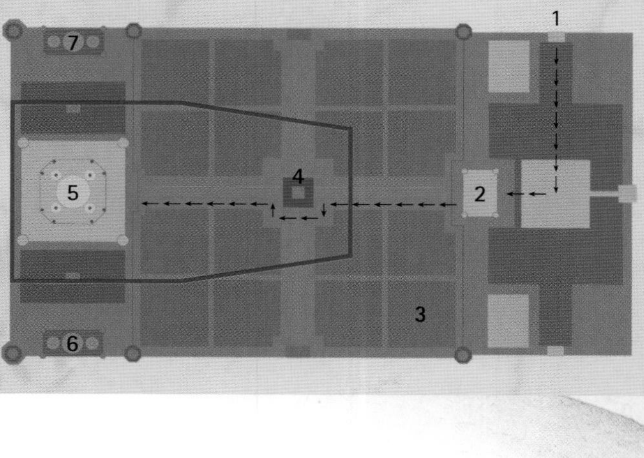

1. Entrance Gate
2. Main Entrance
3. Charbagh
4. Lotus Pool
5. Taj Mahal
6. Masjid
7. Mehman Khana

← Path to Taj Mahal
☐ Area illustrated above

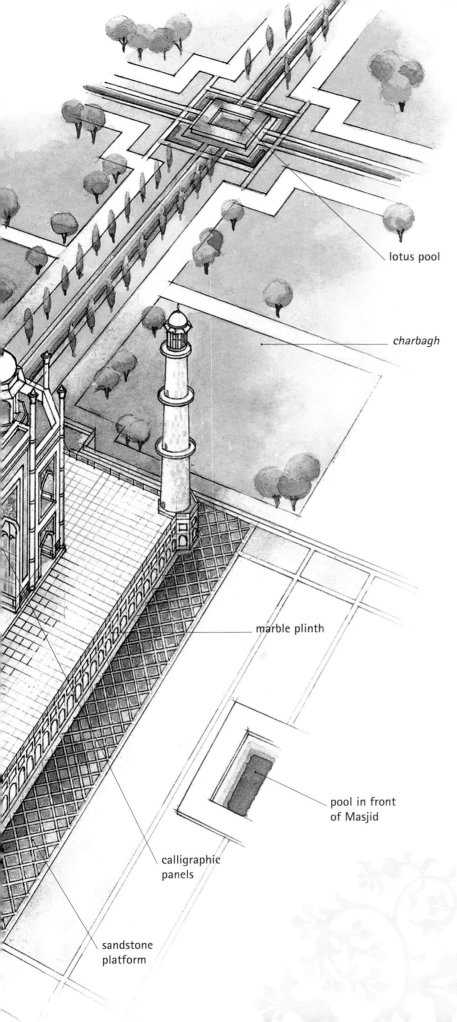

lotus pool

charbagh

marble plinth

pool in front of Masjid

calligraphic panels

sandstone platform

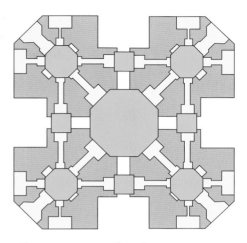

Octagonal plan

The plan of the mausoleum is based on the *hasht-bihisht* (eight paradises) plan employed by the Mughals for tomb design. In this system, a square plan is divided into an octagonal central chamber with four spaces in the centre of each elevation and four rooms at the corners.

MATERIALS

The principal building material, white marble, was brought from the quarries of Makrana in Nagaur, Rajasthan. Red sandstone was brought from Fatehpur Sikri and Rupbas, both near Agra. The colour of the sandstone used in the complex varies from soft red to yellow-tinted red. Garnets from Bundelkhand, jasper from Punjab, jade and crystal from China, onyx and amethyst from Persia, lapis lazuli and sapphire from Sri Lanka, coral and cornelian from Arabia, and diamonds from Panna were used for the inlay work.

MARBLE

SANDSTONE

PRECIOUS STONES

Charbagh

In Islam, four is the holiest of all numbers – most arrangements of the Taj are based on that number or its multiples. The *charbagh* (*char* means "four" and *bagh* means "garden") style is a distinctive feature of Mughal, Arabic, and Persian architecture. Babur, the first Mughal emperor, introduced the *charbagh*-style gardens in India, inspired by Persian gardens that adopt the same principle. They evoke the Islamic image of the four rivers flowing in the Garden of Paradise. The landscape architects perfectly translated this theory to create the *charbagh* at the Taj. The gardens are divided into four equal sections by waterways – one running from north to south, and the other from east to west. Their intersection is marked by a lotus pool.

⚜ SURROUNDING FOLIAGE
Trees such as the cypress, and a variety of fruit trees grow in the garden – cypress trees symbolize death while fruit trees symbolize life.

GEOMETRIC PATTERNS

Tessellated designs (mosaic patterns formed without gaps and overlaps) depicting octagonal figures and stars decorate the pathways, the red sandstone base, the ceilings of the sandstone structures, as well as the flooring in the mausoleum. Similar patterns can be seen on the lawns lining the walkways.

MARBLE ON SANDSTONE BASE

BLACK STONE ON FLOORING

lotus design

⚜ FOUNTAIN
Copper vessels placed below the fountains control the pressure of the flow of water.

⚜ REFLECTION
The pool and the waterway running from north to south mirror the Taj in their clear water.

Lotus pool

Like the *charbagh*, the lotus pool, too, is divided into quarters by shallow canals of water, lined by wide walkways. These are further divided into smaller quarters by broad causeways. Water is brought to the waterways and the pool through underground copper pipes from the Yamuna. The pool contains five fountains and its corners are decorated with floral designs. In 1907, Lord Curzon added a marble bench on each side. This is a particularly popular setting for tourists who wish to be photographed with the Taj as a backdrop.

STEPS TO POOL ⚜
The elevated pool is reached by steps. It is said that originally, excess water cascaded down the steps.

Foundation and plinth

The foundation of the Taj Mahal was laid on a solid base to support its massive weight. Workers were made to dig till they reached the water level and then the space was filled with lime mortar and stone. The red sandstone platform was constructed on this foundation, which takes the weight of the marble plinth (upon which the mausoleum and minarets rest), the Masjid, and the Mehman Khana.

STEPS UP TO THE MARBLE PLINTH

⚜ STAIRWAY TO THE MARBLE TOMB
The marble plinth can be reached through an internal staircase.

⚜ GARDEN VIEW
The red sandstone terrace features balconies with jaalis (lattice work) and marble-inlay geometric patterns on its flooring.

ETHEREAL GLOW AT DUSK
*The subtle colours of the marble reflect
the changing sky above, even as the Taj
is reflected in the river Yamuna.*

Marble plinth

The secondary square plinth, about 95m (300ft) long, is centred on the red sandstone base. It is faced entirely with marble. This plinth supports the mausoleum and the minarets. Decorative motifs are minimal yet elegant – the base of the plinth is decorated with simple floral carvings, which also appear on the white marble cladding of the mausoleum.

PERFORATED SCREEN

Jaali (latticed) screens present on all sides except the front of the plinth allow air and sunlight into the lower tomb chamber.

MARBLE CLADDING

PIETRA DURA

Meaning "inlaid work in which pieces of coloured stones are cut and fitted into marble", the pietra dura technique was developed in Florence, Italy. In all, 28 kinds of rare semi-precious, and precious stones were used to embellish the Taj. Some flowers have been created with as many as 60 pieces of different stones.

FLORAL MOTIF

DETAIL OF PIETRA DURA INLAY WORK

Central doorway

The frame of the mausoleum's main *pishtaq*, the vaulted entrance, is decorated with an inscription of a Quranic verse in the Thuluth script (a style of Islamic calligraphy). The triangular portions on either side of the arch are filled with an inlaid mirror-symmetrical pattern in pietra dura. The arch of the frame is outlined with rope-like mouldings. At the *pishtaq's* highest point is a linear floral pattern in pietra dura that runs between two pilasters (shallow rectangular columns). This design of an arch within a rectangle has been used repeatedly in the complex to emphasize symmetry.

⚜ INLAID THULUTH SCRIPT
Created by Persian calligrapher Amanat Khan, the script is engraved with jasper inlaid in marble.

⚜ CARVED MARBLE WORK
Realistic bas-relief depictions of flowers in white marble are found on the lower walls of the tomb, highlighting the texture of the polished marble.

Pishtaqs

The main *pishtaq* is flanked by smaller *pishtaqs*. The arched alcoves at the corners of the tomb are of the same size too, but are semi-octagonal in shape, while the ones on the façade are rectangular. It is this unique shape that allows the alcoves to be viewed from any angle, which would not have been possible otherwise. Each section of the façade is framed by pilasters covered with chevron (V-shaped) motifs.

PATTERNED PILASTERS

Majestic dome

Sheathed in white marble, the dome of the Taj derives its shape both from Hindu temple design and Persian Timurid architecture. The dome is accentuated as it sits on a cylindrical base, which is ornamented with coloured inlaid work emphasizing its whiteness. From here, it widens to a gentle fullness till it tapers to form the base of the finial (crowning element of the dome), which is decorated by carving in an inverted lotus design. The gilded bronze finial (originally made of gold) combines Persian and Hindu decorative elements. Although the dome reaches to about 45m (150ft) up to the apex of the finial, this extraordinary height is not evident to visitors viewing it from the interior, as the dome is double-shelled. The first surface outlines the monument on the exterior while the second serves as a ceiling to the hall inside.

inscription with the holy word "Allah" embossed in Urdu

SUBLIME PEAK
The bronze finial is crowned by the crescent, a typically Islamic motif, while the kalash *(pot-shaped) motif suggests the Hindu influence.*

bronze finial

lotus carving

main dome

Chhatri

Four octagonal *chhatris* flank the main dome of the mausoleum. They replicate the design of the dome in miniature, complete with the inverted lotus motif and a gilded finial, and serve to balance the extraordinary height of the dome. They also echo the design of the *chhatris* on the four minarets.

RAJASTHANI INFLUENCE
The use of the chhatri *illustrates the influence of Hindu (specifically Rajasthani) architecture on Mughal monuments.*

Minaret

Four detached minarets flank the mausoleum, one at each corner of the plinth. They frame the mausoleum, highlighting the perfect symmetry of the Taj Mahal. Each of these is more than 47m (154ft) tall and is topped with a *chhatri*, which is supported by multi-cusped arches and eight pillars. Each minaret is divided into three equal parts by two balconies that ring the tower. The *chhatri* and balconies are accessible by a spiral staircase within the tower, though they are not open to the public. Minarets are distinctive features of Islamic architecture, but they were not used in Mughal structures until the 17th century. The call to prayer was traditionally given from the *chhatri* at the top.

chhatri

PORTAL FINIALS

Tall, minaret-like finials rise from the sides of the arched portals and openings on the Taj Mahal's façade. A geometric, herringbone pattern in black-and-white marble adorns each of these slender structures, which are capped by a marble *guldasta* (bouquet) and a brass finial. Since these portal finials extend beyond the roof, they also emphasize the height of the mausoleum.

BALCONY DETAIL
Each of the balconies has marble carvings beneath, along with bands of pietra dura in floral and geometric patterns.

LEANING MINARET
All the minarets have a slight outward tilt, believed to be an architectural design measure to protect the mausoleum from any damage if a minaret collapses.

Funerary chamber

The mausoleum of the Taj Mahal houses an octagonal chamber within which lie the marble cenotaphs of Mumtaz Mahal and Shah Jahan. The actual graves, in a dark crypt below, are closed to the public (see box, p.253). The dome-shaped ceiling is decorated with pietra dura. *Jaali* screens fitted on the external walls allow natural light and air into the hall. The muted light lends an aura of serenity, heightened by the magical glow of the almost translucent marble. Each chamber wall is decorated with bas-relief, lapidary inlay (engraving with precious stones), and refined calligraphy panels, reflecting the design elements on the exterior. At the corners of the chamber are four octagonal rooms.

✍ ILLUMINATING THE SEPULCHRES
Lord Curzon presented a brass lamp in 1909, fashioned after a model which hung in a Cairo mosque.

✍ ORNATE CASKETS
The cenotaphs of the emperor and his queen are inlaid with precious and semi-precious stones. The pen-stand (for men) and writing tablet (for women) are traditional funerary symbols.

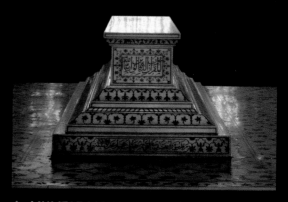

✍ MUMTAZ MAHAL'S CENOTAPH
Mumtaz Mahal's casket contains calligraphic inscriptions from the Quran. A raised rectangular surface on the casket symbolizes a writing tablet.

calligraphic inscriptions

✧ CEILING
The decorated marble ceiling above the cenotaphs uses pietra dura to depict the sun.

FINIAL TOPPING THE SCREEN JOINT

Screen

The delicate marble screen that currently surrounds the cenotaphs of Shah Jahan and Mumtaz Mahal was set up in 1643 in place of the original gold-enamelled one. Each side of this octagonal screen is divided into three panels; only one opens into the cenotaph. All panels have been delicately carved and inlaid with semi-precious stones in extremely intricate detail, forming graceful vines, fruits, and flowers.

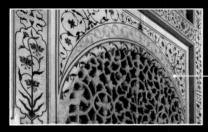

inlay work in gold

CRESCENT ON SCREEN PANEL

✧ SHAH JAHAN'S CENOTAPH
A symbolic pen-stand sits atop Shah Jahan's cenotaph, which is similar in decoration to Mumtaz Mahal's casket, but slightly larger in size.

CRYPT

In accordance with Muslim tradition, which forbids elaborate decoration of graves, the actual graves of Mumtaz Mahal and Shah Jahan are laid in a relatively plain crypt beneath the chamber. The bodies are buried with their heads turned towards Mecca. Clad in marble, the crypt has an undecorated ceiling. The graves are lightly decorated as compared to the highly embellished cenotaphs on the upper storey.

✧ TOP VIEW
Mumtaz Mahal's cenotaph is placed at the precise centre of the inner chamber.

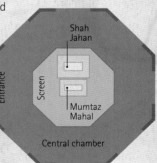

Entrance

Screen

Shah Jahan

Mumtaz Mahal

Central chamber

SECTION VIEW ✧
A staircase to the south of the cenotaphs leads to the graves below but it is now closed to the public.

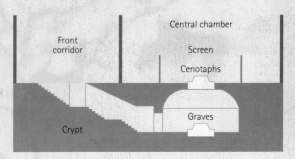

Front corridor

Crypt

Central chamber

Screen

Cenotaphs

Graves

chhatri

finial

marble dome

Masjid

The Masjid (mosque) on the left of the Taj lies on the sandstone plinth. It is capped with three domes, the central dome being the largest. All three are placed on cylindrical bases decorated with a geometric pattern of alternating white marble and red sandstone. The ceiling of the Masjid is decorated in the sgraffito technique (layers of plaster tinted in contrasting colours). A coat of red plaster is laid over a white one and floral designs are carved through the red layer, to appear in white. The floor of the mosque is patterned in outlines of 569 prayer mats in black marble. The Masjid has a *mihrab* (niche for prayers) in its *qiblah* wall (indicating the direction of Mecca). The Masjid's basic design is similar to the other mosques built by Shah Jahan, particularly the Jama Masjid in Delhi.

❧ ORNAMENTAL FAÇADE
The central pishtaq *is flanked by smaller "blind" arches on either side. The façade is decorated with pietra dura and alternating red and white patterns.*

❦ RITUAL PURIFICATION
An ablution tank lies in front of the Masjid. An integral part of any mosque complex, it is used by devotees to cleanse their hands and feet before praying.

OUTLINE OF FINIAL

A 9.5m (31ft) high replica of the brass finial topping the main dome has been engraved in black stone near the entrance of the Mehman Khana (guest house). This stone replica gives visitors an idea of how massive the finial actually is, which is difficult to gauge otherwise.

BLACK STONE REPLICA

⚜ **DECORATIVE DETAILS**
The floor of the mosque is patterned to look like prayer mats. Intricate floral designs in the sgraffito technique adorn the ceilings.

⚜ **PAVILIONS**
Four identical tower pavilions stand at the corners of the sandstone base. Each of these are octagonal in plan.

⚜ **AN ILLUSION**
The geometric pattern makes the pilasters appear to have many sides.

Mehman Khana

Identical in design to the Masjid, the Mehman Khana is also called the *jawab* (response) as it was built opposite the mosque to establish architectural balance in the complex. The red sandstone of the Masjid and Mehman Khana provide the perfect contrast to the white marble of the Taj Mahal. It is believed that the Mehman Khana was used to accommodate guests during Mumtaz Mahal's *urs* (death anniversary). To maintain symmetry, this guest house also has a corresponding tank. There is, however, no *mihrab* in the Mehman Khana and the floors lack the prayer-mat designs.

POOL IN FRONT OF THE MEHMAN KHANA

TAKING THE SCENIC ROUTE
India's railways connect even the remotest parts of the country. This "toy" steam train is on its way to Darjeeling, in the state of West Bengal.

In the vicinity

The monuments shown in this book are but a fraction of the heritage of this vast country. If you are planning to vist India, see the quick tips below on how to reach the monuments. As each monument also has numerous lesser-known sites in the vicinity that are equally rich in heritage, these listings offer an additional selection of fascinating places that are well worth including in your visit.

Sanchi

GETTING THERE **By Air:** Bhopal, which is 250km (155 miles) away, is the closest airport. **By Rail/Road:** The nearest station is also at Bhopal, which is connected to most cities. From Bhopal, a taxi or bus service is available.

SEE ALSO **Udaigiri Caves**, 20km (12 miles) north of Sanchi, have fine examples of 5th century CE caves carved into the hillside. Cave 5 is the most notable, with its impressive sculpture of Varaha, the incarnation of Vishnu as a boar, rescuing the Earth goddess from the churning ocean. **Raisen Fort** straddles a hill-top, 23km (14 miles) southeast of Sanchi. Its 13th century gates, palaces, temples, and pavilions have lain in ruins ever since a devastating attack in the 16th century by the Sultan of Gujarat, but the site is still hauntingly atmospheric.

Mamallapuram

GETTING THERE **By Air:** Chennai, which is 60km (37 miles) away, is the closest airport. **By Rail/Road:** The nearest station is also at Chennai. From Chennai, a taxi or bus service is available.

SEE ALSO **Tiger Cave**, also known as the Yali Mandapam, is 5km (3 miles) from Mamallapuram. This rocky outcrop has a central stage, surrounded by 11 tiger faces. It may have been a meeting place or a spot from where the king watched festivals or other cultural events. **Mukunda Nayanar Temple** is on the way to Tiger Cave. Its outer walls are completely without ornamentation, but it has a Somaskanda panel on the rear wall of the *garbagriha*. A *lingam*, probably a later addition, is installed in front of the panel.

Khajuraho

GETTING THERE **By Air:** Khajuraho is linked to all major cities of India. **By Rail/Road:** Jhansi is the nearest railway station, located about 175km (109 miles) away. A number of buses and taxis go to Khajuraho from Jhansi, and from other cities of Madhya Pradesh, such as Gwalior, Bhopal, and Indore.

SEE ALSO **Panna National Park**, located about 40km (25 miles) from Khajuraho, is home to a large variety of wildlife, including panthers, wild boars and deer. Its picturesque gorges, waterfalls, and thick teak forests are an added attraction. **Ajaygarh**, a 13th-century fort, is perched on a plateau approximately 80km (50 miles) from Khajuraho. A former centre of the Chandellas, it contains the ruins of palaces, temples, and many other forgotten monuments.

Qutb Minar

GETTING THERE **By Air:** Delhi can be reached by air from all major international cities, as well as cities within India. **By Rail/Road:** Delhi is connected to all cities in India by rail. To get to the Qutb complex, autorickshaws and taxis are available for hire within the city.

SEE ALSO **Mehrauli Archaeological Park** lies to the south of the Qutb complex. It covers an expanse of more than 100 hectares (250 acres) and contains the ruins of numerous monuments including mosques, tombs, water tanks, and gateways. The remarkable monuments here range from the 13th-century tomb of Sultan Balban, the Jamali Kamali Mosque and Tomb, and the Dargah Qutb Sahib, to later structures such as Jahaz Mahal, Adham Khan's Tomb (built by Akbar), Muhammad Quli Khan's Tomb, and the Madhi Masjid.

GANDHAK KI BAOLI (STEP-WELL), MEHRAULI, DELHI

Konark

GETTING THERE **By Air:** Bhubaneswar, which is 62km (38.5 miles) away, is the closest airport. **By Rail/Road:** The nearest station is Puri, which is 31km (20 miles) away and is connected to most of India's cities. From Puri or Bhubaneswar a taxi or bus service is available.

SEE ALSO Bhubaneswar has temples built over a period of about 500 years, including the famous Lingaraja Temple and the majestic Muktesvara Temple, an architectural gem. **Puri**, 64km (40 miles) from Bhubaneswar, has one of the most sacred pilgrimage centres in India – the Jagannatha Temple. This 11th century temple is dedicated to Jagannatha, a form of the Hindu god Vishnu. **Udayagiri** and **Khandagiri**, also near Bhubaneswar, are twin hills with rock-cut caves. They were carved out as living quarters for Jain monks in the 2nd century.

MUKTESVARA TEMPLE, KONARK

Hampi

GETTING THERE **By Air:** Bangalore, which is 335km (208 miles) away, is the closest airport. **By Rail/Road:** The nearest station is Hospet, which is 11km (7 miles) away and is connected to most cities. From Bangalore and Hospet, a taxi or bus service is available.

SEE ALSO Anegondi is across the Tungabhadra river and can be reached by a basket-boat or coracle from Hampi. There are several ruins of fortresses, buildings, and temples in this town, which was the capital city of the Vijayanagara empire before Hampi. **Kamalapuram** has the remains of an early Vijayanagara fort. It also has a large tank that is fed by an old canal from the Tungabhadra river. **Anantasayanagudi**, 1.5km (0.9 miles) from Hospet, is famous for a large Vishnu temple built in 1524. **Kadirampuram** is well known for several 15th-century domed structures. Some of these are tombs because Vijayanagara rulers employed many Muslim architects and artisans.

VITTHALA TEMPLE, HAMPI

JAHANARA'S TOMB, NIZAMUDDIN'S DARGAH, DELHI

Humayun's Tomb

GETTING THERE **By Air:** Delhi can be reached by air from all major international cities, as well as cities within India. **By Rail/Road:** Delhi is linked to all the major cities of India by rail and road. Once in the city, hire autorickshaws, taxis, or luxury coaches to get to Humayun's Tomb.

SEE ALSO Hazrat Nizamuddin's Dargah (shrine) lies in a settlement across the road from Humayun's Tomb. Named after Sheikh Hazrat Nizamuddin, a medieval Sufi saint who could grant wishes and answer prayers, the settlement also contains tombs of the famous poet Amir Khusro and Jahanara Begum (Shah Jahan's daughter). **Purana Qila** (Old Fort), to the east of Humayun's Tomb, contains the remains of Dinpanah, a city founded by Humayun.

ITMAD-UD-DAULAH'S TOMB, AGRA

Fatehpur Sikri

GETTING THERE By Air: Delhi, which is 240km (150 miles) away, is the closest airport. **By Rail/Road:** Agra, which is 40km (25 miles) away, is the closest railway station. From Agra, bus services and taxis are available.

SEE ALSO Agra Fort is a 16th-century citadel that stands in the city of Agra, and encompasses the imperial city of the Mughals. **Taj Mahal** (pp.236-255). **Itmad–ud–Daulah's Tomb**, close to the Taj Mahal, is an elegant two-storeyed tomb decorated with stone inlay, and was built by his daughter Nur Jahan, Jahangir's favourite wife.

Amber Fort

GETTING THERE By Air: Jaipur, which is 11km (9 miles) away, is the closest airport. **By Rail/Road:** Amber is situated on the Delhi-Jaipur highway, 261km (162 miles) from Delhi. Trains to Jaipur run from all the major cities in India. You can also travel by buses and luxury coaches or hire a taxi from any of the nearby cities.

SEE ALSO Jaipur is the capital of Rajasthan. Also known as the Pink City, it is a fascinating labyrinth of opulent palaces and vibrant bazaars. **Jaigarh and Nahargarh** are two of the most spectacular forts that guard the approach from the north to both Amber and Jaipur.

Red Fort

GETTING THERE By Air: All airlines have flights to Delhi. **By Rail/Road:** Delhi is connected to most cities. Autorickshaws, taxis, and luxury coaches are available for hire in the city.

SEE ALSO Chandni Chowk, one of the oldest markets in Delhi, lies opposite the Red Fort, and was the primary commercial hub of the ancient city of Shahjahanabad. It has shops selling jewellery, wedding accessories, spices, metal products, and local food. **Jama Masjid** sits on a rocky outcrop to the west of the Red Fort. Made of marble and sandstone, this mammoth mosque has a prayer hall surmounted by black and white marble domes.

Taj Mahal

GETTING THERE By Air: Delhi, which is 203km (126 miles) away, is the closest airport. **By Rail/Road:** You can take a train to Agra from any of India's major cities, then hire a taxi or autorickshaw to the Taj Mahal.

SEE ALSO Fatehpur Sikri (pp.170-193). **Sikandra**, on the outskirts of Agra, is home to Akbar's tomb. The stately gateway, Bulund Darwaza, leads to a walled garden containing the tomb. In accordance with the custom of his time, Akbar designed the tomb himself.

NAHARGARH FORT, AMBER

Glossary

Amalakha A fluted circular stone, usually found at the top of a temple spire. It is shaped like the fruit of the *amalaka*, the primordial tree, which in Hindu mythology is associated with regeneration.

Anda Literally an "egg"; the dome-shaped part of a stupa, which rises from the low, cylindrical base. In Buddhist architecture, it represents the dome of heaven.

Antarala A small foyer or antechamber between a temple's main hall and the inner sanctum.

Arabesque An Islamic style of surface decoration, using intricate flowing lines and geometric patterns.

Ardha-mandapa An entrance porch or chamber that leads to the main hall (*mandapa*) in a temple.

Bada The wall portion of a temple, below the curvilinear spire or pyramidal roof.

Badgir Persian word for a tall tower, designed to catch the breeze.

Bagh Persian word for garden.

Baithak Hindi word meaning a meeting hall.

Bali–pittha A sacrificial altar outside Hindu temples.

Baoli An underground rectangular stone or brick structure built around a circular or octagonal well. The well is reached by flights of steps that are surrounded by galleries or chambers.

Baradari A pillared portico or pavilion.

Bas-relief A carving that projects from a flat background.

Capital The topmost feature of a column; often highly decorated.

Chaitya A rock-cut Buddhist shrine.

Chaitya-griha A prayer hall in a rock-cut Buddhist shrine.

Charbagh A Persian-style formal garden that is divided by paths or canals into four main parts.

Chajja An overhanging eave.

Chhatra An umbrella-like disc; part of the *yasti* on top of a stupa.

Chhatri Literally an "umbrella"; a small, dome-shaped pavilion usually found on the roof. An essential feature of Rajput architecture, it was later incorporated by the Mughals.

Corbel A projection of stone or timber jutting out from a wall to support a beam or other weight.

Dargah Persian word for a shrine or tomb built over the grave of a Sufi saint.

Darwaza Literally "door"; also a large gateway.

Deul The generic name for a temple in Orissa.

Diwan-i-Aam A hall for public audiences in Mughal palaces.

Diwan-i-Khas A hall for private audiences in Mughal palaces.

Double dome A dome composed of two shells, with a space between the vaulting and the exterior; a feature of Mughal architecture.

Dwarapala Literally "doorkeeper"; a guardian deity usually placed near a Hindu temple doorway.

Finial The small ornamental feature at the top of a dome or a temple spire.

Gandi Literally elephant's "trunk"; the curvilinear spire or pyramidal roof of a temple.

Garbha-griha The innermost sacred chamber of a temple, housing the main deity.

Ghusal khana Persian word literally meaning a bathroom.

Gopi A milkmaid companion of Lord Krishna.

Gopuram A towering gateway in a south Indian Hindu temple complex.

Gothic A medieval European architectural style characterized by high stone vaults, spires, pointed arches, and flying buttresses.

Hammam The royal bathhouse, usually consisting of a group of rooms.

Harmika A small, often square, railing enclosing the finial at the top of a stupa.

Hasht-bihisht Persian for "eight paradises"; also refers to the design of Mughal tombs, such as the Taj Mahal.

Hujra A cloistered prayer hall in an Islamic building.

Iwan An arched recess, often containing an entrance.

Jaali An ornamental pierced or latticed stone screen.

Jagamohana An assembly hall that leads to the sanctum of temples in Orissa; similar to the *mandapa* in other parts of India.

Jharokha A decorative protruding balcony.

Kabr A grave.

Kalasha Literally "water jar"; describes a finial in the shape of a pitcher or vase, which is used as a symbol of plenty or immortality.

Khiyaban Persian word for a path in a garden.

Khwabgah Literally "chamber of dreams" in Persian; the sleeping-pavilion of a Mughal emperor.

Kitab khana Persian word for a library.

Lingam The phallic symbol of the Hindu deity Shiva.

Lintel A structural beam placed over an opening to support the load above.

Madrasa An Islamic theological school, especially one associated with a mosque.

Maha–mandapa A large assembly hall adjoining the *mandapa* in a temple.

Mandapa A hall with pillars, usually in front of the sanctum of a temple.

Mandir A Hindu temple.

Maqsura A screen or arched façade of a mosque, demarcating the space enclosed for prayer.

Mardana Persian word for men's quarters in a Islamic palace or house.

Mastaka Literally the "head"; the crowning elements above the *gandi* (spire) of a temple.

Meenakari A style or method of decorating metal with enamel work.

Mehman khana Persian word for *a* guesthouse.

Mihrab A niche or arched recess in a mosque or Islamic tomb, pointing to Mecca, towards which worshippers turn for prayers. In India, it is found on the western wall.

Minar A high tower, usually attached to a mosque, from which a muezzin calls Muslims to prayer.

Monolith A single block of stone, carved in the form of a column or monument.

Muqarnas A type of decorative bracket in Islamic and Persian architecture.

Naga A mythical creature with a human bust and a serpent tail and hood; common to both Buddhist and Hindu mythology.

Namazgah Persian word for an open-air venue where Muslims gather for prayers.

Naqqar khana Literally a "drum-house"; the place where musicians played to announce prayers or herald the arrival of royalty.

Natmandir A dance pavilion.

Pabhaga The lowermost portion of a temple *bada*.

Pietra dura Inlaid work in which pieces of coloured stone are fitted into marble to create decorative patterns.

Pilaster A rectangular pillar projecting slightly from the wall, as opposed to a free-standing pillar.

Pishtaq Persian word for an opening in the façade of a building; consists of a high arch set within a rectangular decorated frame.

Pol A fortified gateway.

Potala A tier on the roof of a temple.

Pradakshina A path for circumambulating a temple or sacred deity.

Qiblah The wall in a mosque that faces Mecca.

Qila Persian word for fort.

Ratha Literally "chariot"; a type of shrine or temple designed like a chariot for the patron deity.

Sarcophagus A stone coffin, sometimes elaborately decorated.

Shikhara The spire above a temple's sanctum.

Torana An elaborately carved ceremonial gateway; originally with posts and crosspieces in front of a stupa.

Vedika A balustrade.

Vihara A Buddhist monastery.

Vimana A multi-tiered pyramidal spire above a temple's sanctum.

Yakshas A class of demigods that are common to Buddhist, Jain, and Hindu mythology; in feminine form they are known as *yakshis*.

Yasti A finial with three *chhatras*; the topmost element on the dome of a stupa.

Zenana Persian word for the area in a palace or house where women live in seclusion.

Index

Acknowledgements

The publisher would like to thank the following for their kind permission to reproduce their photographs:

(Key: a-above; b-below/bottom; c-centre; f-far; l-left; r-right; t-top)

2-3 Getty Images: WIN-Initiative (c). 6 Getty Images: Robert Harding (cr). 7 Getty Images: Bridgeman Art Library (br); Ursula Gahwiler (bl). 8 DK Images: Amit Pasricha (ftr). Getty Images: Indian (br); Alison Wright (bl). 9 Corbis: Bettmann (fbl). Getty Images: Indian School (fbr). 10 Corbis: Atlantide Phototravel / Massimo Borchi (fbr). Getty Images: Indian School (fbl). 11 Corbis: Frederic Soltan (fbr); Luca Tettoni (fbl). 12 Corbis: Luca Tettoni (bc). Getty Images: Travel Ink (tc). 13 Corbis: Angelo Hornak (fbl); Frederic Soltan (fbr). 14 Getty Images: Vladimir Pcholkin (fbl); Travel Ink

(fbr). 15 Corbis: Jim Zuckerman (fbr). 15 Shefali Upadhyay (bl). 16 Corbis: Paul Almasy (fbl); Brooklyn Museum / Manohar (ftr). Getty Images: Travel Ink (fbr). 17 Corbis: Diego Lezama Orezzoli (fbl). 18 Corbis: Philip Spruyt (cb). 19 Corbis: Frde10 Soltan (fbr). Getty Images: R H Productions (fbl). 20 Corbis: Jeremy Horner (fbr). Getty Images: Sir David Wilkie (ftr); WIN-Initiative (fbl). 21 Corbis: PictureNet / Fariburz Sahba (cb). 29 Romi Chakraborty (ftr). 34 Romi Chakraborty (bl). 41 Romi Chakraborty (bl). 46-47 Glenda Fernandes (cb). 94 Robert Lankenau (br). 95 Shefali Upadhyay (cl). 96 Shefali Upadhyay (c/b). 113 British Library: British Library Board/ X 472 plate 3 (crb). 114-115 Corbis: Richard A. Cooke (c). 154 Getty Images: Time & Life Pictures (crb). 155 Wikimedia Commons (public

domain) (ca). 172 Corbis: John Henry Claude Wilson (crb). Wikimedia Commons: (public domain) (tr). 173 Wikimedia Commons: Altons Aberg (tr); (bcl/bcr). 181 Wikimedia Commons: (br). 196-197 Rohan Sinha (bc). 197 India Picture Agency: (cr). 198-199 Rohan Sinha (bc). 201 Rohan Sinha (cra/tr). 202 Rohan Sinha (cra). 205 Rohan Sinha (cr). 206 Rohan Sinha (bl). 206-207 Rohan Sinha (t). 208-209 Rohan Sinha (br/cr). 209 Rohan Sinha (cla). Bryn Walls (b). 210 Rohan Sinha (bl). 211 Rohan Sinha (bl/br/c/tr). 239 Corbis: Robert Harding World Imagery (fbr). 246-247 DK Images: Rowan Greenwood (c). 251 Tannishtha Chakraborty (cb). 256 Getty Images: Sybil Sassoon (c). 258 Corbis: Charles & Josette Lenars (fcl). 259 Getty Images: Caroline von Tuempling (ca); WIN-Initiative (fbr).

Jacket images: Front and Back: Mack Wong: (sky). Front: Tobias F. Leeger.

All other images © Penguin India / Dorling Kindersley For further information see: www.dkimages.com

Dorling Kindersley would like to thank the following institutions and people for their invaluable help in preparing this book: the Archaeological Survey of India (ASI) for helping to access the monuments; Razia Grover, Dr Narayani Gupta, and Ranjana Sengupta for reviewing the text so painstakingly; and the production team at Penguin India for proofing the book.

ML

1/10